KT-511-719

MONOGRAPHS OF THE
SOCIETY FOR RESEARCH IN
CHILD DEVELOPMENT

Serial No. 257, Vol. 64, No. 2, 1999

THE STORIES THAT FAMILIES TELL: NARRATIVE COHERENCE, NARRATIVE INTERACTION, AND RELATIONSHIP BELIEFS

University of Hertfordshire

Learning and Information

Barbara H. Fiese
Arnold J. Sameroff
Harold D. Grotevant
Frederick S. Wamboldt
Susan Dickstein
Deborah Lewis Fravel

IN COLLABORATION WITH
Kathleen Marjinsky
Dean Gorall
Joyce Piper
Martin St. Andre
Ronald Seifer
Masha Schiller

WITH COMMENTARY BY
Philip A. Cowan

MONOGRAPHS OF THE SOCIETY FOR RESEARCH IN CHILD DEVELOPMENT
Serial No. 257, Vol. 64, No. 2, 1999

CONTENTS

ABSTRACT

FIESE, BARBARA H.; SAMEROFF, ARNOLD J.; GROTEVANT, HAROLD D.; WAMBOLDT, FREDERICK S.; DICKSTEIN, SUSAN; and FRAVEL, DEBORAH LEWIS. The Stories That Families Tell: Narrative Coherence, Narrative Interaction, and Relationship Beliefs. With Commentary by PHILIP A. COWAN. Monographs of the Society for Research in Child Development, 1999, **64**(2, serial no. 257)

Personal narratives are receiving considerable interest as reflections of important psychological processes. Less attention, however, has been paid to how narratives are constructed among family members and serve as markers of family relationship functioning that directly affect child development. As a group activity, the telling of family stories may be one way that families regulate social interactions. As reflections of individual and family beliefs, family stories also may be a way that representations of relationships are passed down across generations. The Family Narrative Consortium was formed by a group of family researchers who aimed to devise a system by which family stories could be coded reliably. The consortium members were interested in how narratives about personal experiences could be considered a central aspect of the family's attempt to make sense of their social world and to share representations of relationships with their children.

The narratives used in the collaborative project came from family interviews conducted with four different samples using four different interview protocols. The data sets were originally part of larger research projects aimed at studying a variety of family processes including intimate couple formation, family rituals, family adoption, and effects of parental psychiatric illness on the family. Three dimensions were proposed as part of the coding scheme: Narrative Coherence, Narrative Interaction, and Relationship Beliefs. Family narratives are proposed to involve the process of creating a coherent statement about family events, the exchange of information among family members, and attribution of meaning to family experiences. Analyses conducted across the samples and within each site provided support for the reliability and validity of the narrative scales.

The consortium members conclude that narratives provide access to the insider's view of the family, can detect interactional and representational aspects of family process, and are important markers of family functioning. Furthermore, the study of family narratives emphasizes how the meaning-making process comes to life in family interaction and transacts with representations of family relationships.

Picture a family gathering. Perhaps the family is sitting down for dinner or preparing to meet the eldest son's fiancée. During the course of the conversation someone may begin . . . "Remember when we all . . . ," or "That reminds me of the time I had to. . . ." As the story is being told, other family members may jump in with their own perspective, or nod in agreement, endorsing a shared perspective of a family event. The same scene with another family may look strikingly different. The individual who started the story may be struggling to make his or her point, other family members may become impatient or even overtly angry, and the interchange may wind up being cut short after disparaging remarks. Whether it is an active shared process or a grappling of misunderstood statements, families do tell stories (Fiese, Hooker, Kotary, Schwagler, & Rimmer, 1995; Miller, Wiley, Fung, & Liang, 1997).

Now picture a gathering of family researchers. The researchers are faced with the challenge of developing a framework that would allow for testing hypotheses about continuity and discontinuity of family process across generations. As we began to discuss how family process could be transmitted from parents to children, we, as researchers, began to tell stories. We shared stories of families that we had come to know through either research projects or clinical work. Vivid images of family process came to life. A story was told of a family whose strong religious convictions had transformed the process of adopting a child into the belief that the child was genetically related. Another investigator told of a young woman who readily saw the "craziness" in her family of origin, but discounted the problems in her fiancé's, even though there was a family history of serious depressive episodes. A story was told of a mother diagnosed with Obsessive Compulsive Disorder (OCD) who recruited her son into a complex system of handwashing. Another story was told of a father who refused to eat dinner with his family because they "were animals." He preferred, instead, to eat at the coffee table in front of the television as his father had before him. We came to realize that the families we had been trying to understand through questionnaires and structured interview techniques were telling us unique stories that were powerful expressions of family process, containing important information about intergenerational transmission. This realization led this group of researchers to establish a narrative consortium to better understand what we were observing.

The Family Narrative Consortium (FNC), developed through the synergistic efforts of this group of family researchers, was brought together by the John D. and Catherine T. MacArthur Foundation Network on Early Childhood Transitions. Over a period of 5 years, the group tackled the thorny issues of how best to understand families and their effects on children's development, through an analysis of family stories. The group brought to the table a variety of perspectives, including human development, psychiatry, family therapy, and systems theory. Our efforts were focused on developing a framework that would allow for testing hypotheses about the relative continuity and discontinuity of family process across generations and the transactive interplay between family process and human development. The group had little difficulty in generating ideas about how intergenerational processes also may affect relationships in the current family. When faced with how to create a methodology to actually study family process across generations, however, we encountered many obstacles. We began to construct intergenerational histories of families we knew through our research and clinical endeavors. From the stories we told we came to realize that one path into intergenerational family process was to understand how families create their histories through the narratives they tell of family experiences.

The FNC was truly a collaborative and multidisciplinary (e.g., psychiatry, clinical psychology, human development, and family therapy) endeavor, aimed at developing a general understanding of basic family processes from a narrative perspective. During the first 2 years of the project, we focused our efforts on identifying central dimensions of family process associated with child development and family adaptation. Given a broad-based multidisciplinary theoretical framework, we faced the methodological challenge of measuring family narratives. Over a period of 3 years we concentrated our efforts on developing a coding manual. The coding scheme underwent three major revisions, in an attempt to develop a language that could be understood by multiple disciplines and applied to diverse data sets from different research settings. The principal investigators represented four different approaches to studying family process, but shared a common methodology of interviewing families directly about their experiences. It was hoped that a general coding scheme could be applied by researchers to test their own specific hypotheses about family process.

In addition to the core members of the FNC, several individuals made a significant contribution to this project and we would like to acknowledge their effort. Robert Emde served as the Director of the MacArthur

Foundation Early Childhood Network, providing invaluable moral support throughout the project. Howard Markman consulted with the group on coding couple interaction, providing vivid images of how couples face the task of communicating with each other. David Reiss consulted with the group on family belief systems, giving us much to contemplate about in the complex endeavor of studying families.

Studying families is a personal endeavor; not only did we share stories about our research families, but those of our own families as well. A lengthy project of this sort involves patience, not only on the part of the investigators, but also that of spouses and children. At this point we are glad to share our work with the professional community and suspect that perhaps our own families might want us to create some new stories.

I. THE FAMILY NARRATIVE CONSORTIUM: A MULTIDIMENSIONAL APPROACH TO NARRATIVES

Barbara H. Fiese and Arnold J. Sameroff

It is a truism that families affect children's development. Understanding how this occurs, however, is becoming an increasingly complex enterprise. Current conceptions of the family's effect on children involve an interlocking set of social contexts. Bronfenbrenner (1977) described the ways in which a child's development is embedded in the system of the family, which is itself embedded in systems of neighborhoods, social institutions, and schools. Attempts at understanding how the family system may affect the child's development have explored direct as well as indirect influences. Patterson and colleagues (Dishion, French, & Patterson, 1995; Patterson, 1982) have demonstrated that identifiable patterns of parent-child interaction are directly related to the child's social adjustment. Models of family functioning have been proposed, in which distress in the marital system has an indirect effect on child adjustment (Downey & Coyne, 1990). Even more distal to the child's experience may be the ways in which parents create representations of past relationships, which in turn moderate current relationships (Benoit & Parker, 1994; Crowell & Feldman, 1988; Main & Goldwyn, 1984). Family system influences on child development range from directly observed proximal factors, such as parent-child interaction patterns, to more distal factors, such as the parent's family of origin experiences. These family influences are seen as part of a transactional process that interlocks parents, children, and the caregiving environment (Sameroff, 1987; Sameroff & Fiese, 1990, 1992). Although the complexity of family influences on child development has been long recognized, suitable methods for studying the family have lagged behind theoretical advances.

Families are considered rule-governed systems that change over time. Inherent in the family system are rules of organization and process that allow the family to carry out tasks that insure the growth and well-being of its members (Sameroff & Fiese, 1992; Walsh, 1993). These include

1

nurturance and care of young offspring, support for emotional development, social and cognitive competencies, moral and spiritual growth, and engagement in culture and community (Landesman, Jaccard, & Gunderson, 1991). The principles of family organization often include rules of interaction (Minuchin, 1974; Watzlawick, Beavin, & Jackson, 1967) and beliefs (Reiss, 1981). These rules are not necessarily articulated by the family, but may be accessed indirectly through how members interpret family behavior and come to a consensus about family organization. The process of interpreting family behavior may be carried across generations, providing links between the family of origin and current family functioning. One approach that may incorporate both proximal and distal influences, as well as focus on the family's interpretation of family events, is the study of family narratives.

In this chapter, we will provide an overview of the theoretical rationale for the study of family narratives and how the consortium devised a multidimensional coding scheme. Furthermore, we will present analyses conducted across four study sites including data on interrater reliability, confirmatory factor analysis, and the relation among narrative dimensions.

NARRATIVE FRAMEWORK

There has been a burgeoning interest in the study of narratives over the past 10 years. Some have gone so far as to propose that narratives are a new paradigm for psychology (Howard, 1991) and clinical practice (cf. White & Epston, 1990). In reality however, the study of narratives has a long history in both. Indeed, Freud's case studies are accounts of individual narratives and the struggle to make sense of personal experience. A focus on narratives necessitates a focus on experience and meaning. Over 50 years ago, Henry Murray (1938) proposed that in order to truly understand individual lives it was necessary to chart individual experiences across the life course, often using a narrative approach to grasp the meaning of experience. There is a long tradition of considering narratives from the perspective of the individual.

Much of the current interest in narrative psychology stems from using talk as a window into cognitive processes of the individual (Bruner, 1987). How the individual puts together the pieces of his or her life story may reflect important aspects of individual identity (McAdams, 1993). As they recount personal experiences, they are creating their autobiographies. But this is not necessarily a factual accounting of person, place, and time. Rather, it is a constructive process in which past events are viewed in light of current context (Riessman, 1993). Indeed, Bruner (1987) describes the process of talking about one's life as an "interpretive feat" (p. 13). Interpreting personal experiences provides the elocutionary force to individual narratives and a coherent account of how and why something has happened. Whereas there has been considerable focus on narratives and the creation of an individual's autobiography, there has been less attention paid to how narratives may be constructed among family members and reflect family relationship functioning. Some aspects of the study of individual narratives may be directly applicable to the study of family narratives, such as the struggle with meaning-making and the organized structure of the narrative. There are additional dimensions, however, to the study of family narratives, which include the exchange of information among family members and regulation of close relationships.

Family narratives move beyond the individual and deal with how the family makes sense of its world, expresses rules of interaction, and creates beliefs about relationships. The process of creating family narratives and the themes inherent in the stories may be shared across generations, regulating family beliefs and interaction patterns. These narratives become a scrapbook of family history resulting from a process of meaning-making in the family. When family members are called upon to recount an experience, they set an interpretive frame reflecting how individuals grapple with understanding events, how the family works together, and how the ascription of meaning is linked to beliefs about relationships in the family and social world.

Meaning-making in the family is associated with family adaptations to stressful conditions, such as chronic illness (Patterson & Garwick, 1994), alcoholism (Wolin, Bennett, Noonan, & Teitelbaum, 1980), or having a child kidnapped or mysteriously missing (Fravel & Boss, 1992). Meaning-making also has been found to be associated with normal transition points, such as the development of adolescent identity (Fiese, 1992; Grotevant, 1993), and relationship formation (Wamboldt & Reiss, 1989; Wamboldt & Wolin, 1989).

Although the vitality of meaning-making in the family has been recognized, reliable and ecologically valid methods for ascertaining meaning in the family have been scarce. An examination of family narratives highlights the process of meaning-making and takes as its core the interpretation of experiences from the family's perspective. The Family Narrative Consortium (FNC) was organized to devise a research methodology that could capture some of the richness of family narratives along reliable dimensions that could be related to family interaction patterns, marital satisfaction, and child adjustment. The material used in the collaborative project came from family narratives in four different data sets. Each of these sets was originally part of larger research projects aimed at studying a variety of family processes, including early intimate couple formation, family rituals, levels of openness in adoption, and the effects of parental psychiatric illness on the family.

Although the projects had different aims, used different samples, and employed different interview techniques, we endeavored to develop a common multidimensional coding scheme that would allow for reliable coding of family narratives.

Dimensions of Narrative and Language

The consortium began its efforts by identifying a number of components we believed central to the study of family narratives: narrative coherence, narrative interaction, and relationship beliefs. On the individual level, the relative coherence of each family member's narrative may be related to his or her individual identity and life history. As a group activity, constructing a narrative reflects how the family works together and is linked to each member's relationship history. As a set of beliefs, family narratives reflect how much trust can be placed in relationships within and outside the family.

Although narratives are clearly communications, they have rarely been studied along the multiple dimensions that characterize other communication forms such as language. Language typically is considered a multidimensional phenomenon, broken into syntax, semantics, and pragmatics. Syntax refers to how language is organized. Semantics refers to the meaning of language. Pragmatics refers to the conversational nature or act of using language and may include such features as affective tone and the process of turn-taking. According to Halliday (1973), three conditions must be met to interpret meaning in language: the textual or structural aspect or *how* a narrative is said, the ideational function or *what* is said, and the interpersonal function or what role *relationships* are expressed. We are proposing that family narratives include three analogous dimensions: (a) *Narrative Coherence reflects* the ways in which individuals considered separately and together organize the narrative, or the syntax of the narrative; (b) *Narrative Interaction reflects* the ways in which two or more family members construct the story, or the pragmatics of the narrative; and (c) *Relationship Beliefs reflects* the implicit beliefs about the trustworthiness of relationships, or the semantics of the narratives. These three dimensions are proposed to reflect the "deep structure" of family narratives and may make unique contributions to the understanding of family process from a narrative perspective.

Narrative Coherence

The first component we identified was the *Coherence* of the narrative. Coherence refers to how well the individual is able to construct and organize a story. The ways in which an individual's story makes sense, how clauses and thoughts are organized, the willingness of the individual to consider differing perspectives, and the match between affect and content are all considered part of the coherence of an individual's story or narrative.

As part of a constructive process, narratives may be viewed from the perspective of the individual and how the story is put together. But narratives also involve relationships and relating to others. Whereas the coherence of the story may be linked to the individual's struggle with meaning-making, narratives also include important markers of relationship functioning and the meaning of an interaction between two or more people. We labeled this second component *Narrative Interaction.*

Narrative Interaction

This next component refers to how the couple or family works together in putting together their story, the *act* of storytelling.

When individuals construct a story, they must also tell it. Within the context of the family, family members co-construct the meaning of their relational worlds (Berger & Kellner, 1964; Gubrium, Holstein, & Buckholdt, 1994; Wamboldt & Reiss, 1989). The process of co-construction involves a history of interaction in which the meaning of relationships is negotiated over time. This process is clearly illustrated in the formation of marital relationships. The ways in which couples create meaning in their relationship is reflected in the narratives they tell about their relationship and is related to how satisfied they are together (Buehlman, Gottman, & Katz, 1992; Veroff, Sutherland, Chadiha, & Ortega, 1993; Wamboldt & Reiss, 1989). Not only do narratives reflect aspects of individual identity, but they also reflect important aspects of the family's relational world.

Relationship Beliefs

This third component includes themes about the trustworthiness of the social world and expectations for rewarding relationships. Narratives are not only told by someone about some event, but also told to someone. Qualities of the narrative reflect beliefs about the "telling" relationship as well as the family. Family belief systems reflect the family's shared value system and provide meaning to family interactions (Reiss, 1981). As narratives deal with the "vicissitudes of human intention" (Bruner, 1990), family narratives serve to verify beliefs about family members' intentions and actions. Implicit in many family stories are beliefs about the trustworthiness of relationships. The ways in which family members describe each other often include whether there is an expectation for reward and satisfaction or whether there is an expectation to be disappointed or even harmed.

These stories also include family beliefs about the workings of the social world. Some families are very secure in their interactions with the social world and embrace the opportunity to "tell their story." Other families, however, are reticent to share either with each other or with the social world.

Reiss (1981) proposed that families differ in their perceptions about the relative safety of relationships within the family and relationships with the outside world. The relative trustworthiness of relationships has been found to be related to engagement in psychotherapy and psychiatric status (Costell, Reiss, Berkman, & Jones, 1981). The distinction between inside and outside the family also has been noted in the narratives described by Bruner (1987). Bruner describes the "psychic geography of the family" (p. 25) as evident in narrative accounts of one family's perception of the relative safety of the home in contrast to the unpredictable nature of the "real world." The stories constructed by the family also must mesh with their beliefs about the social world. Ultimately, the narrative must include an understanding of what it means in the context of the community and culture in which it takes place (Polkinghorne, 1988).

Distinguishing Between Narratives and Stories

Thus far, we have used the concepts of narratives and stories interchangeably to highlight their theoretical significance in the study of families. It may be important, however, to distinguish between them for methodological purposes. For our purposes, narratives are the form and stories are the content. Narratives, as a construct, reflect a mode of thinking that is often contrasted with paradigmatic thought (Baumeister & Newman, 1994; Bruner, 1986). In this regard, telling stories, or recounting experiences in a narrative framework, provides a window into the personal and emotional lives of individuals (Grotevant, 1993; McAdams, 1989; Oppenheim, Nir, Warren, & Emde, 1997). Inherent in the narrative process is a recounting of past experiences. Indeed, narrative processes have been defined as the "language of memory" (p. 137, McCabe, Capron, & Peterson, 1991). On the one hand, narrative studies may focus on how memories are formed and organized (e.g., Neisser, 1994). On the other hand, they may focus on how personal experiences are related to interpersonal relationships (Main & Goldwyn, 1984).

Stories are told within a narrative framework and involve a verbal recounting of a past event. Family stories may include a recital told over and over in a particular family (Byng-Hall, 1988; Martin, Hagested, & Diedrick, 1988), a newly constructed story about past interpersonal experiences (Main & Goldwyn, 1984), the mapping of relationships over time (Buehlman et al., 1992; Veroff et al.,1993), or the imparting of personal, family, or cultural values (Emde, 1994; Miller, Wiley, Fung, & Liang, 1997). Regardless of the substantive focus of the narrative study, stories involve talk about past events.

The consortium defined family stories as the verbal accounts of personal experiences that are important to the family, and typically involve the creation and maintenance of relationships, depict rules of interaction, and reflect beliefs about family and other social institutions. The stories described in this *Monograph* were drawn from interviews conducted with individuals, couples, and families. In some cases the families were asked "to tell a story" about a family event (Fiese & Marjinksy), in other cases the individuals or couples were asked to talk about how relationships were formed (Grotevant et al., and Wamboldt) or in still others to describe family practices (Dickstein et al.). In all cases, the focus was on how a past family event made sense, provided meaning, or included rules of interaction for the family.

THREE DIMENSIONS OF FAMILY NARRATIVES

A multidimensional view of narratives requires that the specific qualities of each dimension be identified. In what follows we will overview the qualities of each dimension.

Narrative Coherence

The central dimensions of an individual's identity are captured by personal narratives (e.g., Grotevant, 1993; McAdams, 1988; Polkinghorne, 1991). Narratives have been found to be particularly useful in studying identity, emphasizing how the construction of a life story is part and parcel of who we are (Erikson, 1963). The coherence of the narrative is considered a benchmark for evaluating integrity of the self. Coherence implies the pulling together of different domains or the glue that holds the pieces together. When considering personal identity, a life story may include the domains of occupation, gender, race, and family values (Grotevant, 1993). When considering the development of attachment relationships, the life story may include the domains of parental responsiveness, trust, and responses to rejection and loss (Main & Goldwyn, 1984). When considering resilience of the self, the domains of adverse past events, future expectations, and coping strategies are integrated into a coherent whole (Cohler, 1991). Regardless of the domain being examined, the coherence of the narrative is seen as pivotal to the integrity of the story.

Attachment researchers have generated considerable interest in the link between narratives and working models of relationships that are important for child development. Using the Adult Attachment Interview (AAI), several studies have found that the ways in which parents reflect on their caregiving relationships are related to markers of mental health and child attachment classifications (for meta-analytic reviews, see van IJzendoorn, 1995; van

IJzendoorn & Bakermans-Kranenbrug, 1996). A central aspect of AAI research is the measurement of coherence. Indices of discourse coherence are then used to assign attachment classifications. Coherence has long been identified as an important aspect of discourse processes (Agar & Hobbes, 1982; Labov & Waletzky, 1967; McCabe & Peterson, 1991) as well as a marker of individual adaptation (Antonovsky, 1979; Cohler, 1991; Grotevant, 1993).

The narrative consortium also found coherence to be an important aspect of family narratives. Rather than attempt to develop a categorical classification system, however, we have kept the coherence construct continuous. Furthermore, the consortium attempted to keep beliefs about the trustworthiness of relationships on a dimension distinct from the discourse coherence of the narrative. Our thinking was based, in part, on family systems theory and previously published work on discourse processing and storytelling in the family context. From a family systems perspective, we were less convinced that categorizing families would be a worthwhile venture. Previously designed typologies have not meaningfully described family functioning in relation to child adaptation (Christensen & Arrington, 1987). Moreover, our interest in narratives was in line with social constructionist perspectives on family process (e.g., Berger & Kellner, 1964; Gergen & Gergen, 1988; Reiss, 1981). In this regard, we wanted to link individual characteristics (narrative coherence) with family systems regulations (narrative interaction) and understandings about how systems of relationships work (relationship beliefs). Our goal was to access the insider's view of the family through family narratives and to compare these views to directly observable patterns of family interaction.

Coherence is seen as an integration of different aspects of an experience that provides a sense of unity and purpose (McAdams, 1989). The transformation of individual sequences into a unified whole creates the coherent plot of the story (Polkinghorne, 1991). There have been a variety of ways to evaluate coherence, including linguistic approaches based on story grammars (e.g., McCabe & Peterson, 1991), computational models based on computer simulation (e.g., Lehnert & Vine, 1987), and discourse analysis (Agar & Hobbs, 1982). When the focus of the study is on meaning-making and identity, however, coherence analysis should focus on how the story is put together, the steps taken to present a unified whole, the degree to which the story makes sense, and the way in which the pieces of the story match the affect of the storyteller. Therefore, four qualities of narrative coherence need to be considered: the relative consistency of the narrative, how the narrative is organized, the incorporation of multiple perspectives, and the modulation of affect.

Internal Consistency

Internal consistency refers to the completeness of the narrative. A coherent narrative is considered to be internally consistent when the different parts of the story "hang together" to form a whole. Story construction, like theory construction, involves creating a rationale for why events are linked together. A coherent narrative includes an internally consistent theory that is supported by sufficient detail to allow the listener to determine whether actions were justified and conclusions warranted. Narrators can bolster the internal consistency of a story through the use of synthesizing statements that draw together information about physical laws, personal dispositions and character, responses to actions, and the process of deliberation in making decisions (Polkinghorne, 1991). Narratives that include contradictions are less internally consistent and often leave the listener confused. For example, one husband reported that he had no family, that he was all alone in the world, and then gave a fairly complete listing of the aunts, uncles, cousins, and siblings that had been important in his upbringing. It could be argued that his subjective feeling of loneliness and abandonment was consistent with his definition of family. The details that were provided to support his feelings of "no family," however, were inconsistent with kinship definitions of family that include aunts, uncles, and siblings. Contrast this story with a similar theme but different supporting details. "I felt alone when I was growing up. My father had left the family and mother was always working. She tried to take good care of us but it was more than shelter I was looking for." Internal consistency contributes to coherence by integrating and synthesizing details to support the theory inherent in the story.

Organization

The second quality of narrative coherence we considered was organization. Organization refers to how the individual structures the narrative. A sense of order is considered a key component to a coherent narrative (Polkinghorne, 1988). An organized narrative provides the listener with a sense of orientation of context, and a clear sense of referents (who, what, where, when, and why). Intelligible narratives are both "recountable" and "followable" (Cohler, 1991). A sense of order is implied in the comprehension of any speech. "The dog barked loudly" is understandable, whereas "the loudly barked dog" is not. In constructing a narrative, organization includes the ordering of thoughts in a clear chronology so that the listener can understand the point the storyteller is trying to make. Well organized narratives may include the use of orienting statements to create a context for the listener to understand the meaning of the story. These statements are typically succinct and to the point, whereas poorly organized narratives include stops and starts, incomplete thoughts, or excessive repetitive language. Organization contributes to the coherence of the story by ordering sequences and orienting the listener.

Flexibility

The third quality of narrative coherence is flexibility. Narratives are threaded with cause and effect. The storyteller relates what happened in the story and why he or she thinks the events occurred in the way they did. Causal relationships expressed in narratives include the intentions of others as well as the actor (Burke, 1950). Flexibility refers to the narrator's ability to explore new ideas and alternatives. The flexible storyteller is able to view issues as they might be seen by others and recognizes that there is more than one side to a story. The coherence of a narrative includes the degree to which the individual holds convictions about his or her statements (Cohler, 1991), but convictions need not be rigid to be coherent. The more flexible the individual is in considering multiple viewpoints, the more likely elaboration will lead to a coherent life story. The recognition of two or more alternatives indicates a willingness to consider the complexity of relationships, while maintaining personal integrity. Flexibility contributes to the coherence of the narrative by including multiple perspectives.

Congruence of Affect and Content

The fourth quality of narrative coherence included was the congruence of affect and content. In some sense, affect can be considered in the domain of pragmatics rather than syntax, but as a paralinguistic aspect of language it is an exceedingly important part of the communication process. The congruence of affect and content addresses the "fit" between actions or thoughts and the emotions expressed with regard to them. Affect has been considered a regulating feature of narratives linked to the goals of the story (Mandler & Johnson, 1977) and the creation of an overall tone (McAdams, 1988). In addition, there is considerable evidence that the emotions expressed about relationships are related to psychological functioning in the family (e.g., Goldstein & Strachan, 1987; Hooley & Teasdale, 1989).

Affect is used in narratives to highlight important parts of the story. A statement made about "a wonderful experience" may be bracketed with a smile and increasing intonation reaffirming the positive nature of the event. If the statement is made with clenched teeth and a falling intonation, however, it may signify sarcasm. Affect can be used to clarify or distort a narrative. This process includes a combination of content and affect. Affect varies not only in tone but also intensity. It is possible to have a mismatch of intensity with content as well as a mismatch between content and tone. Bland or flattened affect may be appropriate when discussing a neutral event such as writing a grocery list, but would be mismatched when discussing a traumatic event such as loss of a loved one. Mismatch also may occur when there are signs of nervous laughter or inappropriate crying. Congruence of affect and content contributes to the coherence of the narrative by clarifying the emotional significance of an event.

Narrative Interaction

Whereas there has been little precedence for studying families from the perspective of narrative coherence, there is a relatively long tradition of examining family process in regard to family interaction patterns. Consistent with the focus on building meaning in narrative coherence, narrative interaction focuses on the couple's co-construction of this meaning within the dyadic context of husband and wife. The central features of the narrative coherence dimension were designed to include the ways in which the individual family members struggle with meaning-making and preserve the integrity of their narrative. Narratives are told in context. To the previously studied context of narratives, such as individual characteristics of gender (e.g., Fivush, 1991), age (e.g., McCabe & Peterson, 1991), and culture (Riessman, 1993), we must add the marital relationship and how the couple comes to place meaning on shared events. This perspective is consistent with the social constructivist model proposed by Berger and Kelner (1964) and empirically supported by recent research (Buehlman et al., 1992; Oppenheim, Wamboldt, Gavin, Renouf, & Emde,1996; Veroff et al., 1993; Wamboldt & Reiss, 1989). In this model, the biographies of the husband and wife are reconstructed in light of their current relationship and their future goals. Just as narrative coherence focuses on struggles with individual identity, narrative interaction focuses on the couple's identity. The ways in which the couple put together the pieces of their story reflects their relational world (Wamboldt & Wolin, 1989) and linkages with the social world (Fravel & Boss, 1992). Although previous family interaction research has focused primarily on couple conflict resolution (e.g., Gottman, 1993; Markman, 1992), the narrative approach presented here focuses on how the couple constructs a meaningful story. The co-construction process may, or may not, involve conflict. Families are faced not only with solving problems, but also with managing issues that involve reaching social consensus (Berger & Kellner, 1964; Wamboldt & Reiss, 1989, 1991). The creation of a family narrative reflects, in part, the consensus that the family has reached in co-constructing its definition of family. The family may use these "practices" of co-construction to impart values to other family members and to reaffirm its beliefs (Reiss, 1989).

Thus far, we have discussed theoretically how the family works together in creating narratives about family experiences. We operationalized these concepts by focusing on how couples co-constructed family stories as an indication of family narrative interaction. Although the consortium focused on couple interaction, we believe that the same principles will hold when other family members are included in the storytelling process (cf. Fiese & Marjinksy, this volume). The narrative interaction dimension included four separate qualities: how the couple co-constructs the narrative, how the couple works together, and the degree to which the husband and wife either confirm or disconfirm each other's story.

Couple Narrative Style

Couple narrative style describes how the couple conjointly produces the narrative. This quality includes both the content of the story and the couple's storytelling process. Previous research has reinforced the notion that couples differ in regard to how they contain or modulate affect and conflict (Fitzpatrick, 1988; Gottman, 1993; Gottman & Levenson, 1992). Some couples are positively engaged with each other, whereas others choose to distance themselves from each other, remaining aloof and uninvolved with their partner. In the latter case, these couples present parallel stories that do not differ in facts but are told separately by husband and wife. Couples also may differ in regard to how they negotiate conflict. Some spouses use conflict as a way to disrupt their partner's effort at telling his or her story. These narratives are frequently difficult to follow, involving multiple differences of opinion that create a lingering negative affect.

Conflict also may be expressed but contained. Couples may be able to produce a coherent story with some discrepancies or differences of opinion about the facts, but the differences do not disrupt the process of constructing the narrative. At a more optimal level, some couples are able to tell a story that "hangs together" well, expressing similar facts, and the partners are pleasantly engaged with each other. The most collaborative effort is seen when a couple not only is able to construct a unified story, but the story told together is much richer than if told by one individual. Couple narrative style highlights both the process and content of narrative co-construction.

Coordination

Coordination includes an evaluation of how the couple or family works together, with regard to their ability and willingness to develop shared solutions and perceptions. We drew heavily from Reiss's (1981) proposition that families differ in the ways in which they are willing to share information, affecting their ability to work together. In some families, problems are solved as part of a group process, in which input actively is sought from all members and evaluated prior to coming to a decision. Other families, however, may reach a conclusion based on the perspective of one individual, often discounting another family member's contribution in the process. Some families believe that all members may make significant contributions to problem solution, whereas other families believe that members are placed in a hierarchy, and decisions are weighted by position in the hierarchy.

Coordination extends beyond the family's simple agreement about facts or beliefs. Rather, it reflects the family's shared assumption that reaching an agreement would be possible and that there are ways in which the family may share information in order to reach a consensus. From a narrative perspective, coordination involves the weaving together of the separate threads of a family's story. At one extreme, family members are seen as separate and unrelated individuals, presenting separate and unrelated threads of the story. At the other extreme, families present as a group and actively call for input from each other. Typically the entire family reinforces this input. The family presents a strong unified front, pressuring others to interpret events in a similar manner. In the mid-range, there is a balance between separateness and connectedness in family relationships. Coordination contributes to the narrative interaction dimension by highlighting how the family works together and presents the story as a group or individual process.

Husband and Wife Confirmation/Disconfirmation

Couples who actively validate each other's opinion in comparison to couples who withdraw or become hostile during problem solving are more likely to remain married (Gottman, 1993), report fewer illnesses (Gottman & Levenson, 1992), and are more satisfied in their marital relationship (Markman, Floyd, Stanley, & Storaasli, 1988). The confirmation of another's opinion typically relies on signs of nonverbal as well as verbal communication. Acknowledgement can be expressed through direct eye contact, whereas disconfirmation may be evident when a spouse "rolls their eyes" in response to their partner's comments. From a narrative perspective, confirmation reflects the ways in which family members share the facts and perspectives of the story.

The confirmation/disconfirmation dimension ranges from overtly disconfirming comments, which may include put-downs and strong power moves, to actively confirming ones, which may include recognition, acknowledgement, and endorsement of the partner. An example of an extremely disconfirming comment would be, "What you have just heard is a fantasy, now I'm going to tell you the real story." An example of an actively confirming comment would be, "You know that's funny, I had forgotten about some of the things that happened. Now that you mention it, we did talk a lot about our plans." Confirmation/disconfirmation contributes to the narrative inter-action dimension by highlighting the ways in which the facts and perspec-tives of one partner are either acknowledged or rejected by the other partner.

Relationship Beliefs

Families have beliefs that represent the way they construct the social world and are reflected in the narrative content and style of the interview. Reiss (1981) has proposed that the ways in which families work together and share information is multidetermined. On the one hand, observable interac-tion patterns can facilitate or disrupt effective problem solving and family management. These patterns of support and validation, information ex-change, and collaboration are reflected in narratives. Whereas patterned fam-ily interactions may be relatively proximal to the experience of its members, more distal factors may actually regulate and affect the directly observable patterns. In an initial set of studies, Reiss and colleagues noted that the family constructs their view of the laboratory and the research setting based on their expectations of rewards, whether the environment can be mastered by the family as a unit, and whether they will or will not meet success in their inter-change with the environment. These expectations, based in part on a long family history, sometimes spanning generations, were reflected in the ways in which the family interacted in the laboratory and solved a relatively ambigu-ous card-sorting procedure (Reiss, 1981). Based on the way in which the card-sorting task was approached, Reiss identified different family groups that differed in regard to the paradigms that they held about themselves and the social world. At the crux of the paradigm typology were the dimensions of mastery of relationships and trust in the outside social world. For some fami-lies there was an excitement in tackling new problems, challenges were met with enthusiasm, and the outside social world was embraced. For other fami-lies, however, relationships were seen as confusing, with few guidelines or rules for mastery. The outside social world may be seen as either dangerous or threatening or a place that did not warrant the family's attention.

The conceptual framework for Reiss's paradigms include two dimen-sions that may reflect what Reiss labeled as the family's working models of their family relationships and the social world. Inherent in this framework is the notion that families hold beliefs about relationships and develop rules of interaction to conform to these beliefs. In this regard, the interaction itself is seen as an indicator of family belief systems.

From a narrative perspective, the ways in which the family views the relative safety and rewarding features of relationships is expressed in the tone of the narrative and statements of satisfaction with relationships. When relationships are seen as manageable, reliable, and safe, the beliefs that are constructed include an expectation that relationships will bring rewards and are opportunities to feel successful and satisfied. Reiss proposes that these beliefs may then moderate interactions, which reaffirm the constructed belief system. For example, a family member who expects relationships to be rewarding may be more likely to seek actively the opinion of other family members and respond to overtures with positive affect. Should the interaction confirm the belief, then there is personal evidence to retain the shared assumption that family relationships are rewarding. If, however, beliefs are held that relationships are dangerous and threatening, there may be a greater likelihood to withdraw from the interaction and perhaps become hostile to overtures from others.

Families not only create beliefs about the workings and rules of their family; they also create beliefs about the workings of the outside social world. Bruner (1990) describes a family that created several stories contrasting the themes of "home" and the "real world." The distinction drawn between home and the outside world points to the creation of family beliefs that "created tension for the children about 'safe versus dangerous' environments" (p. 133). Family beliefs about the relative safety of the outside social world may serve to regulate how family members engage with others and the degree to which they will share details about their lives with others. In the family described by Bruner it was often the conflicts between the "home" rules and "real world" rules that created tensions and problems for the children in the family.

From a narrative perspective, beliefs about the social world may be evaluated indirectly by the ways in which the family interacts with the interviewer. The interviewer is, after all, a representative of the outside world relatively unknown to the family. The family approaches the interview context with expectations about the intentions of the interviewer, which are aligned with their knowledge of the workings of the social world. These two aspects are part of the narrative beliefs domain: the relative manageability of family relationships and interactions with the outside social world.

Relationship Expectations

Relationship expectations refer to whether the family views relationships as manageable, reliable, and safe. Two aspects of relationships are considered important in understanding relationship expectations: safety and mastery. Relationships may be seen as relatively safe or threatening and dangerous. Relationships also may be seen as something that can be mastered and rewarding or as overwhelming and confusing. Frequently these narratives will include statements of confusion and dissatisfaction in regard to relationships. At the other end of the dimension, relationships are seen as rewarding, safe, reliable, and fulfilling. These narratives may include statements about the creation of opportunities to form and maintain relationships and a sense of confidence about the durability of relationships. Relationship expectations add to the understanding of narrative beliefs by highlighting the relative safety and mastery of family relationships.

Interviewer Intimacy

Interviewer intimacy examines the degree to which the family is open and willing to share personal and affectively sensitive experiences with the interviewer. Families differ in the degree to which they actively engage the interviewer in the conversation, are warm with the interviewer, and elaborate personal details. From the narrative perspective, attention is paid to how the family incorporates personal details into the recital and how potentially sensitive material such as embarrassing moments, family secrets, or other affectively charged material is presented. Families that view the social world as threatening may remain distant from the interviewer by being hostile, cold, or closely guarded. Families that invite opportunities to engage with the social world may engage the interviewer through warm and positive affect and elaborate "insider" information such as family jokes, nicknames, or family secrets. Interviewer intimacy contributes to the dimension of relationship beliefs by highlighting how the family engages with the social world and their openness to providing personal details in the narrative.

SUMMARY

Family narratives can be considered across three different dimensions: coherence, interaction, and beliefs. These narratives involve the process of creating a coherent statement about family events, the exchange of information among family members, and the attribution of meaning to family experiences. Family narratives are considered part of the dynamic process of imparting family values, family beliefs, and family expectations that will affect family functioning. We have focused most of our discussion on the couple or parent input into narrative construction. But we also are very interested in the relation of such stories to the development of children in the family. The multiple dimensions of narratives may impact directly on the child's development through proximal interaction, or may reflect family process that is more distal to the child's experience but serves to regulate child development indirectly. We are not proposing that family narratives cause adaptive functioning in families. We are proposing, however, that family narratives provide a window into how families come to define themselves and that the active process of family storytelling is linked to important parameters of the family system.

A central goal of the FNC was to create a multidimensional system of narrative analysis that would be sensitive to different domains of family process. The aim was to provide a descriptive foundation for the study of family narratives. Attempts were made to examine both the direct relation between narrative dimensions and family functioning, as well as more indirect effects of family narratives serving a regulatory function. The initial sets of analyses were aimed at determining the feasibility of a multidimensional system of narrative analysis across all sites. Follow-up analyses examined the relation between the three dimensions of family narrative and family functioning within each of the study sites. The consortium's narrative coding system is not linked to a single theoretical bias, but rather is a multidisciplinary system that may be applied by a variety of researchers addressing different aspects of family process. A variety of interview techniques were used across the sites and the coding system was developed to apply to the broad range of questions asked of the families. (The interview protocols are presented in Appendix A. The interview protocol for the Washington, DC study may be found in Wamboldt & Wolin, 1989.) The intent of the project was to create a system that could be applied to various structured and semi-structured interviews.

Although we endeavored to develop a coding system that could be applied across settings and that could incorporate a number of theoretical perspectives, we realized that the coding scheme was embedded within our own cultural understanding of families and family process. Narratives by themselves, however, are not completely constrained by culture, and their analysis may indeed prove to be an approach that can be applied to diverse samples of families (Miller et al., 1997). The definitions and descriptions included in the coding scheme, however, are based on the work of others and ourselves (e.g., Fitzpatrick; 1988; Gottman, 1983; Julien, Markman, Lindahl, Johnson, & Van Widenfelt, 1987; Reiss, 1981) that emphasizes the cooperative interchange between couples and the value of safe and trustworthy relationships. It is possible that in different cultures, or subcultures, different values would be highlighted in the coding scheme (e.g., Markus & Kitayama, 1991).

METHOD

We had two major goals in the initial data analysis: first, would it be possible to identify reliable dimensions of family narratives, and second, would it be possible to validate the dimensions by showing relations to other areas of child and family functioning. Data from the four studies were used in our analyses. Given that the Narrative Consortium was a preliminary step in developing a multidimensional method of narrative assessment, it was advantageous in terms of time and effort to make use of existing data sets rather than design new data collection for our first effort (McCall & Appelbaum, 1991). Although the consortium did not rely on using data collected by individuals other than the principal investigators, several key issues of secondary data analysis were addressed. Because we had access to the raw data, either audio- or videotaped interviews, we were not restricted to the original coding schemes of each study. We were, however, restricted to the use of already collected data. A feasibility matrix of dependent variables was constructed, revealing that measures of marital adjustment were collected across all sites and that child factors (primarily behavior adjustment) were measured in two of the four sites. Therefore, two aspects of family functioning could be evaluated in relation to family narratives: marital adjustment and child adjustment. In addition, we could look at the relation between narrative measures and other aspects of family functioning unique to each site, such as family of origin relationships, family affect, openness in adoption, and psychiatric status. Additionally, these studies, as a group, comprised multiple "samples" across the family life cycle.

The unique aspects of each study are reported in the following chapters. Because there were differences in the thematic goals of the studies, sampling procedures, and age of children across the studies, we did not combine the data sets when examining the relation between the narrative dimensions and family functioning. We did choose, however, to combine the data sets to determine reliability of the scales. A brief description of each sample and the procedures used in the individual studies is presented. For more complete sample description, the reader is referred to the individual study chapters in this *Monograph*.

Samples and Procedures

Washington, DC, Couple Formation

Sixty-three premarital couples were recruited for a study on early couple formation. The couples were seen for approximately 4 hours in a larger study on family of origin influences on relationship formation. The couples were conjointly interviewed about their current relationship, as well as their families of origin. The interview portion used for this study focused on the couples' narrative about their relationship, how their family of origin experiences may have affected their choice of partner, and their parents' reactions to their being a couple.

Syracuse Dinnertime Study

Fifty families with at least one child between 5 and 7 years of age participated in the study. Families were videotaped while eating dinner and then interviewed following the meal. The families viewed the videotape of their mealtime and were asked to describe what they saw. The family members were asked to describe how their current meals compared to mealtimes when they were growing up. The parents were then asked to tell their child a story about a dinnertime in their family of origin.

Minnesota Adoption Study

Twenty-seven adoptive families, including the husband, wife, and one target child, were included in the study. The families were evenly distributed across three types of adoptions that differed according to the amount of information and the ways in which it was shared between adoptive parents and birth mothers: confidential, mediated, and fully disclosed. The families were part of a larger study and participated in a home visit that lasted approximately 4 hours. Three interviews were conducted for each family: mothers, fathers, and mothers and fathers conjointly. The interviews focused on the parents' motivation for adoption, experience with the adoptive placement, and experiences and feelings about the level of openness in the adoption.

Providence Family Study

Fifty two-parent families whose youngest child was a toddler were recruited for a study on maternal psychiatric illness and family functioning. Approximately one half of the mothers in the sample were diagnosed with a major depressive disorder and the other half had no diagnosable mental problems. The families were interviewed in their homes and asked about their family of origin traditions, current family practices, and perceptions about their child's development.

Narrative Measures Applied to All Sites

The consortium's narrative dimensions are rated on 5-point scales. Rating scales have been found to be advantageous when attempting to assess broad theoretical constructs such as couple co-construction and family beliefs (Bell & Bell, 1989). The sole use of frequency counts may mask important relations in family process (Bakeman & Gottman, 1987). Implicit in the rating scales was an assessment of *patterns* of interaction, building on existing coding schemes (e.g., Fitzpatrick, 1988; Gottman, 1983; Julien et al., 1987). As pointed out by Markman (1992), global coding schemes are most effective when based on the results of studies that have used microanalytic schemes to identify sequences of behavior.

Coding is based on the use of interview transcripts (checked for accuracy) and review of audio- or videotapes. A three-step process is used in assigning a score to each scale. First, the transcript is fully reviewed. Second, the transcript is rereviewed while viewing the video or listening to the audiotape. Third, specific aspects of the transcript are noted as to behavioral referents for scoring each scale. The assignment of the score follows an evaluation of the list of behavioral referents. Once the behavioral referents have been noted and evaluated, a global code is assigned based on the description provided for each scale point. Each dimension is comprised of several subscales. An abstracted version of the codebook is included in Appendix B.

Narrative Coherence

Narrative coherence refers to how well the individual is able to construct and organize a story. Four distinct qualities are incorporated in narrative coherence: (a) Internal Consistency, (b) Organization, (c) Flexibility, and (d) Congruence of Affect and Content.

Internal Consistency

Internal consistency of the narrative reflects its completeness and how well the different parts of the individual's theory of relationships form a cohesive whole. Narratives range from a disconnected theory full of discrepancies with little rationale to a well developed and integrated theory. Referents noted for internal consistency include unrecognized contradictions, recognized contradictions, explained contradictions, personalized examples, and synthesizing explanations. The scale points include: (a) no theory—none can be identified, (b) unsupported theory—may include some minor unacknowledged contradictions, (c) theory with some support—respondent makes generalizations, (d) theory in process—emergent theory, supported evidence but not integrated, and (e) well-documented theory—must have all indicators of integration.

Organization

Organization refers to the respondent's management of the narrative, with particular attention to statements that convey information as to how points are made within the narrative. An organized narrative provides the listener with a sense of orientation to context and flows smoothly with completed thoughts. Referents for disorganization include scattered comments with no transition, incomplete thoughts, ambiguous referents for who, what, or where, overelaboration, repetitive language, stops and starts, and lack of orienting statements. The scale points include: (a) poor organization—rater has no clear picture of story; (b) moderately poor organization—rater understands most of narrative, based on efforts of the interviewer or other family members to clarify meaning during the interview; (c) moderate organization—rater can understand story, but there may still be some markers of disorganization; (d) moderately good organization—rater can understand story clearly with rare incidence of markers of disorganization; and (e) good organization—individual puts story together in succinct and direct fashion.

Flexibility

Flexibility refers to the respondent's ability to explore new ideas and alternatives. The flexible respondent is able to view issues as others might see them. Positive referents for flexibility include elaboration of alternatives with possibility of action, whereas negative referents for flexibility include rigid statements of conviction. The scale points include: (a) low flexibility (rigid)—individual narrative strongly adheres to one perspective, (b) moderately low flexibility—individual narrative adheres to one perspective with minimal recognition of alternative views, (c) moderate flexibility—individual clearly recognizes more than one perspective, (d) moderately high flexibility—individual elaborates two or more perspectives to issue, and (e) high flexibility (balanced)—individual integrates and resolves two or more perspectives.

Congruence of Affect and Content

This scale assesses the fit between reported actions or thoughts and the emotion expressed in regard to them. Narratives scored high on this scale show a good match between descriptions of events or actions and corresponding emotions, both in the type of affect expressed, and the level of intensity. Tone of voice, facial expressions, and emotional content are major indicators of congruence. Referents for lack of congruence include inappropriate laughter, inappropriate crying, nervous laughter, inappropriate bland or flattened affect, and inappropriate intensity of affect. The scale points include: (a) low congruence—clear mismatch between expressed affect and content of narrative, (b) moderately low congruence—content of narrative and expressed affect frequently do not match, (c) moderate congruence—content and expressed emotions occasionally mismatch, (d) moderately high congruence—content of actions and expressed emotion rarely mismatch, and (e) high congruence—no mismatch.

Narrative Interaction

The Narrative Interaction scales rate how the couple works together in constructing the narrative and are only used when there is a joint interview. We drew upon existing marital coding schemes such as the Rapid Couple Interaction Scoring System (RCISS; Gottman, 1983) and Interactional Dimension Coding System (IDCS: Julien et al., 1987) to aid in forming definitions and to be consistent with previous couple interaction schemes. There are four scales to the Narrative Interaction dimension: (a) Couple Narrative Style, (b) Coordination, (c) Husband Confirmation/Disconfirmation, and (d) Wife Confirmation/Disconfirmation. The Couple Narrative Style and Coordination scales score the couple as a unit. The Husband and Wife Confirmation/Disconfirmation scales are scored separately for each spouse.

Couple Narrative Style

This scale is designed to capture the style and character of the narrative conjointly produced by the couple or family. This code requires attention to the *content* of the story as well as to the couple's storytelling *process*. Negative referents for couple narrative style include discrepancies, differences of opinion, parallel stories, and occasions of anger. Positive referents include additions to the partner's story and synthetic interaction. The scale points include: (a) disengaged—content includes major disagreements and the process is cool and distant, (b) conflictual-disruptive—content includes major disagreements and the process is hot and negative, (c) conflictual-contained—the content includes some discrepancies and the process includes few quickly abated episodes of anger or conflict, (d) cooperative—content includes story that hangs together well and process is pleasant, and (e) collaborative—content includes a story told conjointly richer than told alone and the process is highly collaborative.

Coordination

Coordination is the assessment of how the couple or family works together and the ability and willingness to develop shared solutions and perceptions. Negative referents include disconfirming opinions and exclusions. Positive referents include polite turn-taking, confirmation of opinions, asking for others' opinions, asking for clarification, and "we" statements. The scale points include: (a) very low—family members present as separate and unrelated individuals, (b) low—some separateness among family members, (c) balanced—balance between separateness and connectedness in family relationships, (d) high—family presents itself as a group, and (e) very high—family presents itself as an overinvolved group.

Husband and Wife Confirmation/Disconfirmation

This scale is scored separately for husbands and wives. This scale assesses the degree of confirmation or disconfirmation from each partner in the dyad to the other. In a dyad, individuals differ in conveying a message that the partner and his/her ideas are important, or, alternatively, that the partner and his/her ideas are inferior and unimportant. Negative referents include invalidating behaviors or statements, statements or behaviors that convey indifference, and behaviors or statements that are restrictive of the other's opinion. Positive referents include validating behaviors or statements and behaviors or statements that convey interest. The scale points include: (a) overtly disconfirming—major restriction and/or denial of other's right to think, feel, or speak; (b) moderately disconfirming—moderate restriction of other's right to think, feel, or speak; (c) occasionally disconfirming—occasional mild disconfirmation; (d) occasionally confirming—neutral, polite conversation with no evidence of disconfirmation, but not more than occasional confirmation; and (e) actively confirming—evidence of active confirmation/validation, no disconfirmation.

Relationship Beliefs

The Relationship Beliefs codes represent the way a family's construction of the social world is reflected in the narrative content and style of the interview. There are two scales in the Relationship Beliefs dimension: Relationship Expectations and Interviewer Intimacy.

Relationship Expectations

The Relationship Expectations scale assesses whether the family views relationships as manageable, reliable, and safe. The husband and wife are scored separately for expectations about relationships in their current family and also for expectations associated with their family of origin. Family of origin relationship expectations are coded for how the husband or wife reports relating to his or her family of origin at the time of the interview. Negative referents include statements that relationships are dangerous and unfulfilling, interaction with the social world is avoided, and the family dichotomizes relationships into good or bad. Positive referents include statements that relationships are safe, satisfying, understandable, and opportunities are made to interact with the social world. Scale points include: (a) very low—expectations that relationships are dangerous, threatening, or overwhelming; (b) low—relationships are seen as precarious, trying, or unreliable; (c) moderate—relationships may be met with success, but family tends to categorize into good or bad, black or white; (d) high—relationships are relatively understandable, safe, successful, usually rewarding, and reliable; and (e) very high—relationships are safe, reliable, and fulfilling.

Interviewer Intimacy

The Interviewer Intimacy scale assesses the degree to which the family is open and willing to share personal and affectively sensitive material with the interviewer. Families scoring higher on this scale will characteristically engage the interviewer in a way that leaves the interviewer feeling as if he or she were an old friend of the family. Referents to this scale include hostile comments, an unexplained referent (e.g., naming a person without clarifying relationship), sensitive material mentioned but not elaborated, sensitive material elaborated, and family invites interviewer to participate in conversation. Scale points include (a) hostile—at least one member of the family is overtly hostile to the interviewer, (b) cold—family members present just the facts, (c) stoic—family is polite and responsive but few details are provided, (d) moderately warm—family provides a few details on sensitive or affectively charged experiences, and (e) warm and inviting—family actively includes interviewer in conversation.

TRAINING OF RATERS

Prior to training raters, the principal investigators (PIs) jointly coded a series of transcripts to identify problem scales and to clarify decision rules. Once the PIs were able to reach consensus on a set of transcripts, arrangements were made to train naive coders. The raters and PIs from each site attended a 2½ day workshop. The workshop entailed a general orientation to narrative analysis, an overview of the Consortium narrative scales, and practice at rating a common set of narratives. The PIs originally coded two interviews from each site and a master rating was reached through consensus. The master ratings then were used to train the naive raters to the coding scheme. The raters were advanced graduate or postdoctoral students in either psychology, family studies, or child psychiatry. The raters had considerable clinical experience with families and were chosen, in part, because of their sensitivity to family interaction patterns and ability to detect subtle nuances in couple communication. Following the training workshop, site specific training was conducted and interrater reliability was established at each site. Training at each site included a careful examination of the interview protocol, discussions about the interpretive task associated with the interview, and the expectable range of interview responses at each site. The site-specific training was conducted over several weeks and averaged approximately 20 hours of training beyond the workshop. At three of the four sites, interrater reliability was established between the site PI and graduate assistant. At the Minnesota site, interrater reliability was established between two graduate assistants across all the interviews. In all cases, the raters had not been involved in the initial data collection and were naive to characteristics of the families other than that revealed in the interviews.

Interrater reliability was determined at each site based on paired ratings of 10–27 cases. Cohen's κs are presented in Table 1. In three of the four sites, the interrater reliability was based on interviews conducted with the couple. At the Minnesota site, two sets of interrater reliability estimates were calculated. The first set was calculated according to interviews conducted

TABLE 1

INTERRATER RELIABILITY AT FOUR SITES (COHEN'S κ)

	Site				
	Washington, DC	Syracuse	Minnesota		Providence
Interview Setting	Couple	Couple	Couple	Individual	Couple
Narrative Scale					
Narrative Coherence:					
Husband					
Internal Consistency	.74	.72	.82	.85	.92
Organization	.83	.85	.76	.77	.87
Flexibility	.75	.79	.89	.80	.91
Congruence	.88	.90	.86	.78	.67
Wife					
Internal Consistency	.72	.70	.82	.85	.81
Organization	.80	.82	.76	.77	.71
Flexibility	.78	.80	.89	.80	.87
Congruence	.90	.85	.86	.78	.89
Narrative Interaction:					
Couple Narrative Style	.94	.91	.90		.96
Coordination	.93	.90	.87		.94
Husband					
Conf/Disconfirmation	.89	.79	.84		.89
Wife					
Conf/Disconfirmation	.87	.85	.84		.81
Relationship Beliefs:					
Relationship Expectations					
Husband Current Family	.91	.88	na		.74
Husband Family of Origin	.82	.79	na		.82
Wife Current Family	.90	.88	na		.93
Wife Family of Origin	.83	.84	na		.57
Interviewer Intimacy	.83	.80	.86		.83

na—Sample size too small to complete rating for this scale.

with the husband or wife alone, and the second set was calculated according to conjointly conducted interviews. Across all sites, interrater reliability estimates were in the good to excellent range (Fleiss, 1981).

RESULTS

We used a two-step data analytic strategy to explore the narrative scale scores. Our first strategy was to consider the reliability of the narrative scales and the relation among scales. For these analyses, the data across the four sites were pooled to examine the overall structure of the coding scheme. The second data-analytic strategy was site specific. Each site conducted analyses to determine the relation between the narrative scales and local measures of child and family functioning. The site-specific findings are linked to the theoretical perspective and objectives of each research project. These data are presented in individual chapters that follow.

The first cross-site analysis we conducted was primarily descriptive. Frequency distributions for each scale were examined to determine whether the scales were distributed normally and whether all scale points had been used. Descriptive statistics are presented in Table 2. In most cases all points of each scale were used and the distributions were relatively normal, although somewhat positively skewed. In almost every instance all scale points were used by all sites, indicating that there was sufficient variability used in each scale (see Table 2).

Summary scores were calculated for Narrative Coherence and Narrative Interaction. The internal consistencies of these summary scores were examined. Narrative Coherence summary scores were comprised of the ratings on Internal Consistency, Organization, Flexibility, and Congruence of Affect and Content. Narrative Interaction summary scores were comprised of the ratings on Couple Narrative Style, Coordination, Husband Confirmation/Disconfirmation, and Wife Confirmation/Disconfirmation. Alpha coefficients are presented in Table 3 for each site and the four sites combined. In general, the scores on individual scales were relatively consistent within dimensions. There were two exceptions, however, that deserve comment. By site, the lowest alphas were found in Washington, DC, for husband and wife narrative coherence. Wives' narrative coherence, in particular, was marked by little to nonexistent correlation among individual scales. Because the same pattern did not hold across sites, we were led to believe that the narratives of the wives in the Washington, DC, sample were somehow different than in the other sites. Upon reflection, it became apparent that the beginning couples in the Washington, DC, sample were just beginning to put together the story of their relationship and in this respect did not have, nor

TABLE 2

Scale	Range	Mean	Standard Deviation
Narrative Coherence:			
Wife			
Internal Consistency	1–5	3.20	1.19
Organization	1–5	3.30	1.00
Flexibility	1–5	2.77	1.07
Congruence	1–5	3.89	1.01
Husband			
Internal Consistency	1–5	3.34	1.17
Organization	1–5	3.25	1.04
Flexibility	1–5	2.60	1.12
Congruence	1–5	3.83	1.03
Summary Score			
Wife	5–20	13.23	2.81
Husband	5–20	13.09	3.18
Narrative Interaction:			
Couple Narrative Style	1–5	3.60	0.74
Coordination	1–5	2.98	1.09
Wife Confirmation	1–5	3.81	0.86
Husband Confirmation	1–5	3.80	0.84
Summary Score	6–20	14.41	2.97
Relationship Beliefs:			
Wife			
Current Family	1–5	3.82	0.98
Family of Origin	1–5	3.32	1.11
Husband			
Current Family	1–5	3.83	1.02
Family of Origin	1–5	3.13	1.13
Interviewer Intimacy	1–5	3.43	0.82

TABLE 3

SCALE RELIABILITY (CRONBACH'S α) FOR EACH SITE

	Site					
	Washington, DC	Syracuse	Minnesota		Providence	Combined
Interview Setting	Couple	Couple	Couple	Individual	Couple	Couple
Narrative Scale:						
Husband Coherence	.50	.70	.77	.67	.99	.71
Wife Coherence	.06	.53	.58	.76	.87	.57
Narrative Interaction	.71	.80	.73		.93	.78

would we expect, a well developed and thus coherent account of their journey together. The chapter by Wamboldt further addresses this issue.

The second aspect of the alpha analysis that deserves comment is that wives' narratives, overall, tended to be less consistent within the coherence dimension. The relative variability within the subscales of Narrative Coherence for wives was noted and further analyses took this variability into account.

As discussed in this chapter, the coding scheme was derived to incorporate three dimensions: Narrative Coherence, Narrative Interaction, and Relationship Beliefs. We considered the Narrative Coherence and Narrative Interaction dimensions to reflect process level aspects of narrative constructions. On the level of coherence, the process of constructing a story and providing evidence to support the story was evaluated. On the level of interaction, the ways in which the couple worked together to tell their stories was evaluated. Relationship Beliefs, on the other hand, are more strongly content based than the other dimensions. The degree to which the content of the narrative reveals details of family life to the interviewer and the degree to which the content of the narrative included depictions of rewarding and trustworthy relationships is evaluated on this dimension. Therefore, we were unsure whether Relationship Beliefs would be related to the other process dimensions.

We sought to establish a measurement model that would reflect the separate dimensions of the coding scheme and their interrelationships by conducting a confirmatory factor analysis (Bollen, 1988). We constructed a measurement model and tested it separately for husbands, wives, and the couple. We reasoned that since narrative coherence is considered a property of the individual, husband and wife narrative coherence would not necessarily be related to each other. Alternatively, because the narratives were constructed between the husband and wife, then interaction could influence the coherence of the narrative. Therefore, a couple's model was tested incorporating husband coherence, wife coherence, and narrative interaction. We did not include a third strategy that would have compared husbands and wives. When we examined the descriptive statistics, there were few differences between men and women in terms of mean level and variability in the narrative measures. Furthermore, in this preliminary analysis we did not have any hypotheses that would predict systematic differences between men and women.

Our initial task was to determine whether Narrative Coherence, Narrative Interaction, and Relationship Beliefs constituted three distinct aspects in the measurement of family narratives. Following the recommendations of Bollen (1988) and Loehlin (1987) we used a confirmatory factor analysis approach to determine our measurement model. Furthermore, because each site had used a different sampling technique and did not have comparable

TABLE 4

INTERCORRELATIONS OF NARRATIVE SCALES FOR HUSBANDS

	Narrative Scales							
	(1)	(2)	(3)	(4)	(5)	(6)	(7)	(8)
(1) Internal Consistency		.74	.50	.12	.09	.06	.19	−.14
(2) Organization			.39	.11	.10	.01	.21	.06
(3) Flexibility				.34	.28	.26	.32	.05
(4) Congruence					.46	.49	.45	.29
(5) Coordination						.60	.46	.49
(6) Couple Narrative Style							.50	.46
(7) Husband Confirmation/ Disconfirmation								.40
(8) Wife Confirmation/ Disconfirmation								

demographics we used the covariance among measures as part of the measurement model (Bollen, 1988; Loehlin, 1987).

We attempted to test the measurement model including Narrative Coherence, Narrative Interaction, and Relationship Beliefs as separate latent variables using LISREL as our statistical package. The three-factor measurement model could not be successfully fit for husbands ($\chi^2(26) = 60.49$, $p = .0001$, $N = 126$), wives ($\chi^2(26) = 61.22$, $p = .0001$, $N = 126$) or husbands and wives combined ($\chi^2(26) = 80.86$, $p = .0002$, $N = 126$).[1] We examined the residuals and determined that Relationship Beliefs were, indeed, not systematically related to the overall model. Therefore we dropped Relationship Beliefs and conducted further model testing using only the scores from the Narrative Coherence and Narrative Interaction scales.

The correlation matrix for the husbands of the combined sites is presented in Table 4. For husbands, the initial measurement model of Narrative Coherence and Narrative Interaction was confirmed by the factor analysis, $\chi^2(13) = 11.95$, $p = .53$, $N = 166$, Goodness of Fit Index (GFI) = .98, Adjusted Goodness of Fit Index (AGFI) = .96, Root Mean Square Residual = .04. A schematic representation of the model is presented in Figure 1.

The correlation matrix for the wives of the combined sites is presented in Table 5. The same measurement model was run for wives as for husbands, and resulted in a poor fit, $\chi^2(19) = 61.22$, $p = .0001$, $N = 165$. We examined the standardized residuals and modification indices indicated by LISREL and it was apparent that the subscales of Flexibility and Congruence of

---

[1] The sample size for the model including Relationship Beliefs is smaller than in the other models due to the coding restrictions at the Minnesota site for the couple interview.

29

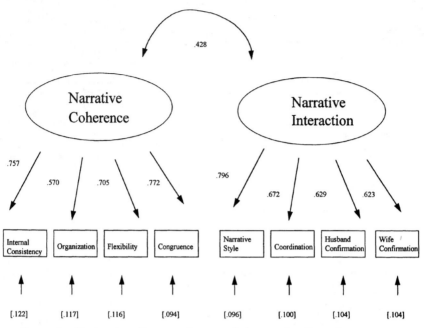

FIGURE 1.—Husband confirmatory factor analysis narrative dimensions.

TABLE 5

INTERCORRELATIONS OF NARRATIVE SCALES FOR WIVES

	Narrative Scales							
	(1)	(2)	(3)	(4)	(5)	(6)	(7)	(8)
(1) Internal Consistency		.40	.37	.15	.17	.28	.12	.26
(2) Organization			.15	.13	.22	.30	.22	.12
(3) Flexibility				−.11	.03	.14	.04	.25
(4) Congruence					.18	.35	.34	.25
(5) Coordination						.81	.44	.41
(6) Couple Narrative Style							.74	.74
(7) Husband Confirmation/ Disconfirmation								.47
(8) Wife Confirmation/ Disconfirmation								

Affect and Content did not fit the latent variable of Narrative Coherence. The model was run again, dropping the two indicated scales and a good fit was found, $\chi^2(8) = 9.68$, $p = .29$, $N = 165$, GFI = .97, AGFI = .97, Root Mean Square Residual = .03. A schematic representation of the model is presented in Figure 2.

A third measurement model was tested combining the scores of the husband and wife. The covariance matrix is presented in Table 6. Because the model for wives did not include Flexibility and Congruence of Affect and Content, these scales were dropped for the combined model. The model resulted in a good fit, $\chi^2(17) = 22.78$, $p = .16$, $N = 165$, GFI = .97, AGFI = .93, Root Mean Square Residual = .04. We were somewhat concerned that one of the parameter estimates (Husband Internal Consistency) slightly exceeded a value of 1.00. According to Bollen (1988) a parameter estimate slightly greater than 1.00 can occur when there is a relatively small sample size or if the model is overspecified. In the case of overspecification, the Non-Normed Fit Index (NNFI) should provide an indication of whether the model is indeed a reasonable fit (Bollen, 1988). The NNFI for the model was .97, suggesting that the model was a reasonable fit given the relatively small sample size. A schematic representation is presented in Figure 3.

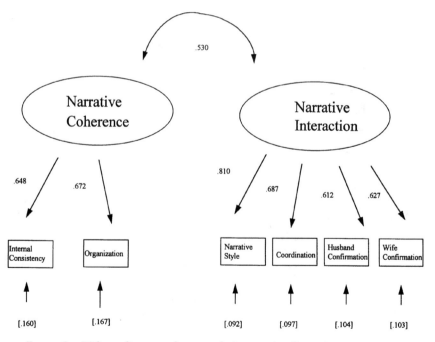

FIGURE 2.—Wife confirmatory factor analysis narrative dimensions.

31

TABLE 6

COVARIANCE MATRIX FOR HUSBAND AND WIFE MODEL

	Narrative Scales							
	(1)	(2)	(3)	(4)	(5)	(6)	(7)	(8)
(1) Couple Narrative Style	1.05							
(2) Coordination	0.63	1.17						
(3) Husband Confirmation/ Disconfirmation	0.39	0.38	0.69					
(4) Wife Confirmation/ Disconfirmation	0.43	0.35	0.31	0.70				
(5) Husband Internal Consistency	0.34	0.21	0.25	0.17	1.41			
(6) Husband Organization	0.21	0.12	0.22	0.14	0.66	1.05		
(7) Wife Internal Consistency	0.38	0.23	0.11	0.23	0.46	0.28	1.37	
(8) Wife Organization	0.34	0.24	0.17	0.08	0.33	0.20	0.49	0.94

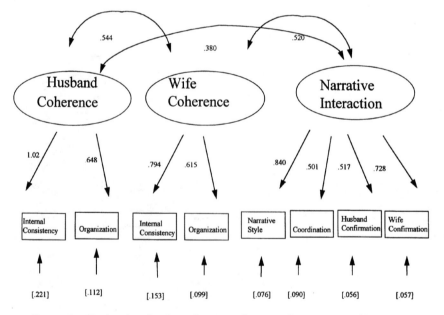

FIGURE 3.—Husband and wife confirmatory factor analysis narrative dimensions.

The results of the confirmatory factor analyses suggest that separate dimensions of Narrative Coherence and Narrative Interaction could be identified. Furthermore, the individual measures of narrative coherence were related to how the couple interacted together to construct their stories.

We were interested in whether these narrative process dimensions also might be related to the ways in which relationships were depicted in the stories. Correlations were generated between Relationship Beliefs and the Narrative Coherence and Narrative Interaction dimensions. These correlations are presented in Table 7. For the husband, the relative coherence of his story was only moderately related to how trustworthy he depicted relationships in his current family, positively related to how rewarding his wife depicted relationships in their family, and to how open and inviting the husband was with the interviewer. For the wife, a similar pattern was found in that the coherence of her story was related to how rewarding she depicted relationships in her family and how open she was to the interviewer. Couples who are able to construct a coherent account of family experiences tend to share this information more readily with an outsider, the interviewer, and tend to describe family relationships as sources of pleasure and reward.

In addition to how the individuals create coherent accounts of their families, the ways in which the couple works together to tell their stories was

TABLE 7

INTERCORRELATIONS OF NARRATIVE DIMENSIONS

		Narrative Scales						
		(1)	(2)	(3)	(4)	(5)	(6)	(7)
	Narrative Coherence:							
(1)	Husband							
(2)	Wife	.41***						
(3)	Narrative Interaction	.31***	.37***					
	Relationship Beliefs							
	Relationship Expectations:							
(4)	Husband Current Family	.19*	.11	.28***				
(5)	Husband Family of Origin	.05	.01	.14	.19*			
(6)	Wife Current Family	.28***	.33***	.37***	.55***	.23**		
(7)	Wife Family of Origin	.16	.21*	.17	.22*	.07	.40***	
(8)	Interviewer Intimacy	.43***	.33***	.37***	.27**	.07	.21**	.05

* $p < .05$.
** $p < .01$.
*** $p < .001$.

related to how open they were with the interviewer and their expectations for rewarding relationships in the family. Comparatively, there were few positive relations between how husbands and wives described their family of origin and other narrative measures. An interesting exception was a positive relation between how rewarding wives considered relationships in their family of origin with their expectations for rewarding relationships in their current family.

The results of the confirmatory factor analysis revealed that whereas Congruence of Affect and Content and Flexibility were associated with the latent variable of Narrative Coherence for husbands, the same pattern did not hold for wives. To examine whether Congruence of Affect and Content and Flexibility may be related to the other narrative dimensions, correlations were generated (see Table 8). For wives, Congruence of Affect and Content was related to all of the narrative dimensions except for Relationship Expectations of the husband's family of origin and minimally related to Interviewer Intimacy. For husbands, a similar pattern was evident but the strength of the correlations were considerably weaker than for wives. Flexibility was related to the dimensions of Narrative Coherence and Interviewer Intimacy for both husbands and wives, but to Narrative Interaction only for husbands.

TABLE 8

CORRELATIONS BETWEEN NARRATIVE DIMENSIONS AND CONGRUENCE OF
AFFECT AND CONTENT AND FLEXIBILITY FOR HUSBANDS AND WIVES

	Congruence of Affect and Content		Flexibility	
	Husband	Wife	Husband	Wife
Narrative Coherence:				
Husband	.37***	.23**	.76***	.20**
Wife	.15	.18*	.38***	.72***
Narrative Interaction	.36***	.34***	.30**	.12
Relationship Beliefs:				
Relationship Expectations				
Husband Current Family	.17	.35***	.14	.10
Husband Family of Origin	.23**	.04	.03	−.10
Wife Current Family	.23**	.31***	.17*	.18*
Wife Family of Origin	.18*	.31***	−.01	.02
Interviewer Intimacy	.24**	.18**	.38***	.21**

* $p < .05$.
** $p < .01$.
*** $p < .001$.

34

SUMMARY

The cross-site data analyses support, in general, our assumption that the Consortium's coding scheme could be reliably applied to four different samples that had been interviewed using four different strategies. A notable exception was the low level of internal consistency found in the coherence scales for the Washington, DC, site. All of the scale points were used across the sites and the distribution of scores was relatively normal. We were encouraged that, despite different interview formats and different samples, it was possible to reliably identify distinct dimensions of the narrative process. Furthermore, measures of coherence based on individual accounts of family experiences (i.e., Narrative Coherence) were related to the directly observable way that couples constructed their stories (i.e., Narrative Interaction). In this regard, the private insider's view of the family could be ascertained in a way that also was reflected in how the family behaved with each other. The relative tensions between the insider and outsider view of the family (e.g., Sigafoos, Reiss, Rich, & Douglas, 1985) has been of considerable concern to family researchers for a long time. Although we cannot address all the subtle nuances of this debate, we are encouraged that when an individual is called upon to interpret family experiences, the coherence of these accounts also is related to how the couple behaves with each other.

We encountered some difficulties in identifying a measurement model that could be applied equally to husbands and wives. For men, the four coherence subscales were interrelated, but the coherence of the wives' narrative appeared to be comprised of two distinct aspects, organizational and affective. We were unable to combine these features when considering the wives' narrative coherence. Furthermore, the different aspects of coherence that we are proposing did not reliably combine together when wives were telling stories about newly developed family relationships in the Washington, DC, sample, as opposed to more long-term relationships in the other groups. This may be a weakness in the measure, or our conceptualization of the different aspects of coherence. It also may be that the narrative process is more homogeneous for men than for women and is susceptible to developmental influences in family relationships. Men and women may also differ in the ways in which they create coherent narrative accounts, with women emphasizing relational and affective bonds and men emphasizing instrumental acts (Gilligan, 1982; Tannen, 1994). Future research may be directed toward examining gender differences in family narratives. Further discussion of this point is included in Chapter 2.

The relatively small sample size precluded us from testing additional models that may provide more insight into the structure of the narrative dimensions. Future efforts are warranted to include larger samples where issues of gender and method variance may be reliably assessed.

The Relationship Beliefs scales were found to be related to the Narrative Style and Narrative Coherence scales; however, in the overall analyses, it is difficult to determine whether Relationship Beliefs are making a contribution above and beyond coherence and interaction in the assessment of family narratives. Site specific analyses will more clearly address the possible mediating role of Relationship Beliefs.

From a developmental and family systems perspective, we had expected the depiction of family of origin relationships to be more closely related to other aspects of the narrative. In devising the scales, we felt that it was important to distinguish between how relationships were described in the current family as contrasted with the family of origin. We had hoped to identify how current family representations might provide a buffer from harmful family of origin representations. When we examined the relations between family of origin expectations and other narrative indices, however, we found few significant correlations. It may be that the representations of family of origin experiences are too far removed from the task of creating a coherent account of family experiences. It also may be that the types of interviews used in these studies did not delve into enough depth when considering how the family of origin may affect current family representations.

We conducted the cross-site analyses to establish the reliability and structure of the narrative scales before we moved to test their validity. Now that we have a reasonable picture of how the scales interrelate with each other, we can move on to determine how they relate to other developmentally important domains. The following chapters will report the relations between the narrative scales and the measures of child and family functioning found in each of the four projects in our collaboration.

II. CO-CONSTRUCTING A MARRIAGE: ANALYSES OF YOUNG COUPLES' RELATIONSHIP NARRATIVES

Frederick S. Wamboldt

Marriage, without doubt, is an embarkation of enormous developmental importance. It seems especially probable that the social cognitions, relationship schemas, and interactional patterns constructed early in a new couple's relationship are key determinants of the outcome of this voyage. In this chapter, I present results obtained using the Consortium's rating scales on narrative data previously collected from a sample of premarital couples to examine how the Narrative Coherence, Interaction, and Relationship Beliefs scales relate to other aspects of the young couples' families of origin and developing relationships.

Perhaps the most developed proposal concerning the role of narrative processes in early marital development is contained in Berger and Kellner's (1964) stimulating and provocative essay, "Marriage and the Construction of Reality," in which they proposed that the central task of early marriage is to engage in a transformative narrative. Specifically, the two individuals' developmental task is to communicate, share, and conversationally redefine the "realities" they brought with them into their relationship, and thereby, construct a new, co-constructed "reality." In their view, this new reality is a perceptual consensus that defines for the couple the nature of the world in which they live as well as their own place and identity within that world. Furthermore, they proposed that this consensus is gradually and painstakingly constructed through an active, transactional process in which each person contributes his or her perception of events, including events from each person's past as well as those currently happening, with the couple repeatedly "talking through" any perceptual disparities present as part of their reality constructing "conversation." This essay concludes with the authors proposing that the outcome of the couple's effort to construct such

37

an intimate consensual reality is the primary determinant of the psychosocial outcome for not only the individuals but also the relationship they form.

The Berger and Kellner proposition for "reality construction" within marriages is a complex one, in that it suggests that both individual-level and couple-level processes are at work. First, individuals should vary in their ability to "get their minds around" and articulate to their partner key aspects of the socioemotional representations of their prior "realities" or relationship experience, especially those from their families of origin. In other words, individuals who can more coherently articulate their past and present "reality" should be better at promoting the development of a shared, conjoint "reality" with their partner. Similarly, individuals who view relationships as more safe and masterable should be more prone to engage in such "conversations" with their partners than those individuals who view relationships as more risky or unpredictable. Second, couples should vary in the degree to which their modes of interactional process allow and foster such co-constructive "conversations" to proceed. In other words, couples whose interactional process is more collaborative should be more able to co-construct a marriage. Accordingly, we propose that the Consortium's Narrative Coherence and Relationship Belief scales appear analogous to these individual-level processes, whereas the Narrative Interaction scales should tap into these interpersonal processes. All are predicted to be associated with aspects of couples' concurrent relationship status.

Berger and Kellner's propositions have received some support from several recent studies examining aspects of marital narratives and marital/family outcomes. Three studies have examined characteristics of conjointly produced narratives. Buehlman, Gottman, and Katz (1992) used data from a conjoint marital interview to predict the couple's subsequent marital status. Both linguistic (e.g., the coded level of "we-ness" expressed) and thematic (e.g., "Glorifying the Struggle") features of the narratives were found to be associated with marital status 3 years later. Similarly, Veroff, Sutherland, Chadiha, and Ortega (1993) reported that newlywed couples who were coded as using more relationship-oriented (rather than individual) emotional expression in their narratives were more satisfied with their marriage when followed up 2 years later. Finally, Oppenheim, Wamboldt, Gavin, Renouf, and Emde (1996) found that couples whose conjoint narratives of their child's birth were more emotionally coherent and expressive had higher concurrent and longitudinal marital satisfaction.

A final study (Owens et al., 1995) examined individuals' narratives in a unique fashion and provides perhaps the most direct test to date of the "reality construction" proposition. They separately interviewed the members of 45 premarital, engaged couples using the Adult Attachment Interview (AAI; Main & Goldwyn, 1984; Main, Kaplan, & Cassidy, 1985) to assess current mental representations of childhood experiences and relationships and a newly developed Current Relationships Interview (Crowell, 1990) designed to assess each person's mental representations concerning attachment to their current partner. They interpreted the findings of greater concordance between partners on the Current Relationship Interview ratings of security/insecurity (78%) as compared with partner's concordance on AAI ratings (56%) as supporting that models of relationship are co-constructed. Furthermore, they found that individuals whose partners had secure attachment ratings were more likely to receive secure ratings on the current relationship than those whose partners had insecure childhood attachment ratings. Presumably this occurred because the presence of one person who could securely and coherently discuss his or her past allowed that individual to help his or her partner with a less secure childhood attachment status to achieve a secure current relationship rating during their conjoint co-constructive conversations. Conversely, an individual with an insecure childhood rating doubled the likelihood that the partner with a secure childhood rating would be rated as having an insecure current relationship.

In this present study, the Narrative Consortium's rating scales were applied to narratives collected from seriously attached and/or engaged premarital couples. The intent of this study was to examine the descriptive statistics and psychometric properties of the Consortium's scales in such couples, as well as to explore further the Berger and Kellner (1964) propositions concerning individual-level and interpersonal processes in marital development. A number of specific predictions were made for this study. First, it was predicted that couples who are able to successfully co-construct narratives about their past and current relationships would be more satisfied with their current relationship. Accordingly, it is hypothesized that greater Narrative Coherence, better Relationship Expectations about the Current Family (i.e., their premarital relationship), and better Narrative Interaction will be associated with greater self-reported concurrent relationship satisfaction and lower relationship instability. Second, it was predicted that individuals who reported more positive family of origin experiences and closer relationships with their parents would be coded as having more trust and security in their family of origin relationships (i.e., coded as showing greater Relationship Expectations for the Family of Origin). Finally on a more exploratory front, we examine whether individuals from more supportive and positive families of origin are more likely to show greater Narrative Coherence and better Narrative Interaction.

METHODS AND PROCEDURES

Sample

Participants in this study were 63 premarital couples recruited through radio, television, and newspaper advertisements in metropolitan Washington, DC. Criteria for inclusion included couples in which both members: were between 18 and 35 years of age, considered themselves "seriously attached" if not actually engaged to be married, and had not previously been married. The mean age for males was 25.5 years (SD = 3.7), for females, 24.4 (SD = 2.8). The mean length of relationship for the couples was 26.8 months (SD = 21.4). Concerning race, 90.5% of the males were White, and the remaining 9.5% of the males were Black; whereas 87.3% of the females were White, 9.5% were Black, and 3.2% were Hispanic. Regarding religion, 44.4% of the men were Protestant, 33.3% were Catholic, 15.9% were Jewish, and 6.4% declared other or no religious affiliation. Among the females, 38.1% were Protestant, 33.3% were Catholic, 11.1% were Jewish, and 17.4% declared other or no religious affiliation. The average education level for males was 16.3 years (SD = 2.1), and for females was 15.9 years (SD = 1.6), with 12.1% of males and 22.0% of females currently being students. Because approximately one fifth of the participants were students, socioeconomic status of males and females was based on their parents' occupation and education. Using the Hollingshead Four Factor Index of Social Status, the males' origin families fell into the following categories: 40.7% in Class I, 37.3% in Class II, and 22% in Class III. Females' origin families were classified as follows: 49.2% in Class I, 33.9% in Class II, 10.2% in Class III, 5.1% in Class IV, and 1.7% in Class V. The marital status of the males' parents was as follows: 65.1% remained married, 23.8% were divorced, and 11.1% had been separated by death. Among the females' parents, 73% remained married, 22.2% were divorced, and 4.8% had been separated by death.

Procedures

Couples first were seen in a laboratory at the George Washington University Center for Family Research for approximately 4 hours of testing. This included a variety of interviews, self-report measures, and videotaped interaction procedures designed to gather information about each individual's origin family as well as the couple's new relationship. Informed consent was obtained from all participants, and couples were paid for their participation.

Measures

Relationship Narratives

All couples were administered a semistructured, conjoint interview that inquired about characteristics of their current relationship as well as each of their families of origin (Wamboldt & Wolin, 1989). Specific probes and follow-up questions were used to gather information from each person concerning the following areas: (1) a brief description of their relationship, including how they met, challenges they weathered as a couple, and the current status of their relationship; (2) their perceptions of the influence of their respective family backgrounds, including relevant similarities and differences between their families, what they would most want to conserve/change of their family backgrounds; (3) given their family background, do they see their partner as a particularly good or meaningful choice; and (4) their parent's/sibling's reactions to their being a couple. Interviews lasted approximately 60 min, with a range of 48 to 92 min.

These conjoint narratives were coded using rating scales developed by the Narrative Consortium. Ten interviews were utilized for coder training. The remaining 53 interviews were coded by the trained coder. Fourteen of these remaining interviews (25%) were coded by a second coder to establish interrater reliability.

Quality of the Family of Origin — The Family Environment Scale (Moos & Moos, 1986)

The Family Environment Scale is a widely used measure of the social environment of families, containing 10 subscales. High internal consistencies have been reported for each subscale, with Cronbach's αs ranging from .69 to .86 (Moos & Moos, 1986). Given that the young adult subjects in this sample were in the process of leaving their family of origin and forming a new family, they were instructed to rate their family of origin as they would have the last time they were regularly interacting with that family (Carpenter, 1984, reviews such use of family questionnaires). Based on a principal components factor analysis, these 10 subscales were combined into two summary dimensions: Positive Family (cohesiveness, expressiveness, conflict, active-recreational orientation, and intellectual-cultural orientation) and Rule-Oriented Family (achievement orientation, moral-religious emphasis, organization, and control). Similar results have been obtained in factor analyses of data from more traditional uses of the Family Environment Scale (e.g., Deal, Halverson, & Wampler, 1989; Plomin, 1986). In this report we use only the Positive Family summary scale. Internal consistency for this scale within this sample was acceptable (α = .69 and .72 for male's and female's reports, respectively).

Closeness to Parents—Intergenerational Solidarity Index (Bengston & Schrader, 1982)

This questionnaire measures two dimensions of perceived solidarity between adult children and their parents: Associational Solidarity—the quality and frequency of talk, shared activities, and mutual aid across the generation; and Affectional Solidarity—the amount of positive feelings such as understanding, trust, respect, and affection across the generation. Participants completed this questionnaire separately for their father and mother. Excellent internal consistencies have been reported for each dimension (αs of .81 and .92, respectively) and were found in this sample (αs of .91/.90 and .73/.80 for Associational Solidarity and αs of .96/.95 and .97/.96 for Affectional Solidarity for fathers/mothers of males and females, respectively). For each parent, the two dimensions were summed, yielding a Closeness to Mother and a Closeness to Father score.

Relationship Satisfaction—The Dyadic Adjustment Scale (Spanier, 1976)

This widely used, 32-item questionnaire is designed to measure the satisfaction with and the adjustment to a marital or serious premarital relationship. Internal consistency has been reported as excellent (α = .96) and was found to be so in this sample as well (α = .88 and .89 for males and females, respectively). Dyadic Adjustment Scale results are reported as the mean for the couple at entry into the study.

Relationship Instability—The Premarital Instability Scale

This scale is a 45-item version of the Marital Instability Scale (Booth, Johnson, & Edwards, 1983), which was modified for use with premarital couples. It inquires about aspects of relationship instability, such as thinking that the relationship was in trouble, considering breaking up, discussing breaking up with outsiders, and so on. Internal consistency of the modified scale was found to be excellent (α = .92 and .91 for males and females in this sample, respectively). Premarital Instability Scale results are reported as the mean for the couple at entry into the study.

RESULTS

Descriptive Statistics for the Narrative Consortium Scales

Prior to testing predictions between narrative scores and relationship measures, descriptive analyses were conducted. As seen in Table 9, the obtained ratings for all the Narrative Consortium scales in this sample

TABLE 9

Descriptive Statistics for the Narrative Consortium Rating Scales at the Washington, DC, Site

Variable	Couple				Women				Men			
	Mean	Range	SD	Reliability	Mean	Range	SD	Reliability	Mean	Range	SD	Reliability
Narrative Coherence:												
Internal Consistency					3.45	1 to 5	1.08	.72	3.62	1 to 5	1.06	.74
Organization					3.70	2 to 5	.80	.80	3.32	2 to 5	.85	.83
Flexibility					2.25	1 to 4	.94	.78	2.38	1 to 5	1.00	.75
Congruence					4.38	2 to 5	.88	.90	4.28	2 to 5	.89	.88
Narrative Interaction:												
Couple Narrative Style	4.08	2 to 5	.70	.94								
Coordination	3.20	1 to 5	1.01	.93								
Confirmation/ Disconfirmation					3.74	2 to 5	.79	.87	3.92	2 to 5	.73	.89
Relationship Beliefs:												
Relationship Expectations												
Current Family					4.00	2 to 5	.86	.90	3.74	1 to 5	1.04	.91
Family of Origin					3.62	2 to 5	.95	.83	3.12	1 to 5	1.09	.82
Interviewer Intimacy	3.38	2 to 5	.66	.83								

were: (a) distributed across at least 4 of the 5 scale points, (b) centered fairly close to the midpoint of the scale (means ranging from 2.25 to 4.38), (c) variable (SDs ranging from .66 to 1.09), and (d) reliably coded (intraclass correlations of the independent ratings by the two coders ranged from .72 to .94).

Despite the expectation that the scales assessing Narrative Coherence all assessed separate yet interrelated dimensions, the actual observed scale scores for male's and female's narratives were poorly correlated (i.e., correlations ranging from −.19 to .25 and .01 to .42, for females and males, respectively). This unexpected independence of these scales also is reflected by the poor internal consistency of the additive summary scales of these ratings (α of .13 and .54 for females and males, respectively). As expected, the Narrative Interaction scales exhibited moderately high intercorrelations ($M = .41$; range of .24 to .63; $\alpha = .73$). Also as expected, the Relationship Belief scales, which were designed to assess beliefs about different, distinct relationships, showed essentially no intercorrelation ($M = .03$, range of −.36 to .32), although 2 of the 10 intercorrelations were statistically significant (Men's Relationship Expectation for Family of Origin and Women's Relationship Expectation for Family of Origin, $r(51) = −.36$, $p = .01$; and Men's Relationship Expectation for Current Family and Interviewer Intimacy, $r(42) = .32$, $p = .04$).

Narrative Ratings and Concurrent Relationship Satisfaction and Instability

Table 10 displays the associations between the narrative ratings and concurrent measures of relationship satisfaction and instability. Contrary to the prediction, no significant correlations were observed between the Narrative Coherence scales and reports of the status of the couples' relationships.

In contrast and as predicted, a number of significant associations were found between the Narrative Interaction scales and relationship status. Couples who coordinated their efforts in constructing their narrative were more satisfied with their current relationship. For both women and men, disconfirmation of the partner's opinions during the interview was related to current relationship instability. On the other hand, women who actively confirmed their partner's opinions were more satisfied with their current relationship.

Finally, as predicted, men and women whose narratives included depictions of their current dyadic relationship as rewarding, predictable, and reliable (i.e., were coded as having more positive Relationship Expectations for Current Family) reported lower relationship instability. Furthermore, men with such narratives also reported that they were more satisfied with their premarital relationship.

TABLE 10

ASSOCIATIONS BETWEEN NARRATIVE RATING SCALE SCORES AND RELATIONSHIP STATUS VARIABLES

	Relationship Measure	
	Satisfaction r ($n = 53$)	Instability r ($n = 48$)
Women's Narrative Coherence		
Internal Consistency	.08	.04
Organization	.03	−.01
Flexibility	−.05	.17
Congruence	−.04	.02
Men's Narrative Coherence		
Internal Consistency	.05	−.08
Organization	−.10	−.08
Flexibility	.02	−.03
Congruence	−.03	.04
Narrative Interaction		
Couple Narrative Style	.22	−.08
Coordination	.33*	−.18
Men's Confirmation/Disconfirmation	.26	−.29*
Women's Confirmation/Disconfirmation	.36**	−.29*
Relationship Beliefs		
Relationship Expectations		
Men's Current Family	.42**	−.32*
Men's Family of Origin	.00	−.10
Women's Current Family	.21	−.31*
Women's Family of Origin	.04	.02
Interviewer Intimacy	.20	−.14

* $p < .05$.
** $p < .01$.

Narrative Ratings and Family of Origin Measures

To examine the associations between the narrative measures and family of origin factors, correlations were generated between the narrative scale scores and each person's self-report of the quality of their family of origin experiences and their perceptions of closeness to their mother and father. These correlations are presented in Table 11.

Only one specific prediction was made concerning these correlations, namely that the ratings of Relationship Beliefs about the Family of Origin would be significantly associated with individual's self-reports of positive family of origin experience and closeness to their mother and father. This, in fact, was observed. Men's ratings of their family of origin experience and

45

TABLE 11

Correlations Between Narrative Rating Scales and Family of Origin Measures[1]

| | Family of Origin | | | | | |
| | Women's Self-Report | | | Men's Self-Report | | |
	POSFAM	CLOSEM	CLOSEF	POSFAM	CLOSEM	CLOSEF
Women's Narrative Coherence						
Internal Consistency	−.04	.03	.12	.04	.10	.08
Organization	−.05	−.13	−.22	−.04	−.21	−.11
Flexibility	.18	.05	.13	−.02	.15	.04
Congruence	.43**	.17	.44**	−.17	−.19	−.15
Men's Narrative Coherence						
Internal Consistency	.25	.27	−.03	.01	.13	.16
Organization	−.14	−.13	−.09	.16	−.02	−.02
Flexibility	.16	.10	.14	.22	.10	−.06
Congruence	.07	−.07	.06	−.07	−.03	.14
Narrative Interaction						
Couple Narrative						
Style	−.03	−.13	−.20	.04	.12	−.12
Coordination	.02	−.11	−.19	.04	.04	.06
Men's Confirm/						
Disconfirmation	−.01	−.05	−.29*	.04	.05	.23
Women's Confirm/						
Disconfirmation	.04	−.04	−.15	−.14	−.19	−.08
Relationship Beliefs						
Relationship Expectations						
Men's Current						
Family	.14	.06	.13	−.09	.02	−.03
Men's Family of						
Origin	−.31*	−.27	−.29*	.49***	.31*	.34*
Women's Current						
Family	−.05	.08	.04	−.03	−.22	−.20
Women's Family of						
Origin	.47***	.47***	.25	−.33*	−.17	−.14
Interviewer Intimacy	.10	.09	.23	.01	.24	.33*

* $p < .05$.
** $p < .01$.
*** $p < .001$.

[1]Positive Family Scores from Family Environment Scale; Closeness to mother and father from Intergenerational Solidarity Index.

relationship with both parents were related to the degree they expressed trust and confidence toward their family of origin in their narrative. Similarly, women's ratings of their family of origin experience and relationship with their mothers were very strongly associated with their Relationship Expectation for Family of Origin scores.

The remainder of the correlations in Table 11 should be considered exploratory analyses. Indeed, overall the most striking finding is the paucity of significant correlations. Several of these, however, merit brief comment. First, with regard to Narrative Coherence, the only consistent set of findings involves the female's narrative congruence. Those women who showed better congruence of their words and emotions rated their families of origin as more positive and reported better current relationships with their fathers. Although only 2 out of the 48 coherence correlations were statistically significant, the fact that both involved the women's narrative congruence and aspects of their family of origin relationships lends some possible credibility to this finding. Second, it is surprising that all six of the cross-correlations (men's narrative Family of Origin Relationship Expectations and wives' self-report; women's narrative Family of Origin Relationship Expectations and men's self-report) were negative (with 3/6 correlations statistically significant).

DISCUSSION

This study examined the performance of the Narrative Consortium's rating scales in a sample of seriously attached and/or engaged premarital couples. Predictions regarding the Relationship Expectations and Narrative Interaction scales were generally supported, whereas there was a surprising and consistent lack of results concerning the Narrative Coherence scales. Overall, the rating scales were well distributed and coded with good to excellent reliability. Accordingly, these differential results will be discussed in terms of the validity of the scales, as well as methodological and conceptual issues related to this particular study.

The Relationship Expectation Scales and Relationship Status

The predictions made concerning the Relationship Expectation for Current Family scales were supported. Specifically, the degree to which men's and women's narratives suggested that they viewed their current relationship to be a safe, predictable, and potentially masterable situation was associated with better self-reported relationship status. These Relationship Expectation scores showed the strongest correlations with relationship instability of any of the narrative measures, and men's scores on this scale also showed the strongest correlation with relationship satisfaction. These findings are particularly intriguing because they move the prediction of premarital development from observations of interactional behavior, per se, to ratings targeted at the individual's perceptions of the relative security/reward potential versus risk/uncertainty of their relationship. These results echo those of Owens and colleagues (1995) using measures derived from attachment theory, and thereby, suggest the need for further research examining the role of beliefs about relationships as predictors of marital development.

The Narrative Interaction Scales and Relationship Status

The predictions concerning the Narrative Interaction scales also received good support, as these scales were consistently related to current relationship status. All these scales showed positive associations with relationship satisfaction and negative correlations with relationship instability. Significant correlations were found for the Coordination and women's Confirmation/Disconfirmation scales with relationship satisfaction, and both men's and women's Confirmation/Disconfirmation scores and relationship instability. These findings appear reminiscent of the well-established linkage between couples' communication practices and their relationship quality and stability (see recent review by Larson & Holman, 1994). Furthermore, as scales reflecting collaborative versus dismissing interpersonal processes appear key, this study leads some credence to Berger and Kellner's (1964) proposition that interpersonal processes that support or undercut couples' efforts at "reality construction" are important to relationship outcome.

Furthermore, because these Narrative Interaction scales are macro-level rating scales that are applied to an entire interpersonal exchange, they are much more simple and time efficient than the microanalytic rating systems typically used in this field of study. Of course, further research is required to assert that these macro-level scales are as good as or better than existing micro-level coding systems (and microanalytic systems will always continue to be the method of choice for certain types of observational research, e.g., when sequential behavioral processes, such as reciprocity or dominance, are examined). Nonetheless, continued efforts toward the development of reliable and valid macro-level rating scales hold promise to open the power of observational methodology to a much broader array of studies in child and family development.

The Narrative Coherence Scales and Relationship Status

Rather striking negative results were found for the Narrative Coherence scales. None were related to the relationship status variables. Furthermore, although these scales were developed with the assumption that they represented separate but interrelated aspects of an overall Narrative Coherence construct, this assumption received only very weak support for the men, and these scales were virtually orthogonal for the women. Why might this be so?

Given the acceptable levels of interrater reliability that were established for the coding process, itself, and the higher internal consistency found for these dimensions at the other consortium sites, it seems possible that coding error may not be the sole explanation. At least four other methodological and conceptual possibilities exist. First, the task used to generate narratives was a conjoint one with no specific steps taken to ensure that aspects of the couple's interactional process did not interfere with the ability of any specific individual to tell his/her story. Owens and colleagues (1995) dealt with this methodological issue by conducting only individual interviews with their couples. Others have argued, however, that in addition to their intrapsychic, representational importance, family narratives when publicly recounted have important social constructive and regulatory functions within relationships (e.g., Berger & Kellner, 1964; Reiss, 1989; Wamboldt & Wolin, 1989). Further work on both the conceptual and methodological fronts needs to be done on the measurement of narrative coherence in conjoint interviews.

Second, there are some indications that this was an atypical sample of premarital couples. Indeed, as a group they appeared somewhat poorly adjusted when compared to community norms for two of the self-report scales used. For example, the couples' mean Dyadic Adjustment Scale scores at study entry (108.8 ± 11.6) approaches the recommended cutoff score of 107 for distinguishing distressed from nondistressed couples (Crane, Allgood, Larson, & Griffin, 1990). Furthermore, when the narrative data were collected, 42% (22/53) of the couples had a Dyadic Adjustment Scale score less than this cutoff score. This almost certainly would increase any confounding between Narrative Interaction and Narrative Coherence (as was proposed in the previous paragraph). In addition, the mean Family Environment Scale Positive Family score for men (17.5 ± 8.5) was significantly below the expected mean (19.8) based on the Family Environment Scale norms (Moos & Moos, 1986). Relationship problems in the family of origin have been shown to lead to worse individual narrative performance on the Adult Attachment Interview (AAI; Main & Goldwyn, 1984; Main, Kaplan, & Cassidy, 1985).

A third, developmental possibility is in line with Berger and Kellner's (1964) reality construction proposition. Specifically, these young couples are telling narratives that are "under construction." It may well be that some individuals have got the organization of their story down but have not thoroughly considered enough of the other possibilities to be considered flexible. Similarly, some individuals may be able to keep their words internally consistent, but not maintain a congruent affect during their story.

Finally, the fact that the intercorrrelations of the Narrative Coherence scales were particularly low for women may be linked to the proposition that women function as the "architects" of their marital relationships. In other words, women's relationship pasts may most influence the rules and regulatory processes that shape the development of their marriages (Chodorow, 1978; Levy, Wamboldt, & Fiese, 1997; Wamboldt & Reiss, 1989; Wamboldt & Wolin, 1989). If such a gender effect is active and at least in some women not fully conscious, their narratives may be the more difficult to fully consolidate, hence the lower internal consistency that was observed.

The Narrative Scales and Family of Origin Variables

As predicted, there was a consistent pattern of associations between how the men and women described the relatively trustworthiness of their family of origin and their own reports about their family of origin relationships. This supports the validity of these particular scales—individuals who rate their families, in general, and relationships with their parents, specifically, in more positive ways were coded as expressing their origin family environments as more safe, predictable, and masterable.

It is surprising, however, that the remainder of the exploratory analyses between the Narrative Consortium rating scales and family of origin measures yielded virtually no other significant correlations. Indeed, several other studies have shown significant associations between family of origin variables and aspects of premarital relationships (Levy, Wamboldt, & Fiese, 1997; Wamboldt & Reiss, 1989). In each of these other studies, however, the measures of the premarital relationships involved in the correlations were totally independent of the couple's self-report, whereas in this study, although coded by independent raters, the raw data were, in fact, primarily verbal reports from the couple. It is possible that a phenomenon similar to the "generational stake" proposition that Bengston and colleagues (Bengston & Kuypers, 1971; Troll & Bengston, 1982) have advanced to explain why parents consistently report closer relationships to their young adult children than the children report with their parents may have distorted either the questionnaire or interview reports of their families of origin by these young adults in ways that restricted the associations between these domains.

Conclusions

Overall, these results should be seen as preliminary, exploratory findings. For example, the most variance explained in this study by a Narrative Consortium scale with a relationship status variable is less than 18%. Although respectable, this is far from overwhelming, given the well-established power of observational measures in contemporary premarital research (see Larson & Holman, 1994). Additionally, this study was not specifically designed to examine the Narrative Consortium's scales and accordingly has a variety of the conceptual and methodological shortcomings as discussed above. Replication and extension of these findings is needed to help resolve a number of important ambiguities.

Nonetheless, when taken as a whole, these results are intriguing for at least two reasons. First, they demonstrate that many of the Narrative Consortium's rating scales have provisional reliability and validity when used to code conjoint interviews of young premarital couples, even though these interviews were not designed to be used specifically with these scales. Second, although most commonly used marital research coding schemes are tied to relatively low-level, molecular behavioral construct (e.g., negative affect, criticism, self-disclosure), the Narrative Consortium's scales for which good validity were demonstrated are more macro-level narrative, and several evaluate understudied, sociocognitive constructs (e.g., the Relationship Expectations scales). As such, these scales may well represent novel measurement strategies for previously hard to tap dimensions of premarital and marital experience. Ongoing efforts designed to further our understanding of the complex set of cognitive, emotional, and interpersonal processes involved in of the role of narrative in early marital development continue to be needed.

III. DINNERTIME STORIES: CONNECTING FAMILY PRACTICES WITH RELATIONSHIP BELIEFS AND CHILD ADJUSTMENT

Barbara H. Fiese and Kathleen A. T. Marjinsky

Unidirectional models of development have been replaced by bidirectional ones, where on the one hand children are affected by the families that raise them and, on the other hand, children actively influence the way they are being raised by their families. From a general systems perspective, both children and families are rule governed systems that seek to maintain stability, at the same time engaging in developmental changes and transitions (Cowan, 1991; Sameroff & Fiese, 1992; Steinglass, 1987). Although the family may consist of multiple subsystems, most attention has been given to the caregiving dyad of parent and child. Notably, the study of attachment relationships has demonstrated that the relationship built between parent and child becomes internalized and regulates the child's behavior throughout childhood (Sroufe, 1983), adolescence (Kobak, Cole, Ferenz-Gillies, Fleming, & Gamble, 1993), and as a parent (Main & Goldwyn, 1984). Stability of the child's behavior and personality is proposed to reside within the individual's internal working models, which serve as templates for future close relationships. From this perspective, representations of the dyad are central to understanding child adjustment and may be accessed through the study of representations of relationships, or "internal working models." These working models frequently are evaluated through a narrative discourse about caregiving relationships as exemplified in the Adult Attachment Interview (AAI; Main, 1991).

An alternative to considering the primary position of the dyad in regulating child adjustment is to consider the family system as a whole. From this perspective, individual child behavior can be understood only as part of broader regulatory processes of the family system aimed at maintaining stability. When considering larger systems, it is important to consider the multiple dimensions inherent in their organization. Such factors as hierarchical organization, delineation of boundaries, role assignment, and affective involvement are seen as family level factors associated with child adjustment (Minuchin, 1974; Wagner & Reiss, 1995). Rather than relying on internal representations of dyadic relationships to explain child adjustment, family systems typically are studied through the direct observation of family interaction patterns. An exemplar of the observational approach is the work of Patterson and colleagues that has identified repetitive patterns of coercive family interaction that are related to antisocial behavior in childhood, adolescence, and adulthood (Dishion, French, & Patterson, 1995; Patterson, 1982).

A focus on either working models of attachment dyads or family level interaction patterns need not be incompatible in understanding the regulation of child behavior. Indeed, they may inform each other. Reiss (1989) has made an important distinction between the represented and practicing family. The *represented* family highlights the internal representation of relationships and how working memories may provide a sense of stability in dyadic relationships. Working models of relationships are developed within the context of the family, are retained in memory, and guide the individual's behavior over time. The *practicing* family, in contrast, stabilizes and regulates family members through observable interaction. The interaction patterns are repetitive and serve to provide a sense of family coherence and identity. Family life not only resides in the minds of individuals, but comes to life in the observed coordinated practices of the group. Reiss has proposed that only through the study of both the practicing and represented family can we truly capture family pathways of adaptation. Indeed, the study of the practicing family calls for conceptualizing working models of relationships not only from the perspective of the dyad but as part of a group practice aimed at preserving family values, beliefs, routines, and rituals.

The study of the practicing family includes direct observation of the family in activities that are repeated over time and serve to provide meaning to family life. The practice of family rituals has been identified as one such powerful organizer of family life (Bossard & Boll, 1950). Family rituals involve not only the practice of routines but also representations of the family's identity and how the family as a system works together (Bennett, Wolin, & McAvity, 1988; Reiss, 1981). The repetitive nature of patterned routines, such as dinnertime, often leads to the creation of distinct images of how family members interact with each other. Empirical support for the regulatory effects of family rituals has been provided by Wolin, Bennett, and colleagues, in a study of families affected by alcoholism. They found that families that preserved distinct family rituals, such as dinnertime, were less likely to have offspring that became alcoholic (Bennett, Wolin, Reiss, & Teitelbaum, 1987; Wolin, Bennett, Noonan, & Teitelbaum, 1980). Family rituals also have been found to be sensitive to developmental changes in the family, for example, marking the transition from the intense caregiving practices with an infant to role assignment and autonomy fostering practices with preschool-age children (Fiese, Hooker, Kotary, & Schwagler, 1993). The practice of meaningful family rituals is proposed to create a sense of belonging that fosters child adjustment and regulates family practices (Fiese, 1992, 1995).

The Syracuse Dinnertime project was aimed at studying how an aspect of the practicing family, family rituals, would be related to child behavior. In addition to the direct observation of family mealtime practices, we incorporated a storytelling task that allowed for an examination of how representations about family practices may be related to marital satisfaction and child behavior. Furthermore, we proposed a model that integrates observable family practices as a mediator of more distal family representations and beliefs. There is considerable evidence that family interaction patterns are related to child behavior (e.g., Patterson, 1982); however, the connection between parent's representations and family interaction has received less attention. We reasoned that the moment-to-moment family interactions close to the child's experience may be directly related to the report of child behavior problems, but that the representation of family relationships would be related to how the family interacted when gathered at the dinner table. We were interested in whether family representations were related to practices, which in turn would be related to child behavior.

The distinction between the practicing and represented family may have methodological implications for the study of family narratives. Previous research on working models of attachment relationships has found a narrative approach useful in understanding child adjustment and continuity of attachment relationships across generations (Crowell & Feldman, 1988; Kobak et al., 1993; Main & Goldwyn, 1984). The representations of secure relationships require a coherent account of the caregiving relationship marked by an openness to process information about self and relationships. The focus of the secure narrative is on the dyad and trustworthiness and felt security between caregiver and child.

Additional narrative aspects may be important when considering the practicing family and family system effects on child adjustment. Because the practicing family includes the coordinated efforts of multiple family members, the narrative task should focus on a family level activity. A distinction can be made between the *act* of storytelling and the images represented in the story. For the practicing family, the act of storytelling includes how the family works together in creating the story and how the family interacts with the social world, as represented by the interviewer. The act of storytelling serves to reinforce the shared social values of the family and support interaction patterns evident across settings. Qualitative aspects of the substance of the story, on the other hand, include markers of narrative coherence and expectations about the rewarding and fulfilling aspects of family relationships.

Incorporating narratives into the study of the practicing family called for three considerations: (a) the nature of the task, (b) connecting narrative practices to observable family practices, and (c) identification of child adjustment factors. First, the nature of the task was devised to focus on a family gathering that would evoke memories of family level processes, not necessarily limited to dyadic relationships. Therefore, the families were asked to tell stories about a dinnertime in their family of origin as well as describe their current dinnertime. Families were observed, unobtrusively, at a mealtime and given the opportunity to review the videotape of their mealtime. Dinnertime, or a representative mealtime, involves the participation of multiple family members, occurs on a regular basis, and serves important functions in the exchange of information in families (Lewis & Feiring, 1982). Dinnertime is considered a patterned family interaction ritual that maintains the family's unique patterns of interaction and organization (Fiese, 1995; Wolin & Bennett, 1984). Second, direct observation of family practices was made consistent with the narrative task. Thus, the narrative task of telling dinnertime stories was compared to the direct observation of dinnertime.

Family interaction patterns may be studied from a moment-to-moment microanalytic perspective or from a more global perspective. When considering family interaction and family practices, it was important to consider existing research on family interaction, family rituals, and child adjustment. Two dimensions have been identified as important in understanding the role of family rituals in fostering child adaptation: routines and meaning (Fiese, 1992, 1995). The dimension of routine includes the ascription of roles and the degree of flexibility in enacting the family ritual. The dimension of ritual meaning includes affective involvement and symbolic significance attached to the family gathering. Observed patterns of affective involvement have been found to be related to marital satisfaction, child adjustment, and family health (Gottman & Levenson, 1992; Katz & Gottman, 1994). For the purposes of this study, the observed family practice of dinnertime was evaluated for the presence of negative and positive family affect.

Child behavior in social settings often is described along internalizing and externalizing dimensions. Internalizing behaviors include social withdrawal, somatic complaints, and feelings of anxiety and depression (Achenbach, 1995). Externalizing behaviors include aggressive behavior, disobedience, and poor impulse control (Achenbach, 1995). These two dimensions have been found to be relatively stable over time, are comorbid in high risk groups, and related to family factors such as marital status and family conflict (Achenbach, Howell, Quay, & Conners, 1991; Katz & Gottman, 1993).

Three questions were addressed in the Syracuse Dinnertime Project. First, would the coherence of the parent's narratives of family practices be

55

related to the report of child behavior problems? The current work of attachment researchers has suggested that the coherence of a mother's narrative about her family of origin attachment relationships is related to her attachment relationship with her child (e.g., Crowell & Feldman, 1988; van IJzendoorn, 1995). A similar question was addressed in this study. It was predicted that parents who tell coherent family stories would report fewer behavior problems in their children. We reasoned that coherent accounts of family practices would signify family stability and order that would be related to child adjustment. Furthermore, we extended this question to examine whether coherence was related to marital satisfaction and family interaction patterns. Preliminary findings suggest that coherence of attachment narratives is related to marital satisfaction (Cohn, Silver, Cowan, Cowan, & Pearson, 1992) and child behavior problems (Cowan, Cohn, Cowan, & Pearson, 1996). We were interested in whether a similar pattern held when directly observing how family members interact with each other.

The second question to be addressed was whether the ways in which the couple worked together in constructing the narrative were related to the ways in which the family interacted at the dinner table. On the one hand, this is a question of external validity. That is, when couples are asked to construct a narrative about family practices, do they use patterns of interaction with each other similar to those that they use when engaged in a routine family event? On the other hand, this question addresses whether dyadic patterns of interaction are consistent with triadic and whole family interactions, a comparison often overlooked in family systems research.

The third question to be addressed was whether expectations about family relationships at routine gatherings would be related to current family practices and child adjustment. Although a direct relation between relationship expectations and child behavior problems might be found, there was also interest in examining the possible mediating role that family practices may have between expectations about relationships and child behavior problems. Current conceptualizations of child adjustment in the family context recognize the multiple pathways by which child behavior is associated with marital and parental factors (Downey & Coyne, 1990; Sameroff & Fiese, 1992). Reiss (1989) proposed that the development of shared beliefs about the family must be supported by the social organization and practices of the family. In this regard, we hypothesized that the shared expectations about relationships would be supported by and mediated by the directly observed affect at the dinner table, which would in turn be related to child externalizing behavior.

METHOD

Sample and Procedure

Participants

Fifty families participated in the Dinnertime Project. The sample was primarily Caucasian (94% White, 4% Black, and 2% Hispanic), which is consistent with community demographics. The sample was primarily middle- and upper-middle-class distributed across four of the five Hollingshead (1975) classifications (6% Class IV, 14% Class III, 36% Class II, 44% Class I). All couples were married. Family size ranged from 1 to 4 children with an average of 2.6 children. The target child in the family ranged in age from 5 to 7 years old, with an average age of 5 years 9 months. Families were recruited through letters sent to parents of kindergarten, first, and second grade children in a predominately middle-class neighborhood, accounting for approximately 80% of the sample. Newspaper announcements also were used as a recruiting strategy.

Procedure

Families were videotaped during the course of a family meal, typically dinner. A research assistant set up the video camera and instructed a family member in the operation of the camera and then left. After the family videotaped their meal, the assistant returned to the family's home and videotaped the family, while they reviewed the tape of their dinnertime. Family members were instructed to comment on the meal and stop the tape when they wished to elaborate on a particular segment. They were asked to pinpoint segments that were fairly typical for their family and segments that might have special meaning to them. Following the viewing of the tape, the family was interviewed about mealtime practices. This interview portion of the study was used for this analysis (see Appendix A). The family was asked to describe their current mealtimes in general, how they compared to other families that they knew, and for the parents, how their current mealtime compared to meals when they were growing up. After the interview, the mother and father were asked to tell a story to their child about a mealtime when the parent was a child. The interviews lasted for approximately 20 min. The interviews were transcribed verbatim and checked for accuracy.

Measures

We used several measures to assess child, marital, and family level functioning.

Child Behavior Checklist (Achenbach & Edelbrock, 1983)

The Child Behavior Checklist (CBCL) is a questionnaire that includes 118 items to assess problem behaviors. The psychometric properties of the checklist, as reported in the manual, include high test-retest reliability, high parent agreement, and discrimination between clinic referred and nonclinic referred children. The CBCL has been applied to the study of nonclinical children and has proven useful in examining the range of externalizing and internalizing problem behaviors in relation to marital satisfaction (Katz & Gottman, 1993). Mothers and fathers independently completed the CBCL.

Dyadic Adjustment Scale

The Dyadic Adjustment Scale (Spanier, 1976) is a 32-item scale which assesses degree of marital satisfaction. A total marital satisfaction score was derived by summing responses to all items. Internal consistency for the total score is reported to be .96. The Dyadic Adjustment Scale has been used extensively in the study of marital satisfaction (e.g., Belsky, Spanier, & Rovine, 1983; Hetherington, 1991; Kurdek, 1991) and is completed separately by husband and wife.

Georgia Family Q-sort

The Georgia Family Q-sort (Wampler, Moore, Watson, & Halverson, 1989) was used to rate the family's interaction at the dinner table. The Georgia Family Q-sort consists of 43 items that are sorted into a forced normal distribution. For the purposes of this study, items that dealt with task-related behaviors were rewritten to conform to the dinnertime setting as the family task. The rewording of the items was discussed with one of the principal developers of the Q-sort (K. Wampler) and was determined to reflect the original intent of the Q-sort. Two raters, naive to the purpose of the study and to the family narratives, were trained on the Q-sort procedure. Spearman-Brown correlation between the raters, following a 2-week training period, was found to be .82. For the purposes of this analysis, cluster scores were derived following the guidelines presented by the authors. A score reflecting positive affect was derived by summing scores for the items reflecting positive affect when the family is together such as "warm, affectionate with each other." A score reflecting negative affect was derived by summing scores for the items reflecting negative affect such as criticisms and conflict. The cluster scores of positive and negative affect have been found to be related to Beaver-Timberlawn ratings of family health (Wampler et al., 1989).

RESULTS

Narrative Coherence and Markers of Family Functioning

To address the first question (would narrative coherence be related to report of child behavior problems, marital satisfaction, and family behavior), correlations were generated among Narrative Coherence, CBCL, Dyadic Adjustment Scale, and Dinnertime Affect. The correlations are presented in Table 12.

There were few significant correlations between the parent's Narrative Coherence scores and the outcome measures. The exception was a negative correlation between maternal Narrative Coherence and total CBCL scores. We wondered whether particular aspects of coherence, rather than the global estimate, may be more closely related to markers of family functioning. Because the confirmatory factor analysis of all four samples suggested that the subscale of Congruence of Affect and Content may be distinguished from the other Narrative Coherence subscales, particularly for women, we chose to conduct exploratory correlational analysis using the Congruence subscale. Correlations were generated among Congruence and marital satisfaction, child behavior problems, and family dinnertime behavior. For husbands, the more affectively congruent their stories, the more satisfied they were in their marriages and the less likely were their families to engage in

TABLE 12

CORRELATIONS BETWEEN NARRATIVE COHERENCE AND INTERACTION
AND MARKERS OF FAMILY FUNCTIONING

	Narrative Coherence				Narrative Interaction
	Total Score		Congruence		
	Husband	Wife	Husband	Wife	Couple
Marital Satisfaction					
Husband	.13	.24	.37*	.22	.15
Wife	.04	.29	.25	−.03	.03
Family Dinnertime Affect					
Positive Affect	.14	.14	.22	−.20	.39**
Negative Affect	−.02	−.19	−.35**	−.24	−.45***
Reported Child Behavior					
Internalizing	−.11	−.26	−.06	−.21	−.10
Externalizing	−.01	−.21	−.30*	−.45***	−.28
Total	.01	−.31*	−.19	−.36**	−.14

*$p < .05$.
**$p < .01$.
***$p < .001$.

negative interactions at the dinner table. Mismatch in content and affect is evident in such cases where there is a predominance of nervous laughter or in cases where the bland affect of the storyteller does not match the emotional content of the narrative. In cases where there was such a mismatch in both husbands and wives, their children were perceived to have more externalizing behavior problems. Although the summary scores of narrative coherence proved to have little relation to other markers of family functioning, the mother's and father's appropriate modulation of affect in the narratives was linked to the report of fewer behavior problems in their children (see Table 12).

Couple Narrative Interaction and Family Mealtime Interaction

To address the second question (whether the interaction style observed in the narratives was related to patterns of interaction observed during mealtime), correlations were generated between the Couple Narrative Interaction dimension and family mealtime behavior. The correlations are presented in Table 12. As predicted, scores on the Couple Narrative Interaction dimension were consistent with the observed family behavior at the dinner table. Couples who coordinated their efforts, affirmed each other's position, and worked together to create a family story, were more likely to engage in affectively positive interactions at the dinner table, including positive interactions with and among their children. Thus, patterns of behavior observed during the construction of a family narrative were found to be similar to patterns of behavior observed during a routine family event (see Table 12).

Relationship Beliefs and Markers of Family Functioning

To address the third question (whether beliefs about family relationships in the current family and the family of origin, as expressed in narratives, would be related to markers of family functioning) two sets of analyses were conducted. The first set of analyses was correlational, examining the Relationship Belief scales in relation to marital satisfaction, family mealtime behavior, and child behavior problems. The correlations are presented in Table 13.

Father's expectations for rewarding relationships were related to more marital satisfaction and positive affect at the dinner table. When the father's stories were marked by expectations that relationships would be unfulfilling, however, they reported more externalizing and internalizing behavior problems in their children. For mothers, a similar pattern was found between narrative relationship expectations and family dinnertime behavior and report of child behavior problems. Overall, mothers and fathers who

TABLE 13

CORRELATIONS BETWEEN RELATIONSHIP BELIEF SCALES AND MARKERS OF FAMILY FUNCTIONING

	Relationship Expectations				Interviewer Intimacy
	Current Family		Family of Origin		
	Husband	Wife	Husband	Wife	Couple
Marital Satisfaction					
Husband	.34*	.16	.44**	.29	.08
Wife	.17	.01	.33*	.42***	−.01
Family Dinnertime Affect					
Positive	.61***	.57***	.30	.35*	.38**
Negative	−.67***	−.53***	−.36*	−.16	−.38**
Reported Child Behavior					
Internalizing	−.42***	−.32*	.04	−.04	−.04
Externalizing	−.53***	−.40**	−.19	−.28	.03
Total	−.50***	−.36**	−.10	−.16	.09

*$p < .05$.
**$p < .01$.
***$p < .001$.

expressed positive beliefs about the rewards and fulfillment associated with relationships in their current family also reported that their children had fewer problematic behaviors and engaged in more positive interactions at the dinner table. Conversely, if mothers or fathers saw relationships as either dangerous or rigidly adhered to the belief that relationships are *either* good or bad with little middle ground, there was more negative affect at the dinner table and their children were reported as having more problematic behaviors.

Family of origin relationship beliefs were also examined. Fathers and mothers whose narratives depicted their family of origin as a source of rewarding and/or fulfilling relationships were more satisfied in their marriages and engaged in more positive affect at the dinner table. As another indicator of relationship beliefs, the family's behavior with the interviewer was examined. Families that were warm and inviting to the interviewer expressed more positive affect when they gathered together as a family at the dinner table (see Table 13).

The correlation analyses revealed that both dinnertime affect and the report of child behavior problems were related to Relationship Expectations in the current family. We tested whether the effect of the more distal relationship expectations on child externalizing behavior was mediated by the more proximal dinnertime affect. A series of regression analyses was conducted to test the mediator model (Baron & Kenny, 1986). Because negative affect has been proposed to have a more harmful effect than positive affect has a beneficial effect (Katz & Gottman, 1994), and child externalizing problems have been identified as more pervasive than internalizing problems (Achenbach et al., 1991), the regression analyses were limited to negative affect and child externalizing problems. To establish mediation, three regression analyses were conducted: (a) Negative Affect was regressed on Relationship Expectations, (b) Externalizing scores were regressed on Relationship Expectations, and (c) Externalizing scores were regressed on both Relationship Expectations and Negative Affect. If Negative Affect is a mediator of Relationship Expectations the following conditions must hold: (a) Relationship Expectations must be shown to affect Negative Affect, (b) Relationship Expectations must affect Externalizing scores, and (c) Negative Affect must affect Externalizing scores when Relationship Expectation scores are included in the equation. The effect of Relationship Expectations on Externalizing scores must be less in the third equation than in the second to demonstrate a mediator effect. The regression analyses are presented in Table 14. The mediation model proved significant for wives where unfulfilling relationships affected child behavior through the negative affect at the dinner table. For husbands,

TABLE 14

Regression Analyses Testing Mediator Effect of Negative Affect Between Relationship Expectations and Child Externalizing

Equation	Dependent Variable	Predictor	r^2	B	t	p
Husband						
1	Negative Affect	Relationship Expectations	.45	−.67	5.48	.0001
2	Externalizing	Relationship Expectations	.28	−.53	3.81	.0001
3	Externalizing	Relationship Expectations	.32	−.37	1.96	.05
		Negative Affect		.25	1.33	.19
Wife						
1	Negative Affect	Relationship Expectations	.28	−.53	4.02	.0001
2	Externalizing	Relationship Expectations	.16	−.40	2.85	.007
3	Externalizing	Relationship Expectations	.28	−.19	1.23	.23
		Negative Affect		.40	2.57	.01

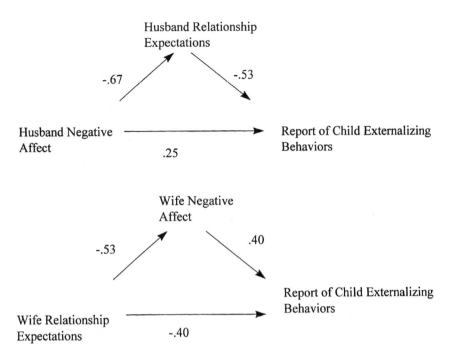

FIGURE 4—Mediational models predicting parent report of child externalizing behavior.

however, the mediation effects were stronger for relationship expectations, where expectations for unrewarding relationships were directly related to child behavior problems and mediated the effects of negative affect at the dinner table. In both cases, the model accounted for at least 30% of the variance associated with child externalizing behavior problems. A schematic presentation of the results is presented in Figure 4. As can be seen in this figure, different patterns of relatedness were found for husbands and wives, with the negative interaction mediating the effects of unrewarding relationship representations for wives and unrewarding relationships mediating the effects of negative affect on child behavior for husbands.

DISCUSSION

In this study we examined the relation between narrative accounts of family of origin and current meal times, observed family interaction and reported child behavior. Of interest is that differential results were found according to which narrative dimension was examined.

In regard to Narrative Coherence, few relations were found between the coherence of the parent's narrative and the measures used in this study. An exception was the negative relation between Narrative Coherence and mother's report of child behavior problems. These relations should be viewed with caution, given the number of correlations that were generated. The lack of findings between narrative coherence and marital satisfaction and family behavior is in contrast to researchers who propose that coherence of a narrative is central to understanding narratives and effects on relationships (Cohler, 1991; Main, 1991; McAdams, 1989).

There were two differences in the methodology used in this study that may warrant consideration. First, the narratives used in this analysis were based on stories that parents told to the interviewer and to their children. The task demanded that the parent not only recount an event but talk about the event in story form, i.e., a beginning, middle, and end. It may be that by using a storytelling task a certain amount of order and organization is forced upon the narrator and masks individual variability. Although this may be a reasonable conclusion that deserves further study, the stories that were told varied in their relative coherence, so a task effect may not be the only explanation for our lack of findings on narrative coherence.

A second methodological aspect of this study that may have affected the relation between coherence and other measures is the inclusion of other family members in the task and the recounting of an event that extends beyond the dyad. It may be that coherence is more closely linked to an individual's struggle with meaning and is more applicable to narratives that relate how one person felt about or interacted with another. Once the story is expanded to include the coordinated efforts of more than two people then coherence may take on a different meaning, not captured in this coding scheme.

The affective regulation associated with coherence may provide one window into how it is related to family relationships. Recently, considerable attention has been paid to the role of affect regulation in developing and maintaining healthy relationships (Gottman, 1994; Katz & Gottman, 1995). Children's exposure to the modulation of affect during the narrative process may be one avenue by which they learn to modulate their own affect and attend to different aspects of family relationships. Parents who present an affectively congruent image of family life may be presenting a more understandable, and thus more memorable, account that may be used in the future to guide the child's behavior.

It is important to consider the nature of the sample when discussing the findings from this study. In this nonclinical community sample, we may not have been able to detect some of the more extreme instances of incoherence. Clinical samples may provide a wider range of narrative coherence and may be more directly linked to child outcome (see Chapter 5 of this *Monograph* for application to clinical samples). Although we are encouraged by the findings of this study, our enthusiasm is tempered by the relatively small and homogenous sample that we interviewed.

The second area to consider is the positive relation between the couple's interaction style in constructing the narrative and family interaction at the dinner table. In some regards this may not be surprising, given that the narrative interaction codes were based on previously established measures of couple interaction (e.g., Gottman, 1983; Julien, Markman, Lindahl, Johnson, & Van Widenfelt, 1987). The findings in this study, however, support the notion that dyadic interaction patterns can be consistent with family interaction patterns that include triads and the whole family. We were fortunate in this study to have independent measures of dyadic interaction (Narrative Interaction) and family interaction (dinnertime behavior) that extended across two contexts. Couples that worked together to tell their story also worked together and with their children in positive exchanges at the dinner table. We think that this finding speaks to more than the notion that good couple behavior is related to good family behavior. The relation between different combinations of family members and their representative interactions is often overlooked in family research (Cowan, 1991; Parke, Power, & Gottman, 1979). These findings also support the generalizability of the narrative measures in a semistructured interview setting to the natural environment of the home.

The third narrative dimension to consider is Relationship Expectations. Both husband's and wife's expectations for rewarding relationships in their own family of origin were related to their current marital satisfaction. Bowen's multigenerational theory of family process proposes that marital relationships are affected by the family of origin, and that patterns of relatedness between parent and offspring are carried into the marital relationship (Bowen, 1966; Papero, 1990). The results from this study appear to support this contention and are consistent with previous reports (Harvey, Curry, & Bray, 1991; Wamboldt & Reiss, 1989; Williamson, 1991). Interestingly, husbands' families of origin expectations were related to wives' marital satisfaction, but the same relationship did not hold for husbands' marital satisfaction. Previous research has suggested that women serve as "relationship specialists" in marriages, often using their family of origin experiences as a guide to their current marital relationship (Wamboldt & Reiss, 1989; Wamboldt & Wolin, 1989). The findings from this study suggest that a husband's family of origin experience may influence not only his marital satisfaction but also his wife's. It may be that when husbands expect family of origin relationships to be unfulfilling there is a cost to the current relationship. Husbands may create a negative perceptual set that spills over into all family relationships. In contrast, wives may recognize previous faults in family of origin relationships and use their current relationship with their husband to create more positive expectations. Belsky and Pensky (1988) have proposed that mothers may be better able to keep family relationships distinct, whereas for fathers, poor marital relationships are related to poor parent-child relationships.

Continuity across generations also was found for observed positive and negative affect at the dinner table. There were notable gender differences, in that depictions of family of origin relationships were related to positive affect for wives and negative affect for husbands. It is possible that the husband's and wife's family of origin experiences regulate different aspects of family interaction. Whereas wives bring to the table a charge to regulate positive affect, husbands may be more likely to be involved in the regulation of negative affect. Although the family of origin has been recognized as an important regulator of current family relationships (e.g., Bowen, 1966), less is known about the mechanisms of regulation.

We tested a mediational model to examine whether the proximal effects of negative affect on child behavior mediated the effects of parental representations on child behavior. Consistent with other gender difference findings in this study, the relation between child behavior and the narrative process in mothers and fathers was different. For mothers, overall, there is a stronger pattern of affect in regulating narratives and their relation to other markers of family functioning. Recently, considerable attention has been directed toward the role of emotion regulation and child adjustment. Eisenberg and Fabes (1992) propose that externalizing types of problem behaviors are the result of difficulties in regulating emotion, which in turn affects social relationships and competence. If we consider the child's role as a storylistener, two possible scenarios develop. Children who have difficulty controlling their impulses and are inattentive may make it more difficult for mothers to tell a story that is affectively congruent. Over time, the mother's storytelling process is woven into an interpersonal process that may include poorly modulated affect, which is related just as much to attempting to keep the impulsive child's attention as it is to her narrative process. Another scenario is also possible. The mother may be presenting the child with an affective model that is marked by poor regulation (e.g., nervous laughter, flattened affect when attempting to highlight an emotional part of the story). The child's exposure to these inconsistent patterns of affect provides a model that is difficult to understand and serves as a poor guide for behavior. It is likely that both scenarios are tenable, and that they act in a transactional manner.

The patterns identified for fathers are somewhat different than those found for mothers, in that the pathway between representations and dinnertime affect was more direct. We are hesitant to conclude that fathers tend to influence child behavior through their representations and mothers influence child behavior through affect. First of all, these findings are purely correlational and cannot address causal relationships. Furthermore, we did not address different patterns according to to whether boys or girls were the target child. Gender differences according to child also warrant further investigation. Given that men and women may develop relationships in different ways (e.g., Chodorow, 1978) and that fathers and mothers may influence the family system in different ways (e.g., Kerig, Cowan, & Cowan, 1993), however, these findings deserve further attention in longitudinal work.

The stories that families create about their practices provide a unique window into examining how family process may be related to child behavior. Whereas some families tell stories filled with images of closeness, laughter, and reaffirmation, other families tell stories marked by distance, hollowness, and expectations for punishment. The following two examples illustrate some of the differences we found in these stories. The first story illustrates images of family life that are unfulfilling.

> I remember—I can remember playing outside and my mother calling us in for dinner and be like, oh man, nobody ever wanted to go in when it was dinnertime. We'd go in and it seemed like my mother made steak every day and when we were little we hated steak and we'd eat cereal all the time. But if we were made to eat, usually if my father was sitting there we had to eat what was on the plate. If we were made to eat, we'd have to sit there until it was bedtime and eat that food. And if we didn't eat the food we went to bed.

In the second story, relationships are described as a source of joy and reward.

> I remember a dinnertime when it was Christmas or something like that and mamma would bring out a huge turkey, and we would have ham, and beets, and homemade biscuits. And we would sit around and eat. And there was my aunt, uncle, grandmother, grandfather, and cousins, too. I remember my uncle would say a prayer before dinner, bless our food and our family. Or my grandfather might say it, my grandfather was a deacon in the church, and I always loved it when my grandfather said the prayer because it was the shortest prayer in the world. Jesus wept. And that was it and we just dove in and that was it. Sometimes there would be other kids over and we would have a little table in the corner where we would eat, the kids, while the adults had the big table to themselves. And I remember that being a specially nice time. A lot of laughing, and cutting, and scraping, and eating and talking and all those kinds of good things.

The description of a family where "oh man, nobody wanted to go in for dinner" can be contrasted with "It was a happy time of laughing, . . . talking, and all those kinds of good things," highlighting how family stories can re-create images and reinforce beliefs. When these children create their own family practices, we are confident that there will be echoes of the stories of their childhood.

IV. NARRATIVES OF ADOPTIVE PARENTS: PERSPECTIVES FROM INDIVIDUAL AND COUPLE INTERVIEWS

Harold D. Grotevant, Deborah Lewis Fravel, Dean Gorall, and Joyce Piper

The transition to parenthood is a watershed event in the lives of many couples. This event simultaneously extends a family into the next generation and brings into play the histories that each partner brings to this event from his or her family of origin. As part of the Narrative Consortium, we are interested in the "meaning-making" process; that is, how individuals and couples construct meanings about phenomena such as parenting and adoption. Both parenting and adoption are events (e.g., birth or placement of a child), but also are long-term processes. The meanings that couples make embody interpretations of these events and interactions and reflect their understandings about the past, their expectations about the future, and their understanding about relationships in which they do or might participate. We also are interested in how those constructed meanings shape subsequent interaction and outcomes. In short, we are interested in how narratives about one's family contribute to reduction of risks or enhancement of strengths passed from one generation to the next.

The portion of the Narrative Consortium to be addressed in this chapter involves data taken from the Minnesota/Texas Adoption Research Project, a study designed to examine variations in levels of openness in adoption (H. Grotevant & R. McRoy, Co–Principal Investigators). "Openness" refers to communication that occurs between an adoptive family and the birthmother after the placement of their adopted child. Openness varies in degree, ranging from confidential adoptions, in which there is no communication after placement; to mediated adoption, in which nonidentifying communication is exchanged through a third party (such as an adoption agency); to fully disclosed adoption, in which there is ongoing, identifying communication and contact.

The transition to biological parenthood occurs for most couples in committed relationships and typically involves a great deal of personal change in the lives of each individual as well as in their relationship with one another. Even under conditions of a planned and eagerly awaited birth of a child, the transition to parenthood can have a disequilibrating effect on the family system (e.g., Belsky & Pensky, 1988; Cowan, Cowan, Heming, & Miller, 1991). When people who want to have biological children are unable to do so, what would have been a normative transition becomes very nonnormative for them. Rather than dealing with the expected pleasure of a pregnancy resulting in a healthy infant, they are instead confronted with seemingly endless and often dehumanizing medical procedures. Eventually, many of these couples are faced with the fact that the only way they can parent a child is through adoption. The decision to adopt, however, is not simply an event; rather, it is a process through which the parties undergo resocialization to adoptive parenthood (Daly, 1992). By the time couples make a decision to adopt, then, their developmental and relational courses have already veered away from those more typically taken. They must enlarge their family in a different way, and this requires them to modify their thinking and adapt their emotions to another way of life.

Because the experiences of infertility and adoption were common to all the couples in this sample, the adoption study provides a forum for examining the way the experiences of these couples have come to have meaning in their lives. In the adoption study, participants were interviewed through questions that invited them to share their adoption stories. In telling their stories, they were faced with a task that required them to explain this turn their lives had taken, to account for or provide a rationale for their status as adoptive parents and their current family situation.

Telling such stories would not be a totally new experience for couples who adopted a number of years prior to participating in this research project. Prospective adoptive couples are typically required to write autobiographical statements as part of the "home study," which evaluates their suitability to parent. In addition, every well-intentioned inquiry from a relative, friend, or stranger occasions the need to tell the story once again. As the story gets told and retold, new and emergent meanings are constructed and revealed.

As we began to examine our research interviews, clear differences emerged in the narratives. Some adoptive parents told a story in some semblance of chronological order, tracing the history from their marriage, to their decision to have a child, to their discovery of infertility, moving systematically on through the adoption of the target child. As they told their stories, the adoptive parents might cry tears of joy when describing the day they received their child. As they revealed their empathy for the birthmother, their stories reflected their ability to take the perspective of another person. In the telling of their stories, there seemed to be a "theme" that ran through their narratives, lending a sense of coherence.

These narratives contrasted strikingly with those of some other parents, for whom the story was told patchwork-style as they jumped around from future to present to past. The storytelling itself seemed to be an exploration: Could it have been this thing at work, or was it another thing? Did I really need to do what I did, or not? Often, in these cases, the adoptive parent would tell a story that lacked congruence between its content and the affect expressed during its telling. For example, an adoptive father might laugh when telling of the three miscarriages he and his wife experienced before they decided to adopt. Some of these parents seemed particularly locked into viewpoints, and their narratives reflected their desire to have things black or white, one way or another.

As we reviewed the different kinds of interviews in our study, it was clear that both the story and the storytelling were important features for our consideration. When things were going well, it seemed that the narratives revealed a sense of coherence and lent meaning to the experience of individuals constructing them. Presumably, these qualities would be associated with psychological well-being and resilience of the parents.

One purpose of this study, then, is to examine family narratives in interviews with adoptive parents. Narratives were assessed in two contexts: an individual interview with each adoptive parent and a conjoint couple interview. This chapter will discuss those interviews, highlighting the ways assessments correspond and differ, both in terms of gender and in terms of the context (individual or conjoint interview). Because of our belief that couple narratives reflect other characteristics of the couple, another purpose of this chapter is to examine the way ratings of the narrative relate to partners' marital satisfaction, as reflected in the Parenting Stress Index.

Research Questions

Six hypotheses supplementing the project's core questions (see Grotevant & McRoy, 1997) guided the work conducted at the Minnesota site.

> 1. The central question in the larger adoption study had to do with differences in family processes, attitudes, and beliefs across levels of openness in adoption. A number of group differences were evident, especially with regard to adoptive parents' views about adoption (Grotevant, McRoy, Elde, & Fravel, 1994). Based on those findings, we hypothesized that narratives of parents in fully disclosed adoptions would be rated highest in coherence, those in confidential adoptions would be rated lowest, and those in mediated adoptions would fall in between.

2.   Because the Minnesota site was the only one in the consortium to have interview data from individuals alone and in interaction with their spouse, we asked whether there was a significant correlation between coherence ratings for each partner when interviewed alone and when interviewed with his or her spouse. We reasoned that there should be correspondence because the same speaker and the same topic were involved; however, the context was different, which should lower the degree of correspondence. Thus, we hypothesized that ratings of individuals alone and in interaction with their spouse would be positively and significantly, but moderately, correlated.

3.   Following similar reasoning, we hypothesized that spousal correlations within the individual and couple contexts would be positive and statistically significant, but moderate.

4.   What are the linkages among narrative coherence ratings in spouses' individual interviews, couple interviews, and characteristics of the couple narrative interaction variables? Because the ratings of individuals in the couple context and the narrative interaction assessments were made from the same transcripts, we hypothesized statistically significant relations among them. We also hypothesized statistically significant correlations between ratings made in the individual interviews and the narrative interaction assessments in the couple interviews, but to a lesser degree.

5.   When one partner's discourse is more coherent in the individual interview than in the couple interview, this suggests that the interaction with the spouse might be pulling the first partner's coherence down when they are together. In these situations, we predicted that higher coherence in the individual than in the couple context would be related to greater marital dissatisfaction for that spouse. Conversely, being rated as more coherent in the couple context would suggest that the person is being scaffolded or benefited by the partner; this should be related to less marital dissatisfaction for that person. This is essentially a between-context comparison.

6.   Husband-wife differences in coherence within the couple and individual interviews could indicate an asymmetrical relationship, one in which one partner "carries" the other conversationally or scaffolds the other's participation more. We predicted that larger asymmetries in coherence would be marked behaviorally in terms of lower couple co-construction, lower confirmation from one spouse to the other, and attitudinally in terms of greater dissatisfaction with the relationship. This is essentially a within-context comparison.

METHOD

Participants

Participants in the study were the husband, wife, and one target child in 27 adoptive families. The sample of families was drawn from the larger Minnesota/Texas Adoption Research Project (Grotevant et al., 1994; Grotevant & McRoy, 1997), which includes 190 adoptive families and 169 birthmothers, recruited with the assistance of 35 private adoption agencies located across the United States. The families in the Narrative Consortium sample were selected using several criteria. The target children were between the ages of 4 and 8, both parents were married to one another and had been so since before the child's arrival in the family, and the children were placed in the adoptive home before their first birthday. Children who were adopted transracially, internationally, or with "special needs" were not included in the sample.

A central purpose of the larger adoption project was to examine differences in individual, relational, and family outcomes for children in three types of adoption arrangements: confidential (in which no information was shared between birth- and adoptive parents after 6 months postplacement); mediated (in which the exchange of nonidentifying information is mediated by adoption agency personnel); and fully disclosed (which involves direct communication between adoptive and birthfamilies and full disclosure of identifying information).

In the consortium subsample of 27 families, one third of the families had confidential adoptions, one third had ongoing mediated adoptions, and one third had fully disclosed adoptions. Within each type of adoption, families were randomly sampled from the larger study, balancing the number of male and female target children.

All parents were married and most were well educated (mean mother's education = 15.3 years, mean father's education = 16.3 years). Mean mother's age was 38.4 years (*range* = 32 to 45); mean father's age was 39.2 years (*range* = 33 to 46). Families had between 1 and 4 children at the time of the interview (*M* = 2.1). In terms of ethnicity, 25 couples were Caucasian and 2 were Mexican American.

Procedure

Each family was seen in its home by a team of two interviewers. The interviewers included adoption agency personnel, social workers, and graduate students in social work or family science programs at nearby universities. All interviewers were trained extensively, completed practice interviews, and received feedback before visiting families. The home visit included individual interviews with the wife and husband, an individual interview with the target adopted child (and occasionally siblings as well), completion of questionnaires by parents and child, and a joint interview with the adoptive parents. The home visit typically lasted 3–4 hours and was scheduled at the family's convenience.

The adoptive parent interview included an extensive set of questions concerning the parent's motivation for adoption, experience with the adoptive placement, and experiences and feelings about the specific level of openness in adoption in which the family is involved (see Appendix A). In most cases, the interviewer was of the same sex as the respondent. All interviews were conducted so that other family members could not hear the respondents' answers when being interviewed separately; all interviews were audiotaped and subsequently transcribed verbatim.

For this study, three separate interviews were coded for each of the 27 families: the adoptive mother's individual interview, the adoptive father's individual interview, and the couple's interview. Thus, a total of 81 interviews form the database for this study. Two graduate students (Gorall and Piper) who established initial reliability and understood the theoretical premises of the Narrative Consortium's work independently coded each interview. Although the same two raters coded both individual and couple interviews, a coding schedule was constructed to ensure that the coding of the three interviews for each case was spread out in time and that a number of other cases were interspersed. Because each coder rated 81 interviews over a period of approximately one year, the likelihood that coders would be biased by a halo effect was minimized.

Consistent with the other studies in the consortium, perceived satisfaction in the couple's marital relationship was of interest. We assessed marital satisfaction by using the Relationship with Spouse subscale of the Parenting Stress Index (Abidin, 1986), which we refer to as the Marital Dissatisfaction scale in this chapter. The Parenting Stress Index is a self-report questionnaire completed independently by each adoptive parent. Higher scores on this scale indicate greater dissatisfaction with the marital relationship. Reliability and validity for this measure are well documented in Abidin (1986). For the Relationship with Spouse scale, Abidin (1986) reports α reliability at .81 and test-retest reliability over a 1- to 3-year period at .96.

One commonality across the consortium was that all the sites had recorded interactional data in the form of audiotapes or videotapes. In the adoption study, raters listened to audiotapes, while following verbatim transcripts of the interviews. In coding narrative coherence in the conjoint interviews, coders listened to the entire audiotape and followed along with the written transcript, but then first coded all the coherence variables for one spouse and then completed the coding for the second spouse.

Training for raters included extensive study of cases from all three levels of openness and extensive practice with the Narrative Consortium codebook. Two raters coded all scales on the adoption interviews, providing a strong assessment of interrater reliability. Reliabilities were computed using Cicchetti's κ for rating scales varying in number of coding intervals in order to control for the possibility of chance agreement. Kappas ranged from .76 to .94 across scales, suggesting excellent interrater reliability. When the four coherence variables were summed, internal consistency coefficients (Cronbach's α) were solid for both husbands and wives in both individual and joint interviews: α ranged from .58 to .77.

RESULTS

Results are discussed in turn for each of the six hypotheses outlined above. First, we examined mean coherence ratings for wives' and husbands' narratives in both individual and couple interviews. We treated level of openness in adoption as the independent variable. The five coherence ratings within each set were first examined with multivariate analyses of variance (MANOVAs) and were followed with univariate F tests. For the ratings of the individual interviews, significant multivariate Fs emerged for both wives and husbands. For wives, the multivariate test was significant [Pillai's trace = 0.65; $F(8, 44) = 2.63$, $p = .019$]; univariate F tests were significant for Internal Consistency, Flexibility, Congruence, and the Total Coherence rating (see Table 15 for details). For husbands, the multivariate test also was significant [Pillai's trace = 0.98; $F(8, 42) = 5.09$, $p < .001$]; univariate F tests were significant for Internal Consistency, Flexibility, and the Total Coherence rating. For the couple interviews, multivariate F tests were significant for neither wives nor husbands. The pattern of means for couple interview ratings, however, was identical to that found with the individual interviews; namely, the most coherence was seen in the fully disclosed adoptions, the least coherence was seen in the confidential adoptions, and an intermediate level of coherence was noted in the mediated adoptions.

The second hypothesis focused on cross-context correlations for participants. We expected positive but moderate correlations between a person's rating on any particular scale in the individual interview, and his or her rating on that same scale in the couple interview. Ratings of coherence in the individual and couple interviews were positively and significantly correlated on most of the coherence scales for both husbands and wives (see Table 16). Correlations on the Total Coherence score were .59 and .50 for wives and husbands, respectively. Cross-context correlations on the Internal Consistency and Flexibility scales were moderate, positive, and significant for both wives and husbands. Additionally, for husbands, ratings on the Organization scale

TABLE 15

Mean Coherence Ratings Across Levels of Adoption Openness

Narrative Scales	Level of Adoption Openness			
	Confidential	Mediated	Fully Disclosed	F
Individual Interview				
Wife				
Internal Consistency	2.8	3.4	4.8	14.61***
Organization	3.3	3.4	3.9	0.88
Flexibility	2.4	3.0	3.9	4.96*
Congruence	3.2	3.9	4.9	8.77**
Total Coherence	11.8	13.8	17.4	13.79***
Husband				
Internal Consistency	3.4	4.4	4.6	4.46*
Organization	3.4	3.6	3.7	0.12
Flexibility	2.2	4.4	3.7	25.27***
Congruence	3.7	3.8	4.4	2.72
Total Coherence	12.8	16.1	16.3	6.85**
Couple Interview				
Wife				
Internal Consistency	3.1	3.1	4.2	4.99*
Organization	3.0	3.3	3.9	2.83
Flexibility	2.6	3.0	3.3	2.12
Congruence	3.4	4.1	4.2	2.79
Total Coherence	12.1	13.6	15.7	8.70**
Husband				
Internal Consistency	2.9	3.6	4.1	4.49*
Organization	3.3	3.6	4.1	2.64
Flexibility	2.2	2.9	3.0	3.07
Congruence	3.4	3.9	4.2	1.76
Total Coherence	11.9	13.9	15.4	5.36

* $p < .05$.
** $p < .01$.
*** $p < .0001$.

TABLE 16

Correlations of Person in Individual Interview/Same Person in Couple Interview

Coherence Scale	Interview Context and Comparison	
	Wife in Individual Interview, Correlated with Wife in Couple Interview	Husband in Individual Interview, Correlated with Husband in Couple Interview
Internal Consistency	.43*	.57***
Organization	.10	.42*
Flexibility	.69***	.37*
Congruence	.31	.03
Total Coherence	.59***	.50**

* $p < .05$.
** $p < .01$.
*** $p < .001$.

were moderately, positively, and significantly correlated across contexts. Neither husbands nor wives showed cross-context consistency for Congruence of Affect and Content. This suggests that, despite the give-and-take that must occur in a conversation as opposed to an individual interview, each of the spouses in these couples generally had similar narrative coherence regardless of the situation. A notable exception to this pattern was little to no consistency for husbands in their affective congruence across situations. The affective match with the content of the story being told by husbands was altered in some way when they were interviewed with their wives.

Third, we found that husband-wife correlations on the coherence scales, when assessed within the couples interview (*range* = .53 to .90), were generally higher than those from individual interviews (*range* = .13 to .44). Z tests for the difference between spousal correlations in the two contexts were significant for Congruence of Affect and Content ($z = 3.43$, $p < .001$) and the Total Coherence scale ($z = 2.05$, $p < .05$; see Table 17). These results suggest that similarities between characteristics of husbands' and wives' narratives are enhanced when they are together. This is not surprising in a volunteer sample of nonclinical families.

Results for the fourth hypothesis linking narrative coherence ratings with characteristics of the couple narrative interaction variables are presented separately for Couple Narrative Style, Wife Confirmation of Husband, Husband Confirmation of Wife, and Interviewer Intimacy (see Table 18).

Couple Narrative Style was positively and significantly correlated with 8 of the 10 coherence variables for husbands and wives when rated from their couple interviews. When rated from their individual interviews, only 1 of the 10 coherence variables (from wives) was significantly and positively correlated with Couple Narrative Style.

TABLE 17

SPOUSAL CORRELATIONS IN COHERENCE

	Husband-Wife Correlation		
Interview Setting	Individual	Couple	Z
Coherence Scale			
Internal Consistency	.33*	.53**	.85
Organization	.13	.54**	1.61
Flexibility	.31	.55**	1.01
Congruence	.44*	.90***	3.43***
Total Coherence	.43*	.79***	2.05*

* $p < .05$.
** $p < .01$.
*** $p < .001$.

TABLE 18

CORRELATIONS BETWEEN NARRATIVE COHERENCE RATINGS OF WIVES AND HUSBANDS IN
INDIVIDUAL AND COUPLE INTERVIEWS AND RATINGS OF THE NARRATIVE INTERACTION

	Interview Setting			
	Wife		Husband	
	Individual	Couple	Individual	Couple
Couple Narrative Style				
Internal Consistency	.24	.13	.00	.32*
Organization	.60***	.34*	−.00	.35*
Flexibility	.09	.25	−.03	.51**
Congruence	.00	.44*	−.04	.46**
Total Coherence	.29	.42*	−.05	.53**
Wife Confirmation				
Internal Consistency	.35*	.16	.26	.46**
Organization	.36*	.20	.06	.36*
Flexibility	.30	.44*	.21	.58***
Congruence	.16	.35*	.13	.37*
Total Coherence	.38*	.40*	.25	.57***
Husband Confirmation				
Internal Consistency	.09	−.03	.05	.39*
Organization	.35*	.24	−.03	.33*
Flexibility	.03	.20	−.10	.52**
Congruence	−.19	.41*	−.21	.48**
Total Coherence	.08	.29*	−.12	.55***
Interviewer Intimacy				
Internal Consistency	.40*	.53**	.27	.41*
Organization	.46**	.30	−.07	.37*
Flexibility	−.05	.20	.11	.29
Congruence	.28	.78***	.21	.79***
Total Coherence	.35*	.67***	.15	.61***

* $p < .05$.
** $p < .01$.
*** $p < .001$.

Wife Confirmation of Husband was positively and significantly correlated with 8 of the 10 coherence variables for husbands and wives when rated from their couple interviews. When rated from individual interviews, 3 of the 10 coherence variables (all from wives) were significantly and positively correlated with Wife Confirmation of Husband.

Husband Confirmation of Wife in the couple interview was positively and significantly correlated with 7 of the 10 coherence variables for husbands and wives when rated from their couple interviews. When rated from individual interviews, only 1 of the 10 coherence variables (from the wife) was significantly and positively correlated with Husband Confirmation of Wife.

Interviewer Intimacy in the couple interview was positively and significantly correlated with 7 of the 10 coherence variables for husbands and wives when rated from their couple interviews. When rated from individual interviews, 3 of the 10 coherence variables (all from wives) were significantly and positively correlated with Interviewer Intimacy.

In sum, the coherence ratings made from the conjoint couple interviews were highly correlated with ratings of the interaction itself. More coherence displayed by each partner in the conjoint narrative was related positively and significantly to the marital partners' greater confirmation of one another in the interview, greater collaborative style in their account, and more warm and inviting interaction with the interviewer.

Coherence ratings made from the individual interviews were moderately related to ratings of the interaction for wives, but not for husbands. In fact, looking down the columns in Table 18, the number of significant ($p <$ .05) correlations between coherence and the couple interaction variables was 8 (of a possible 20) for the wife in the individual interview, 11 for the wife in the couples interview, 0 for the husband in the individual interview, and 19 for the husband in the couples interview.

To examine between-context effects, difference scores were computed between each spouse's coherence ratings in the couple and individual interviews. Positive scores indicated higher coherence in the context of the couple interview than individual interview. These difference scores were then correlated with the Relationship with Spouse scale from the Parenting Stress Index, which measures marital dissatisfaction (see Table 19).

Different patterns of correlations emerged for wives and husbands. For wives, greater overall coherence in the couple context than in the individual context was significantly related to less marital dissatisfaction, as predicted

TABLE 19

CORRELATIONS BETWEEN COHERENCE DIFFERENCES IN COUPLE AND
INDIVIDUAL INTERVIEWS AND SPOUSE'S MARITAL DISSATISFACTION

	Marital Dissatisfaction	
Coherence Difference	Wife	Husband
Coherence Scale		
Internal Consistency	−.43*	−.11
Organization	−.05	−.20
Flexibility	−.38*	−.02
Congruence	−.32	.10
Total Coherence	−.47*	−.08

Note—Higher difference scores indicate greater coherence in the person's narrative when rated from the couple interview than from the same person's individual interview.
* $p < .05$.

($r(23) = -.47$, $p = .011$). This pattern was echoed significantly in two of the four coherence subscales. For husbands, the association between Total Coherence and Marital Dissatisfaction was nonsignificant ($r(24) = -.08$), and it also was nonsignificant for all four of the coherence subscales.

Finally, to look at the correlates of partner asymmetries in the couple interview, husband-wife difference scores for the Total Coherence ratings were computed for both the couple and individual interviews. These difference scores were then correlated with the Marital Dissatisfaction score of the spouse who had the higher coherence rating. Significant correlations were found for both the couple interview ratings ($r(23) = .41$, $p < .05$) and the individual interview ratings ($r(24) = .36$, $p < .05$). Higher discrepancies in coherence ratings were related to higher marital dissatisfaction of the individual whose narrative was rated as more coherent.

Coherence asymmetry was also correlated negatively with Husband Confirmation of Wife ($r(24) = -.51$, $p < .01$), one of the couple interaction variables. That is, greater coherence of the wife than the husband in the couple interview was negatively related to the husband's confirmation of his wife.

DISCUSSION AND CONCLUSIONS

The narrative analysis of interviews from adoptive parents in this study proved quite revealing. The first finding, that individual interviews conducted with adoptive parents in more open adoptions demonstrated greater narrative coherence than the individual interviews of adoptive parents in confidential or mediated adoptions, was quite consistent for both parents and across subscales.

Several possible explanations for this finding could be entertained. Was there a self-selection process in the sample, whereby individuals and couples more prone to telling coherent narratives were in more open adoptions? Although it is possible, we think not, for several reasons. First, all couples were not offered a full range of choices for the level of openness in their adoption. Some worked with agencies that only offered one type of adoption or strongly suggested one type and then provided them with education and support relevant to that type of adoption. In addition, almost two thirds of the fully disclosed adoptive families in the larger study did not start out that way (Grotevant et al., 1994). With more extensive data (e.g., personality or cognitive style), we would be able to ask whether couples who ultimately opt for open adoptions see the world in more complex ways than those who do not, and therefore might be prone to develop more coherent narratives about their family situation.

Was there a bias in coding, whereby raters scored narratives about more open adoptions as more coherent? Ideally, such ratings would be made blindly with respect to level of openness, but this was impossible, due to the content of the interviews being coded. We made explicit efforts in training coders to identify transcripts from all three levels of openness that would vary in levels of coherence, wanting to make sure that coherence and openness were not confounded in the rating process. Therefore, we do not believe the findings can be attributed solely to rater bias.

Is it the case that open adoptions are more complex than confidential or mediated adoptions (in term of contacts, diversity of members involved, and so on) and therefore may elicit a more differentiated story, which may be judged as more coherent? Although this is possible, more complex narratives involving more people provide more opportunities for confusion and incoherence to emerge as well.

Although our correlational data preclude determination of causal direction, we are drawn toward the interpretation that there were main effects of openness on coherence ratings, because families with confidential or mediated adoptions have only partial relationships with their child's birthfamily members. Interviews required these adoptive parents to talk about their construction of these relationships. It is difficult to tell a story about an incomplete relationship, because one does not have complete information. Telling a story with incomplete information can push the narrator to make assumptions, to fall back on stereotypes, or simply to "make up" the missing details. It should not be surprising, then, that a story thus constructed might have a less compelling theme, seem one-sided, or come across to the listener as less than coherent; or, in the terms used in this study, to have lower internal consistency, to be less flexible, or to seem less congruent. This finding bears more detailed examination in future work, both in terms of the construction of such relationship accounts, as well as in terms of the consequences of differences in coherence.

For both wives and husbands, coherence ratings made from their individual and couple interviews were moderately and positively correlated, accounting for 25 to 36% of shared variance, when the Total Coherence scores are considered. Interestingly, no cross-context consistency was found for Congruence of Affect and Content for either spouse, suggesting that the degree of Congruence displayed when partners are interviewed alone is altered when the spouses are interacting. Spousal correlations on the coherence scales, however, generally were higher for the couple interviews than for the individual interviews. It appears that the "jointness" of the couple interview contributed to greater spousal similarity in that setting. This was expected, given the volunteer nature of this nonclinical sample. With a clinical sample, husband-wife correlations in the couple context might be lower. Findings regarding this question also could be due to possible halo effects of the same raters coding both the individual and couple interviews.

Safeguards were built into our procedures, however, to minimize this possibility (see Method section).

Coherence ratings made from the conjoint couple interviews also were highly correlated with ratings of the interaction itself. More coherence displayed by each partner in the conjoint narrative was related positively and significantly to the marital partners' greater confirmation of one another in the interview, greater collaborative style in their account, and more warm and inviting interaction with the interviewer. On the other hand, coherence ratings made from the individual interviews were moderately related to ratings of the interaction for wives, but not for husbands. This points to the stronger role that wives might play in setting the tone for the dyadic conversation or at least to the stronger continuity that might exist between wives' behavior in individual and couple interviews. This gender difference should be considered in light of discussion about the role that wives play as emotional gatekeepers in the family. It also is possible that the correlations between coherence in the couple interview and the narrative interaction ratings were confounded to the degree that process and coherence are interrelated.

Differences between an individual's narrative coherence in the individual and couple interview contexts were examined as an aspect of the interaction. We assumed that greater coherence rated in the individual than in the couple interview indicated that the individual was being "pulled down" by the spouse when they were together and that such a situation would predict greater dissatisfaction with the marriage. This hypothesis was upheld for wives, but not for husbands.

Finally, we predicted that spousal asymmetries in coherence within the couple and individual interviews would be associated with lower ratings on Couple Narrative Style, lower confirmation of one spouse to the other, and greater dissatisfaction with the marriage. One interpretation of this set of findings is that one partner was carrying the other partner conversationally or scaffolding his or her participation. As predicted, larger asymmetries were related behaviorally to lower couple co-construction, less confirmation of one spouse by the other, and greater marital dissatisfaction of the partner doing the carrying. Sequential analysis would be necessary to draw causal inferences relevant to this hypothesis. In addition, interpretation of this and other findings must be made with caution because the sample was relatively small and consisted solely of adoptive families; thus, generalizability to other family situations is limited.

Overall, this study has demonstrated that narrative coherence variables provide an interesting and useful window into examining family process and individuals' attitudes about their family. Adults have varying levels of coherence in their individual narratives about their families. Each spouse brings that quality into the marital relationship, in which the coherence can remain the same, be enhanced, or be reduced. The interdependence involved in a long-standing marital relationship suggests that the partners' individual narratives might be enhanced when they are together, as found in the social psychological research on transactive memory (Wegner, 1991).

On the other hand, it is possible that one spouse's coherence would be reduced when with his or her partner. The spouse might be reluctant to state his or her own point of view, especially if it had been devalued in the past. Or one partner might feel that his or her role is to bolster the spouse, even at personal expense. The outcome of such interactions produces an emergent relationship quality, and the data in our study have shown that this quality is related to characteristics of the interaction and attitudes about the relationship itself. This relationship quality is not a simple function of the coherence of the individual spouses; it is more than the sum of the parts and cannot be reduced to components.

Our finding that narrative coherence is consistently related to degree of openness in adoption also was noteworthy. Although causal conclusions cannot be drawn from correlational work, it is likely that the incomplete communication found in confidential and mediated adoptions constrains coherence in narratives about families' adoptions. Interesting gender differences emerged within couples; wives' narratives were more highly related to ratings of interaction and to attitudes about the relationship than were those of husbands. We are now conducting a longitudinal follow-up of these families, so we may be able to bring further clarity to these interpretations once the data have been collected and analyzed.

The data reported in this study fit very well with other recent research that has identified the usefulness of narratives. For example, Main and Goldwyn (1984) and collaborators have been exploring links between adult attachment and current relationship functioning; Buehlman, Gottman, and Katz (1992) found that coded narratives about marriage could predict the likelihood of a couple's subsequent divorce. The robustness of these results also suggests that narrative approaches might be useful vehicles for prevention-oriented family education programs as well as for family therapy. For example, programs preparing couples for adoption could help them think about how to formulate a "story" that is inclusive of the child's full birth heritage. Current interest in the creation of "lifebooks" for such children is a step in that direction. Narrative approaches to therapy (e.g., White & Epston, 1990) also provide promise for working clinically with adopted persons, adoptive families, or birthfamily members, because the assumption of narrative therapy approaches is that the meaning that family members attribute to events, rather than an outsider's assessment of the events or an underlying pathological structure, determines the behaviors and interactions among family members.

V. MATERNAL DEPRESSION, FAMILY FUNCTIONING, AND CHILD OUTCOMES: A NARRATIVE ASSESSMENT

Susan Dickstein, Martin St. Andre, Arnold Sameroff,
Ronald Seifer, and Masha Schiller

Families are the vehicles by which transmission of competence and risk occurs. Normative development, as well as the expression of mental illness, are family matters (Downey & Coyne, 1990; Radke-Yarrow, Nottelman, Martinez, Fox, & Blemont, 1992; Seifer & Dickstein, 1993). Various models have been proposed to explain the mechanisms by which risk (such as depression) and competence are transmitted within the family. These include genetic hypotheses (e.g., Egeland et al., 1987); constitutional considerations (Fish, Marcus, Hans, Auerbach, & Perdue, 1992; McNeil & Kaij, 1987); environmental models that explore factors such as parenting behavior, family composition, and psychological stress (e.g., Billings & Moos, 1983; Coyne & Downey, 1991; Downey & Coyne, 1990; Hammen, 1991); and affect regulation models (Stern, 1985; Tronick, Cohn, & Shea, 1986). The role of family functioning in this process is poorly understood, however, in part due to the paucity of family assessment techniques and theoretical rationale to study families with young children (Cummings, 1995).

One way families understand and establish patterns associated with the transmission of risk and competence is through storytelling. When parents tell stories to children, they convey all sorts of things they believe are important about relationships and family life. Their beliefs, in part, arise from the families they each grew up in, and their desires to carry forward certain patterns and/or to deliberately break with family of origin traditions. Children learn from the stories they are told, and they love to hear them repeated over and over again. By telling stories, couples gain understanding and/or renew struggles about how similar or discrepant their perceptions are about their current family. The manner in which the stories are told (i.e., the cognitive constructions of family life) may reflect and/or influence quality of family functioning. In this report, we examine narrative methodology as a way to understand parents' current cognitive models of their family and the process by which they ascribe meaning in their narratives to determine associations between maternal depression, family functioning, and child outcomes.

The examination of narratives helps us learn how family members make sense of family experiences, how they work together to tell a story about their family, and how their current family experiences may be related to expectations for relationships in other social domains. This is especially important in families with children at risk for nonoptimal outcomes due to the presence of maternal mental illness, specifically in this study where mothers were diagnosed with affective disorder. Thus, we investigate the relative differences in family narratives between mothers with a lifetime diagnosis of depression with and without current depressive symptoms. This approach combines categorical assessment of illness (*DSM-III-R*) with a commonly examined nonspecific illness factor related to depressive disorder, intensity of depressive symptoms (Nurcombe et al., 1989).

Narrative Domains and Maternal Depression

As described in the Introductory chapter of this *Monograph*, three aspects of narrative production are explored, including Narrative Coherence, Narrative Interaction, and Relationship Beliefs. A cautious approach must be taken to the study of narratives within a high risk sample, as several characteristics of the informants may affect their discourse and/or interpretations of events. The implications of these areas for maternal depression are discussed briefly.

Narrative Coherence

Narrative coherence refers to the manner in which the storyteller constructs the narrative. When asking people about their family experiences to assess cognitive perceptions, we must keep in mind that the information provided in narrative form reflects their current understanding of events, not what may (or may not) have actually happened (Zeanah & Barton, 1989). Mental illness may uniquely influence the manner in which experiences are cognitively constructed, the salience of particular experiences that comprise the cognitive construction of a relationship, and/or the extent to which certain experiences might be differentially disclosed during the course of narrative production. Alternatively, the cognitive construction of the narrative and disclosure of salient experiences may have a significant impact on expressed symptoms (Abramson, Seligman, & Teasdale, 1978; Peterson & Seligman, 1984).

A second issue to consider when assessing narratives within a high-risk sample is that the quality of the narratives produced by depressed women may be more impoverished or otherwise compromised by virtue of current depressive symptomatology. That is, the presence of serious depressive symptoms (such as psychomotor retardation, concentration difficulties, and/ or sleep disturbances) may influence the coherence and consistency of the narrative via an expected deficiency in the mechanisms that underlie verbal production. In the current study, we attempted to control for this potential difficulty by not interviewing a subject if her present level of depressive symptoms was serious enough to significantly impact judgment or to warrant hospitalization.

Narrative Interaction

Narrative Interaction refers to how a couple works together to construct the story. The quality of current and significant adult relationships, such as the marital relationship, is an often neglected link in examining the associations between maternal illness and adverse family outcomes. This omission may obscure important connections, since marital functioning has been related to the initiation, maintenance, and recovery from major depressive episodes (Barnett & Gotlib, 1988; Hooley & Teasdale, 1989; Jacobson, Dobson, Fruzetti, Schmaling, & Salusky, 1991; Kowalik & Gotlib, 1987; Rounsaville, Prusoff, & Weissman, 1980). Furthermore, some work has suggested that, within the context of maternal psychopathology, poor quality marital interaction is associated with adverse child outcomes (Fendrich, Warner, & Weissman, 1990; Kaslow, Warner, John, & Brown, 1992). In this chapter, we examine these links by assessing the association of maternal mental illness and couple narrative interaction.

Relationship Beliefs

Relationship Beliefs refer to how the storyteller perceives relationships as trustworthy (or not) in various social domains. Depressed women more often may provide negatively distorted perceptions of their relationships by virtue of the immediate severity of their illness. This may be viewed as troublesome because of the presumed inaccuracy of the reports. This is related to a current debate regarding the accuracy of depressed mothers' judgments about their childrens' problematic behavior (e.g., Brody & Forehand, 1986; Conrad & Hammen, 1989; Richters & Pelligrini, 1989; Rickard, Forehand, Wells, Greist, & McMahon, 1981). In our research, the important issue is that any "distortions" depressed adults might have about their family relationships are a valid (and accurate) indication of their current sense of those relationships. Indeed, such "distorted" perceptions may be a fundamental process in the etiology or maintenance of depression, as well as in the development of maladaptive relationship patterns (Wamboldt & Gavin, 1992). In this chapter, we focus on the association of maternal depression and mothers' and fathers' perceptions of their relationships within their current family and their family of origin as it is recalled from childhood.

Study Questions

We addressed three main questions regarding coding of narratives with the consortium's scales in our study.

Question 1

To what extent do the Narrative Consortium scale dimensions differentiate narratives produced by women diagnosed with depression (with and without current symptoms) and no-illness control groups? To what extent are narratives produced by husbands of women diagnosed with depression different from those produced by husbands of non-ill women? As discussed above, without implying directionality of effect, we hypothesized that the narratives produced by depressed women would be characterized by lower Narrative Coherence compared to their non-ill counterparts; it was expected that narratives of husbands of depressed women also would be characterized by lower Narrative Coherence. We predicted that couples with a depressed wife would have more difficulty engaging effectively in the task of producing a narrative about their family life, reflected in lower Narrative Interaction ratings. Finally, we expected that depressed women and their husbands would maintain less trustworthy Relationship Beliefs, particularly regarding their current families.

Question 2

How are Narrative Consortium scales related to other measures of family functioning, assessed in different contexts and by different raters? The main purpose of this question was to assess convergent and discriminant validity of the consortium scales. We hypothesized that the Narrative Coherence domain should be associated with the quality of whole family functioning, given that it assesses the manner in which family experience is integrated and cognitively constructed. Given the family nature of our hypotheses, we also expected that there should be correspondence between husbands and wives in their Coherence scores. We speculated that any or all of the following mechanisms may be operative based on other data from the PFS larger study including: (a) husbands of ill women are more often ill themselves, (b) the possibility of assortive mating on broad and/or specific cognitive and experiential factors related to cognitive style, and (c) the possibility of direct transmission resulting from repeated interchanges with one's partner regarding the co-construction of experience.

In addition, we expected that the Narrative Interaction domain should be associated with marital satisfaction, given that it taps the couple's style of producing a joint narrative. Finally, we expected that Relationship Beliefs within the Current Family should be related to both quality of family functioning and marital satisfaction assessed in various contexts, although not necessarily to reports of family of origin functioning. We had no specific hypotheses regarding the associations between husbands' and wives' Relationship Beliefs in the Family of Origin and other assessments of family functioning.

Question 3

How are the Narrative Consortium scales related to child outcome measures in our high risk sample? We assumed that the stories produced by parents about the nature of family life would reflect and/or have important consequences for child behavior and development. We hypothesized that there should be an association between child developmental outcomes and the quality of narratives produced about family relationships, especially Narrative Coherence and Relationship Beliefs in the Current Family.

METHOD

The Providence Family Study is a longitudinal investigation of infants and toddlers at risk for psychopathology because their mother has diagnosed mental illness. Families entered the study when their child was 1 or 2½ years old, and were followed longitudinally at 2½ and 4 years old. The overall focus of the project is to examine the early development of at-risk children within both their family and larger social contexts.

Recruitment

Families were identified by several sources, including records of psychiatric hospital admissions, newspaper advertisements, and from prior studies in our laboratory unrelated to the present work (where participants had been approached during the immediate postpartum period). Mothers were contacted by telephone about participation in the study and were provided with written material about the study. Those mothers who tentatively agreed to participate were then screened over the telephone for history of one of the target diagnoses (major depression, bipolar disorder, anxiety disorder) as well as for exclusion diagnoses (current eating disorders, current substance use disorders, and psychotic symptoms not associated with affective disorder). Mothers who passed this screen were then enrolled in the project. Subsequently, all mothers completed a structured diagnostic interview (see below) to evaluate mental health diagnostic status for group assignment.

Description of Families

In this report, we examine a group of two-parent families to compare functioning in Depressed (n = 25) versus No Mental Illness (n = 18) groups. Within each of the groups, families were randomly chosen from the larger sample and ultimately selected if all pertinent data were available. The children included 17 boys and 26 girls. The No-Illness and Depressed families did not differ on level of socioeconomic status (SES; 2.21 and 2.80, respectively, based on Hollingshead 5-point ratings). In order to assess representative family functioning, we saw families at least 2 months following a psychiatric hospitalization, and procedures were delayed when mothers were judged too severely depressed to participate. Still, there was substantial variation in the current depressive symptomatology experienced by the mothers at the time of the study.

Procedures

The Providence Family Study is a large and complex study, and only relevant aspects will be reported here, although a brief overview of the entire study is provided. To summarize the overall study protocol, families participated in a structured home visit, structured diagnostic interviews (mother and father) conducted at the laboratory, a structured family functioning interview conducted at the laboratory, a mother-child laboratory assessment, and an unstructured home videotaping of a family meal. In addition, mothers and fathers each completed several questionnaires about their own psychological well-being, marital satisfaction, family functioning, and perceptions of their child's behavior and development. Longitudinal follow-ups consisted of a similar set of procedures at 2½ and 4 years of age, as well as telephone contacts to monitor the course of each mother's mental status at 6-month intervals. Specific procedures used in the current report are described below.

For this report, data from four domains using multiple informants were utilized, including: (a) narrative assessment based on the Family Traditions Interview protocol, (b) maternal mental health status based on *DSM-III-R* criteria, (c) family functioning based on the McMaster model, and (d) child behavior using maternal checklist questionnaire. In all cases independent raters were used across the four domains of assessment. Specific procedures are described below.

Narrative Assessment

Family Traditions Interview and Narrative Consortium Coding

The Family Traditions Interview was designed by Sameroff and colleagues, and is based on the work of Wolin and Bennett (1984; see Appendix A). This interview was conducted during the first visit with a family in their home. The complete interview has 84 specific questions and takes approximately 2 hours to complete. All interviews were conducted by the Providence Family Study Family Coordinator, who had clinical training that included experience with families.

Relevant portions of the Family Traditions Interview were transcribed for Narrative Consortium scoring. To ascertain individuals' stories, mothers and fathers were asked separately about what it meant to be a member of their own family of origin; in addition, they were asked separately a series of questions regarding their child's development, personality, and expected characteristics. As a couple, parents were asked to indicate together what it meant to be a member of their current family, the plans they had to maintain patterns from their past family relationships, and the deliberate actions they may have taken to change patterns from the past.

The Family Traditions Interview transcripts were coded by one rater who participated in a weekend-long training session in Minnesota, and who achieved reliability with a criterion rater in the Providence lab. We took several precautions to ensure that consortium codes would be independent from other family measures. The primary consortium rater did not administer any of the Family Traditions Interviews (so he did not have access to potentially confounding peripheral information such as the family's resources or economic status). Moreover, the consortium rater was blind to the diagnostic status of the mothers (although, in some cases, the content of the interview revealed evidence of illness). Finally, the consortium rater did not conduct or code any other family protocol. Transcripts that were difficult to code were conferenced with the criterion rater, and scored by consensus. Adequate reliability on all Narrative Consortium scales was established; detailed reliability information is provided in the introductory chapter of this *Monograph*.

Family and Child Assessments

We used a multimethod assessment strategy, evaluating family, marital and child functioning. A list of measures, their format, and group means for the illness and no illness group is presented in Table 20.

TABLE 20
DESCRIPTION OF MEASURES

Construct	Measure	Format	Score	Group Scores [M (SD)]		
				No Illness	Depressed	
					Low	High
Psychopathology	SCID	Interview	Diagnosis Major Depression			
	Hamilton	Interview	Severity of Depressive Symptoms	0.94 (1.11)	1.80 (1.74)	10.11 (3.89)
Family Functioning	McSiff	Interview	Overall Family Functioing	5.72 (0.89)	5.00 (1.25)	3.33 (1.66)
	FAD-Family of Origin	Questionaire	Overall Family Functioning:			
			Wives	1.93 (0.43)	2.39 (0.52)	2.82 (0.24)
			Husbands	2.28 (0.41)	2.30 (0.37)	2.47 (0.69)
	Mealtime Interaction	Observation	Overall Family Functioning	5.50 (1.04)	5.15 (1.14)	4.71 (1.60)
Marital Relationship	DAS	Questionaire	Marital Satisfaction:			
			Wives	111.60 (11.03)	103.07 (12.81)	91.41 (16.12)
			Husbands	109.81 (10.19)	105.88 (14.27)	87.30 (16.25)
Child Behavior	CBCL	Questionaire (mother report)	Total	40.13 (9.85)	48.57 (7.13)	47.17 (7.28)
			Internalizing	41.53 (8.17)	44.93 (6.92)	43.50 (6.44)
			Externalizing	40.47 (9.44)	49.79 (6.85)	49.33 (7.12)

Psychopathology Assessment

Structured Clinical Interview for DSM-III-R Diagnosis
(SCID; Spitzer, Williams, Gibbon, & First, 1990)

The SCID Interview for Clinical Syndromes Axis I (SCID) and Personality Disorders-Axis II (SCID II) were administered to each parent. The full range of lifetime history Axis I and Axis II diagnoses were obtained. Excellent reliability has been demonstrated (Riskind, Beck, Berchik, Brown, & Steer, 1987). In addition to diagnostic information, this interview yields information about severity and chronicity of illness. Thus, mothers within each of these groups varied on the frequency, duration, and recency of their illness episode(s), although all had met *DSM-III-R* criteria at least at one point in time. We report here on mothers who met criteria for Major Depression.

Modified Hamilton Rating Scale for Depression
(MHRSD; Miller, Bishop, Norman, & Maddever, 1985)

The MHRSD is a 17-item clinician-rated interview assessing current severity of depressive symptoms. It was administered by the clinician during the SCID interview.

In order to conduct planned group comparisons to assess effect of severity of current depressive symptoms as a modifier of depression diagnosis, we divided the sample into three groups based on sample means to include: (a) 18 women who were not diagnosed with *DSM-III-R* Major Depression, all of whom also had MHRSD scores less than 6; (b) 16 women who were diagnosed with *DSM-III-R* Major Depression and had low current depressive symptoms indicated by MHRSD scores less than 6; and (c) nine women who were diagnosed with *DSM-III-R* Major Depression and had high current rates of depressive symptoms indicated by MHRSD scores greater than or equal to 6. The average scores for the three groups are presented in Table 20.

Family Functioning Assessment

We relied on the McMaster model of family functioning focused on processes occurring within the family system that generate behaviors disruptive to everyday functioning of the family unit (Epstein, Bishop, & Levin, 1978; Epstein & Bishop, 1981). Family functioning is conceptualized along six dimensions: problem solving, communication, roles, affective responsiveness, affective involvement, and behavior control.

Briefly, the Clinical Rating Scale allows clinicians to assign standardized ratings of family functioning on the above six dimensions using the

McMaster Structured Interview of Family Functioning as a guide for questioning. The Family Assessment Device, a self-report measure, also assesses these six dimensions of current family functioning as rated by individual family members; we modified this questionnaire to have each family member rate the six dimensions of family functioning about their own family of origin as it was recalled from their childhood. We also extended the model to develop the Mealtime Interaction Coding System to code the six family functioning dimensions from observational data of family interaction.

McMaster Structured Interview of Family Functioning (McSIFF; Epstein, Bishop, & Baldwin, 1982)

This clinician-conducted interview yields information from which Clinical Rating Scale scores are assigned in six McMaster domains of family functioning. Overall Family Functioning was rated, which takes into account all information obtained in the interview. Descriptive statistics are presented in Table 20. In previous research, the McSIFF has proven reliable and valid, and distinguished mentally ill from non-ill samples (Keitner, Miller, Ryan, Bishop, & Epstein, 1990).

Mealtime Interaction Coding System (MICS; Dickstein, Hayden, Schiller, Seifer, & San Antonio, 1994)

Family interaction was videotaped during a family meal to assess naturalistic family functioning. This allowed for coding of observed behaviors such as negotiation of conflicting needs, management of the flow of the meal, and behavioral control strategies for children, as well as affective and instrumental availability of family members to one another. We rated these observed family interactions on six modified McMaster Model domains of family functioning: task accomplishment, communication, roles, affect management, interpersonal involvement, and behavior control. An Overall Family Functioning score was provided based on overall quality of family functioning during the observation segment (i.e., the first 20 min of the meal). Scores range from 1 (very unhealthy) to 7 (very healthy) for each of the domains, with scores of 1 to 4 indicating clinical level disturbance. Average scores for each group are presented in Table 20. Raters were reliable, and patterns of association with other observational measures of family functioning and maternal parenting style support construct validity (Hayden, Schiller, Dickstein, Seifer, & Matzko, 1994).

Family Assessment Device for Family of Origin Functioning (FAD; Epstein, Baldwin, & Bishop, 1983)

The FAD is a 60-item self-report questionnaire based on the McMaster Model to assess the six domains of family functioning (listed above) as well as a Total Family Functioning score (Epstein et al., 1983; Miller, Epstein, Bishop, & Keitner, 1985). Respondents rate items on a 4-point scale ranging from very healthy (1) to very unhealthy (4), with *lower* scores indicating better family functioning (see Table 20 for average scores). The FAD distinguishes between families rated by clinicians as healthy or unhealthy (Miller et al., 1985), and between families with a recovered versus nonrecovered depressed member who have rated themselves as healthy or unhealthy (Keitner, Ryan, Miller, Epstein, & Bishop, 1990). We modified this questionnaire to have each family member rate the six dimensions of family functioning about their own family of origin as it was recalled from their childhood and was completed independently by husbands and wives. In the current analyses, the Total FAD Family of Origin Functioning score for each spouse was used.

Dyadic Adjustment Scale (DAS; Spanier, 1976)

The quality of and level of conflict within the marital relationship was assessed using the DAS, a 32-item instrument that has been widely used to assess dyadic satisfaction, cohesion, consensus, and affectional expression within the current partner relationship. This yields an overall Marital Satisfaction score for husbands and wives, with a mean score of 100, and higher scores indicative of increased marital satisfaction (see Table 20 for average scores).

Child Assessment

Child Behavior Checklist (CBCL; Achenbach, 1988)

Mothers completed the CBCL questionnaire regarding their child's behavioral functioning when the child was 30 months of age. The 2–3 year version of the CBCL is a 100-item questionnaire regarding the child's behavior. Three broad band summary scores are obtained, including: Total Behavior Problems, Internalizing Problems, and Externalizing Problems. Raw scores are converted to age- and sex-normed T scores with a mean of 50 and standard deviation of 10. Higher scores indicate increased behavior problems. Table 20 presents T scores for each group.

RESULTS

Results are presented to address the three main study questions indicated above.

Question 1: Do Narrative Consortium Scales Differentiate Between No Illness and Depression Groups?

A consistent pattern emerged from the data differentiating no illness and depressed groups on the three Narrative Consortium dimensions, which is presented in Table 21. Our strategy was to evaluate two orthogonal planned comparisons that together comprise the 2 df overall F test. These contrasts were no illness versus low- and high-depression groups, and low-depression versus high-depression groups. For wives, all of the Coherence scales except Congruence significantly distinguished the no illness from depression diagnosis groups, independent of level of symptom severity. On three of five Coherence scales, husbands of depressed wives were found to do more poorly, again independent of the level of wives' symptom severity. In contrast, and contrary to expectations, none of the Narrative Interaction scales distinguished the groups. Finally, for both husbands and wives, Relationship Beliefs within the Current Family significantly distinguished between the groups, with the presence of depression diagnosis associated with less positive views of the immediate family relationship. This pattern was consistent for wives' beliefs about Family of Origin relationships as well. Although this was expected for wives, it is interesting to note that for husbands of depressed wives, the severity of wives' symptoms was related to husbands' report of less optimal family of origin relationships. There were no group differences for the Interviewer Intimacy scale (see Table 21).

Question 2: To What Extent Were Narrative Consortium Scales Related to Other Family Functioning Measures?

We explored the validity of the consortium's narrative scales by examining associations with other aspects of family life, including marital satisfaction, family functioning as determined by clinical judgment following a structured family interview, and family interaction rated in the context of observed family mealtime behavior. These results are presented in Table 22.

The overall pattern that emerged was that for both wives and husbands, all levels of family factors examined were significantly related to Narrative Coherence. More coherent narratives produced by both wives and husbands were associated with self-report of marital satisfaction, clinician-based

TABLE 21

MEANS AND STANDARD DEVIATIONS IN NO ILLNESS AND DEPRESSED
(WITH LOW AND HIGH CURRENT SYMPTOMS) GROUPS
ON NARRATIVE COHERENCE, INTERACTION AND RELATIONSHIP BELIEFS SCALES

	No Illness (NI)		Depressed-Low (DL)		Depressed-High (DH)		$F(2,40)$	Significant ($p < .05$) Group Contrasts
	($n = 18$)		($n = 16$)		($n = 9$)			
Wife Narrative Coherence								
Internal Consistency	3.39	(1.29)	2.63	(.89)	2.67	(1.32)	2.18	NI vs. DL, DH
Organization	3.61	(.85)	3.00	(.73)	2.89	(1.05)	3.09	NI vs. DL, DH
Flexibility	3.56	(.62)	3.25	(.77)	2.89	(.78)	2.70	NI vs. DL, DH
Congruence	3.61	(.92)	3.44	(.63)	2.89	(.60)	2.75	
Coherence Summary	3.54	(.74)	3.08	(.62)	2.83	(.77)	3.58*	NI vs. DL, DH
Husband Narrative Coherence								
Internal Consistency	3.00	(1.24)	2.69	(1.01)	2.11	(.60)	2.14	NI vs. DL, DH
Organization	2.94	(.94)	2.81	(.66)	2.33	(.87)	1.67	
Flexibility	3.17	(.99)	2.70	(.87)	2.33	(.70)	2.86	NI vs. DL, DH
Congruence	3.50	(.79)	3.12	(.66)	3.00	(.71)	1.64	
Coherence Summary	3.15	(.81)	2.84	(.71)	2.44	(.58)	2.85	NI vs. DL, DH
Narrative Interaction								
Couple Narrative Style	3.89	(.90)	3.50	(1.41)	3.11	(1.45)	1.25	
Coordination	2.89	(.83)	2.94	(.68)	2.56	(1.13)	0.64	
Wife: Confirmation	3.76	(.75)	3.56	(.89)	3.44	(.73)	0.53	
Husband: Confirmation	3.82	(.73)	3.69	(.70)	3.11	(1.05)	2.44	
Interaction Summary	3.52	(.70)	3.35	(.82)	2.98	(.96)	1.35	
Relationship Beliefs								
Wife: Family of Origin	3.44	(.98)	2.71	(.73)	1.88	(.64)	10.03**	NI vs. DL, DH; DL vs. DH
Husband: Family of Origin	3.25	(.77)	3.27	(1.03)	2.38	(.74)	3.21*	DL vs. DH
Wife: Current Family	4.11	(.68)	3.63	(.72)	3.00	(1.00)	6.41**	NI vs. DL, DH
Husband: Current Family	4.11	(.76)	3.81	(.83)	3.11	(.93)	4.44*	NI vs. DL, DH
Interviewer Intimacy	3.67	(.69)	3.63	(.50)	3.44	(.88)	0.34	

* $p < .05$ for overall F test.

** $p < .01$ for overall F test.

TABLE 22

CORRELATIONS AMONG FAMILY OUTCOME MEASURES AND NARRATIVE SUMMARY VARIABLES

| | Marital Satisfaction | | Family Assessment | |
	Wife	Husband	McSiff Interview	Dinner Observation
Wife Narrative Coherence				
Internal Consistency	.34*	.23	.31*	.36*
Organization	.13	.21	.39**	.57**
Flexibility	.22	.30*	.44**	.54**
Congruence	.23	.32*	.28	.26
Coherence Summary	.39**	.33*	.43**	.44**
Husband Narrative Coherence				
Internal Consistency	.13	.21	.39**	.57**
Organization	.16	.36*	.40**	.40**
Flexibility	.37*	.27	.45**	.54**
Congruence	.30*	.31*	.40**	.39**
Coherence Summary	.28	.33*	.48**	.58**
Narrative Interaction				
Couple Narrative Style	.31*	.28	.26	.37**
Coordination	.24	.12	.09	.34*
Wife: Confirmation	.20	.23	.25	.28
Husband: Confirmation	.34*	.28	.36*	.39**
Interaction Summary	.33*	.27	.26	.41**
Relationship Beliefs				
Wife: Family of Origin	.45**	.47**	.45**	.44**
Husband: Family of Origin	.44**	.40**	.49**	.20
Wife: Current Family	.48**	.52**	.61**	.57**
Husband: Current Family	.30*	.40**	.56**	.57**
Interviewer Intimacy	.10	-.05	.06	.31*

Note—These effects remain similar when SES and depression status are partialled from the analyses.
* $p < .05$.
** $p < .01$.

judgments of healthier family functioning, and rater-based observations of family interaction. In general, observational measures (compared with self-reports) were more associated with narrative measures of coherence.

As expected, the observed interaction patterns of families at dinnertime were related to Narrative Interaction during the narrative task, with healthier family functioning observed in those families who were better able to work together to construct a joint narrative. It is particularly interesting to note that observed family interaction at dinnertime was positively associated with husbands' (and not wives') extent of confirmatory behavior during the narrative task.

Finally, also as expected, husbands' and wives' positive Relationship Beliefs within the Current Family were significantly associated with marital satisfaction and healthy family functioning. The same pattern was generally evident for positive Relationship Beliefs within the Family of Origin; however, for husbands, whereas positive beliefs about family of origin experiences were related to marital satisfaction and clinician-based judgments of family functioning, they were not associated with observed family interaction during the dinnertime context.

Convergent and discriminant validity was provided for the Relationship Beliefs within the Family of Origin scale. For both wives and husbands, positive views of family of origin experiences provided in the narrative context were significantly related to self-reports of healthy early childhood family of origin functioning ($r = .72$ and .43, respectively). As expected, there was no evidence for husband-wife correspondence on their views of their own family of origin experiences provided in the narrative context ($r = .18$). Finally, it is interesting to note that self-reports of husbands' and wives' own early childhood family of origin functioning were related to virtually no Narrative Coherence nor Narrative Interaction scales.

Correspondence Between Husbands and Wives

Given the similarity in patterns described above, we explored the extent to which there was correspondence between husbands' and wives' narrative quality, independent of diagnosis. Of the eight scales that were coded separately for husbands and wives, no significant differences were found for five of them (see Table 23). There was evidence that wives overall produced more organized narratives and were able to maintain a more flexible perspective about family issues. There were no significant differences overall between wives and husbands regarding their behavior during the narrative situation (i.e., confirming or disconfirming their partners' comments) nor the extent to which they maintain positive views of relationships.

To assess consistency within couples on these scales, we computed wife-husband correlations on the independently rated Narrative Consortium scales (see Table 23). Wives' and husbands' scores were significantly associated for seven of the eight scales (with correlations ranging from .39 to .73). As indicated above, there was no husband-wife correspondence on the Relationship Beliefs within the Family of Origin scale.

TABLE 23

WIFE-HUSBAND MEAN DIFFERENCE AND CORRESPONDENCE BETWEEN NARRATIVE COHERENCE, NARRATIVE INTERACTION, AND RELATIONSHIP BELIEFS SCALES ($n = 43$)

	Wife		Husband		Wife-Husband	Wife-Husband
					Mean Difference	Correspondence
	Mean	(SD)	Mean	(SD)	(t)	(r)
Narrative Coherence						
Internal						
Consistency	2.95	(1.19)	2.70	(1.08)	1.64	.60**
Organization	3.23	(0.89)	2.77	(0.84)	3.08*	.39**
Flexibility	3.30	(0.74)	2.81	(0.93)	3.74*	.50**
Congruence	3.39	(0.79)	3.28	(0.73)	1.15	.63**
Coherence						
Summary	3.22	(0.74)	2.89	(0.76)	3.84*	.72**
Narrative Interaction						
Confirm/						
Disconfirm[1]	3.62	(0.80)	3.62	(0.83)	0.00	.67**
Relationship Beliefs						
Family Origin[2]	2.89	(1.02)	3.08	(0.95)	0.91	.18
Current Family	3.70	(0.86)	3.79	(0.89)	0.94	.73**

[1] $n = 42$ couples.
[2] $n = 37$ couples.
* $p < .05$.
** $p < .01$.

Question 3: To What Extent Were Narrative Consortium Scales Related to Child Outcome Measures?

We explored the associations among the Narrative Consortium summary variables and child behavior outcomes as rated by mothers when children were 30 months old. Results indicated no significant associations among narrative scales and child outcome measures as rated by mothers.

DISCUSSION

The goal of assessing the utility of the newly developed Narrative Consortium scales to code family narratives in a high risk sample was attained. We found expected associations between presence of maternal depression and narrative coherence and relationship beliefs for wives and husbands, with one exception of the narrative interaction domain. We also found interesting relations between narrative domains and other measures of family functioning, although expected associations with child outcomes were not found.

Narrative Assessment and Depression

We rely on attachment theory (Bowlby, 1969/1982, 1973, 1980) to better understand the mechanisms by which maternal depression may be related to poor family and child outcomes via disturbances in relationship functioning that are incorporated as internal working models (e.g., Cummings & Cicchetti, 1990). Recent methodological developments have facilitated more direct assessment of adults' current working models of their past relationships, termed adult attachment (George, Kaplan, & Main, 1985; Main & Goldwyn, 1984). The narrative methodology used in the current project extends this work by quantifying adults' representations of current family life, which shares the same family context within which maternal depression is expressed. We assume that the narratives provided reflect relationship models that have developed in the course of repeated interactions with significant others, and are used as a lens through which current family relationships are filtered. Thus, narrative coherence is considered to reflect the representational model used by the parent to integrate family relationship experiences. Although beyond the scope of this chapter, it would be important for future work to assess the degree to which our assumptions are valid. We need to better examine the mechanisms by which depression is related to narrative coherence, including possibilities that depression affects internal working models that are then related to narrative quality, that certain types of representational processes predispose individuals to depression, and/or that some underlying factor explains both vulnerability to depression and narrative coherence.

Depression Diagnosis Versus Symptoms

One of the unique aspects of the Providence Family Study is the attention paid to categorical diagnosis of depression (by *DSM-III-R* criteria) and the concomitant assessment of current depressive symptoms, independent of diagnosis. We found that, for the most part, disruptions to narrative coherence for both husbands and wives was related to the presence of depression diagnosis, not necessarily to the severity of the current symptoms. Beliefs about family of origin relationships were, however, related to increased depressive symptoms. This is consistent with other work from the Providence Family Study, indicating that functional impairment and symptom severity of ill mothers provides additional predictive power associated with family functioning above and beyond categorical diagnosis of illness (Dickstein et al., 1998). More clarification regarding impact of categorical diagnosis versus symptom severity is warranted. To the extent that women act as family "gatekeepers" when they are ill, their heightened unavailability from the family may significantly impact the family's ability to function adequately (Parke & Kellam, 1994).

Narrative Assessment and Family Functioning

Family-unit functioning assessed across contexts (i.e., clinician ratings of family functioning during interview and observed family interaction during a meal) were associated with wives' and husbands' overall ability to produce a coherent narrative regarding family life. Also, family functioning was related to the extent to which wives and husbands maintained positive and trusting views of relationships, both in the current family and the family of origin. Thus, representations about family relationships produced in narrative form are consistent with family functioning assessed using clinical and direct observation strategies. This is an encouraging finding, which supports validity of the Narrative Consortium scales. It also is consistent with attachment research, in which association between maternal representations of family life and quality of parent-child interaction is well documented (Benoit, Vidovic, & Roman, 1991; Eichberg, 1987; Fonagy, Steele, & Steele, 1991; Main & Goldwyn, 1996; Ward, Botyanski, Plunkett, & Carlson, 1991).

Thus far, we have discussed the association between narrative production and family-unit functioning. We also assessed family functioning at another level—marital relationship satisfaction. In previous work, the quality of the marital relationship was found to regulate cognitive-affective processes and provide an important basis of social support (e.g., Quinton, Rutter, & Liddle, 1984). We generally did not find marital satisfaction related to narrative coherence nor to narrative interaction domains, although striking associations were demonstrated with relationship beliefs for the current family and family of origin contexts, for both husbands and wives. This is consistent with prior work in high-risk families, showing stronger links between relationship outcomes and family-unit functioning as compared with marital satisfaction.

The only set of outcome measures associated with the couples' interaction while producing a narrative was the family's quality of interaction during the observed dinnertime situation. This supports validity for the consortium's domain in that the nature of family interaction was consistent across measurement strategies. Otherwise, the Narrative Interaction domain seemed least useful for elucidating processes in our high risk sample. This was surprising, given the wealth of high-risk literature suggesting less optimal marital and parent-child interactions in depressed families. It is possible that the method of data collection limited our ability to find associations. That is, the Family Traditions Interview narratives were scored from transcripts of audiotapes, precluding assessment of nonverbal interaction (such as gaze, touch, body posture, and so on), which may have better informed the narrative interaction codes.

Husband-Wife Concordance

We examined the correspondence of narrative domains for husbands and wives. The influence of husbands/fathers has been the focus of remarkably little research in the domain of developmental psychopathology, which is a critical omission given their unique and important role within the family (Crockenberg, Lyons-Ruth, & Dickstein, 1993; Lamb, 1979; Phares, 1992; Phares & Compas, 1992; Russell & Radojevic, 1992). We found the extent to which husbands and wives produced coherent narratives was very similar, explaining approximately 50% of the variance for narrative coherence, confirmation/disconfirmation, and relationship beliefs about the current family. This may be important when considering the association between couples' perceptions about family life and quality of family functioning and child developmental outcome.

Another point of interest is that although wives and husbands agreed on the positive nature of relationships within their current family, there was not correspondence on the extent to which they had these beliefs about their own families of origin. This provides some evidence for discriminant validity of the technique of assessing different representational models for different relationships. As such, it would be interesting to investigate the individual differences nature of relationship perceptions in order to more fully elucidate potential protective and risk factors transmitted to the next generation.

Narrative Assessment and Child Outcomes

No associations were found between the family narratives produced by parents and maternal report of child behavior difficulties. There are at least two possible hypotheses for this unexpected lack of association. First, the children in this sample were very young (1 to 2½ years of age); it is possible that at this early age, child behavior may not be sufficiently problematic for mothers' ratings to distinguish groups. It may be that the effects of narrative style in the context of maternal depression are not reflected in child behavior problems as asked on the CBCL until later in the child's life. Further, the sample was selected for illness in the mothers, with no emphasis placed on child status, perhaps limiting the range of disturbance in these young children.

Second, and more important, it may be that in order to detect child outcomes, especially at this early stage of development, multiple risk factors need to be explored and mediational models need to be developed (Sameroff, Seifer, Baldwin, & Baldwin, 1993; Seifer, Sameroff, Anagnostopolou, & Elias, 1992; Seifer et al., 1996). Families in the Providence Family Study were selected based on presence of maternal mental illness, which often coexists with a host of other risks (such as single-parent status, low SES, etc.). In the Providence Family Study, when children were 1 year old, 91% of the families were intact with fathers living at home. By 2½ years, only 78% remained intact. The subsample selected for the current report may be at relatively reduced risk, due to the decision to include only two-parent families (i.e., 100%) in order to better assess the consortium's scale properties.

Limitations

The results presented in this report need to be interpreted with caution. First, the sample size is relatively small, and there are numerous statistical comparisons made. Whereas this project constitutes a solid initial attempt to determine the effective utilization of the Narrative Consortium's scoring system in a high risk sample, it would be important for future work to use larger samples to replicate patterns. We used a convenient sample, and therefore one should be careful not to generalize the findings from this study to broader based groups. In addition, as noted above, the sample may have a selection bias given the a priori determination to use only two-parent families; this is not representative of families with maternal affective disorder. Finally, the method of data collection (i.e., narratives transcribed from audiotaped interviews) precluded assessment of nonverbal communicative acts that may have limited our ability to adequately assess the narrative interaction scales.

Summary and Future Directions

We examined individuals' narratives about family life within a high-risk sample to more fully elucidate how maternal depression is related to family functioning and child outcomes. The newly developed Narrative Consortium scoring system provided important and unique information. For both husbands and wives, depression was related to decreased narrative coherence and less positive views of relationships, although not to narrative interaction. Family functioning assessed across contexts (i.e., clinician ratings of family functioning during interview, and observed family interaction during a meal) was associated with mothers' and fathers' narrative coherence and relationship beliefs. Family functioning assessed within the interactional context was related to Narrative Interaction scales. No associations were found between any of the consortium's narrative domains and child behavior difficulties.

Future work should focus on more precise characterization of mental illness. That is, we demonstrated that nonspecific depressive illness factors (i.e., severity of depressive symptoms), in addition to depression diagnosis, were associated with narrative production. It would be important to further specify whether findings are unique to depression, related nonspecific illness factors, or best explained by global assessment of family risk. Furthermore, it would be important to determine the extent to which the quality of parental narratives are associated with other categories of maternal mental illness by including clinical comparison groups. Finally, examination of other child outcome factors (such as attachment security) across various stages of child development is needed. Narrative methodology and the newly developed Narrative Consortium's coding system will likely be helpful in elucidating the mechanisms by which mental illness is transmitted across generations.

VI. NARRATIVE CONNECTIONS IN THE FAMILY CONTEXT: SUMMARY AND CONCLUSIONS

Arnold J. Sameroff and Barbara H. Fiese

Families Affect Children

The understanding of child development has required increased attention to the social context in which the child is reared. Initially, the focus was restricted to mother-child interactions as the sole context, but gradually an ecological model has been accepted in which increasing attention is paid not only to other parenting figures, beginning with fathers, but also to other generations of parenting figures. What we are proposing is that a representational aspect of this expanded social model must be assessed as well as the behavioral manifestations. Our entry into this effort is through family narratives.

The ways parents influence child development take many forms. Some of these are direct and can be observed in specific practices aimed at teaching and regulating behavior in domains of cognitive, emotional, social, and civic functioning (Landesman et al., 1991). Some of these are still observable but less direct through examples parents provide in their own behavior and the models they demonstrate for their children (Parke & Bhavnagri, 1989). And some of these are not only indirect but also not easily observable, because they abide in the organization of thought that underlies parent behavior rather than the behavior itself. A further complication is the addition of family behavior to individual parent behavior. When family members are together, their individual behavior often appears quite different than when they are separate. Moreover, behavior may take on different forms and values depending on which subset of family members are present (Reiss, 1989).

To capture this differentiation of family processes, David Reiss (1989) made the distinction between research strategies devoted to assessing the represented family and those assessing the practicing family. The narrative analyses we have proposed in this *Monograph* are devoted to elaborating and validating the various dimensions of psychological functioning embedded in this distinction. The basic difference is between what families do, which is observable, and how they represent relationships, which is detectable but not necessarily directly observable.

For Reiss (1989), the stability and coherence of family practices resides not in the individual, but in the coordinated behavior of combinations of family members. Group interaction beyond the thought of its individual participants "conserves relationships and regulates and perpetuates many aspects of ongoing family life" (p. 193). Indeed, it is not only the creation and maintenance of representations of family relationships that is regulated by the group process, but also the family's interaction with outside members. In our case, the interactions of the family with the interviewer became our window into the openness with which the family can engage the larger social environment. In this regard, an ecological model of childrearing includes not only a recognition that broader social issues influence the family and child, but also that there are different ways in which the family engages its social world.

Although there is a long history and interest in how mental representations affect behavior, especially in psychodynamic traditions, how representations are carried across generations and from individual to individual is of more recent concern. Much of this work in developmental research is associated with attachment theory and its attention to internal working models as a form of mental representation (Main & Goldwyn, 1984). From this perspective, family interactive and relationship behavior arises from representations in the parent, influenced by relationships with his or her parent, and are absorbed or internalized by the young child to form a new generation of working models. For Reiss (1989), the important core of this perspective is that coherence of family interaction patterns is both represented by such working models and maintained by them. Furthermore, the coherence of family relationships spreads across several domains pertinent to family life including, but not limited to, the formation of new relationships through marriage, normative transitions such as birth of a child or sending a child to school, and nonnormative events such as family illness.

The Empirical Task

The Family Narrative Consortium (FNC) has attempted to demonstrate that separate dimensions of family narratives can be identified, have different relations to the family of origin, have implications for the status of the couple relationship, and may influence the development of children in the family. To achieve this, the FNC developed a methodology to investigate family practices and representations through the analysis of narratives produced by parents and young couples.

We have made our task financially easier, but empirically more difficult, by doing a secondary data analysis of family narratives already collected in four separate research projects undertaken by different investigators with quite disparate hypotheses and goals. If we can demonstrate that the analytic strategy is robust across such disparate data sets, then it could be applied to the analysis of other narratives collected by still other investigators with still other hypotheses and goals.

We demonstrated that the system could be used reliably across sites and that adequate validity could be established by comparing FNC narrative scores with other measures of family functioning. In addition to addressing the psychometric qualities of the system, we were interested in how the construction of family narratives would be affected by social context. In this regard, we explored discrepancies across the sites as well as consistencies. Separate analyses of data from the four FNC sites allowed us to examine the context of individual versus family constructed narratives, newly constructed versus frequently told stories, differences between husbands and wives, and the effects of mental illness.

The Washington, DC, study of couple formation, the Syracuse study of family routines, the Minnesota study of child adoption, and the Providence study of maternal depression differed in interview formats, duration of couple relationship, existence, age and adoption status of children, and mental health of the mothers. What they had shared was that they all involved couple narratives about family life. What the FNC added to this was a common analytic strategy based on three dimensions: (1) Narrative Coherence, (2) Narrative Interaction, and (3) Relationship Beliefs. We hypothesized that these dimensions would be related in many different ways both conceptually and empirically. Conceptually, we believed that family representations could be assessed by the coherence and relationship belief dimensions and family practices could be assessed by the interaction dimension. Empirically, we believed that scales could be designed to assess these dimensions and that coherence and interaction could be distinguished as part of a narrative model. Four aspects of coherence were proposed to comprise the FNC subscales of the coherence dimension and four other aspects of the narrative were proposed to comprise the FNC subscales of the interaction dimension. We expected these dimensions to be moderately related to each other. The third dimension, relationship beliefs, was considered to be a more complex indicator of the represented family and potentially could serve as a moderator in maintaining family practices. The FNC relationship belief subscales included narrative representations associated with the current family, family of origin, and the interviewer. Because of the focus on content, it was considered separately from the other dimensions that focused more on the narrative process.

Reliability of Narrative Dimensions

To establish the usefulness of our narrative assessment scheme, we had to demonstrate three things: first, that the FNC scales could be reliably coded; second, that the three narrative dimensions had internal consistency; and third, that these dimensions were related to other aspects of the behavior of family members.

Data analyses performed within and across the four sites led us to believe that we were successful in our first goal of creating a reliable measure of family narratives. The FNC scheme could be applied to a wide variety of interview formats and contexts. Raters were successfully trained at each site to code reliably each of the proposed dimensions.

To answer the question of internal consistency, scale reliabilities were calculated at each site. The resulting coefficients were high enough for the coherence and interaction dimensions to indicate that we were reasonably successful in this goal. There was variability across sites, however, primarily between the Washington, DC, site and the other three. The primary difference among the samples in the sites was that, in Washington, DC, we were dealing with couples who were in the beginning stages of dyadic adjustment, still getting to know each other and actively working out many aspects of a dynamic relationship without a clear conclusion. In the other sites, all couples were married and had children who were at least preschool age, and usually older. These data led us to consider that the length of relationship can affect the consistency of our narrative dimensions. Because these couples were at the beginning stage of their relationship, they did not have the interactional histories expected of the married couples at the other sites, and they generally had a shorter history of shared couple experiences. It is not possible with this data set to determine whether length of relationship or extent of shared experiences made it easier or harder to construct a coherent relationship narrative. An alternative hypothesis can be generated when considering the characteristics of the Washington, DC, sample. In general, these couples were less satisfied in their relationships than would be expected from a random sample of young couples. It may be that couples who start out a relationship with complaints and dissatisfaction present a less coherent account of their journey together rather than the newness of the relationship affecting coherence. Further research is needed to test this alternate hypothesis.

The overall internal consistency of the FNC relationship beliefs subscales was relatively low at all sites. It would appear that there was no single dimension to the individual beliefs about relationships. The current family, family of origin, and interviewer intimacy scales were relatively uncorrelated, which was not surprising. There is no inherent reason why beliefs about the trustworthiness of one's relationship with one's spouse should be the same as one's family of origin, or with some stranger doing an interview with you. The correlation between beliefs about the most distal relationships, narratives concerning the family of origin, and the interviewer intimacy scale were essentially zero. The more temporally proximal relationships, current family and interviewer scales, had higher intercorrelations averaging in the twenties.

Not surprisingly, husbands' and wives' narrative beliefs about the trustworthiness of relationships in their current family were highly correlated. Given that the couples were describing shared family experiences, there was a consistency in how they represented their general satisfaction with these relationships. Researchers and clinicians interested in what makes couples satisfied with their relationship have long recognized that a shared consensus or worldview should be related to more marital satisfaction (Berger & Kellner, 1964; Stephen & Markman, 1983). Across the sites in this study, husbands and wives tended to describe their family life in similar ways, such that expectations for both rewarding and unrewarding relationships were shared by husbands and wives.

Husbands and wives differed, however, in the degree to which beliefs about family of origin relationships were related to current family relationships. For wives, there was a relatively strong link between their family of origin and current family beliefs. For husbands, the link was relatively weak. Women have been proposed to be the "kinkeepers" in extended family relationships (Oliveri & Reiss, 1981), often determining the extent to which current family relationships are affected by extended family relationships. In this regard, women who hold the belief that their family of origin relationships are rewarding may be more likely to form similar beliefs about their current family relationships. These findings are consistent with Bowen's theory of the multigenerational influences on relationships. As proposed by Bowen (1978), the current family is formed as part of a generational process, whereby representations of the family of origin are infused into the current family. When the family of origin has provided supportive and accepting models, the family of procreation can be blended successfully with past images of family life.

A more comprehensive approach to assessing the dimensional structure of the FNC assessment was to undertake a confirmatory factor analysis of the scales using data from the four sites. We were partially successful in this effort; it worked for the narrative interaction dimension, but not completely for narrative coherence. In both separate and combined analyses of mothers' and fathers' recitals the four FNC subscales of narrative style, coordination, husband confirmation, and wife confirmation fit well on the narrative interaction dimension. The four subscales of the FNC narrative coherence dimension, however, held together only for husbands. For the wives and the combined analysis, only the internal consistency and organization subscales were common components of the coherence dimension.

These findings point to a further exploration of gender differences in narrative coherence. There has been considerable attention paid to the differential ways in which men and women use language to describe relationships (Gilligan, 1982; Riessman, 1993; Thompson & Walker, 1989). From the perspective of the FNC coding scheme, internal consistency and organization of the narrative were central components of coherence for men and women. These two subscales note how well the facts of the story are organized and whether supporting evidence fits with the overall theory of the story being told. Flexibility and congruence of affect and content were found to be distinct aspects of coherence for women. These two subscales include the expression of multiple perspectives in relationships and the regulation of affect during the storytelling process. For women, it may be that these more affectively laden and relationship-focused scales are not as closely linked to the organizational aspect of constructing a narrative. For men, the relational aspects were more tightly connected to the organizational aspects.

Finally, we examined the intercorrelations among the coherence and interaction dimensions and the belief subscales. Here we again found that the more proximal interviewer and current family relationship beliefs were more related to coherence and interaction dimensions than the more distal family of origin beliefs. In general, there was more consistency for wives between their family of origin beliefs and the other narrative dimensions. These findings again raise the issue of generational effects on family narratives, particularly for women.

Individual Versus Joint Interviews

The Minnesota study permitted another perspective on the narrative analysis, in that we were able to compare couple's behavior when together with the narratives they gave when interviewed separately. In accord with Reiss's (1989) analyses of family paradigms, we expected that performance as a family would be different from performance as individuals. Indeed, these were the findings. The correlations between husband and wife coherence in the joint interview were higher than between husband and wife in the individual interviews. It also was possible to examine whether the act of constructing a narrative as a couple was related to relationship satisfaction. Wives, who were able to construct a more coherent narrative in the presence of their husband than when interviewed alone, were more satisfied with their marital relationship. This finding is consistent with the notion that the marital relationship has the potential to scaffold individuals to more competent behaviors (Wamboldt & Reiss, 1989). Because our coding schemes were based on global estimates of interaction and coherence, we were unable to do sequential analysis to determine whether positive interaction between husband and wife led to more coherence in the narrative. Longitudinal or microanalytic strategies could more accurately assess the potential of the marital relationship to scaffold (or deteriorate) narrative coherence.

The Minnesota analyses comparing couples together and separately throws light on the Washington, DC, data, in which there was especially low coherence in the women's narratives. The dyadic adjustment scores and positive family scores on the Family Environment Scale indicated that there were more than average adjustment problems in these Washington, DC, couples. If this were the case, then in the joint interview we would expect to see a reduction in the coherence that the women would have produced had they been interviewed alone, as found in the Minnesota study. Here is an example where diverse methodologies in this collaboration help to explain anomalies in the data of any particular study.

Summary of Reliability of Narrative Dimensions

From our analyses of the narrative scores across the four sites we conclude that we have identified a set of reliable dimensions that can be used to interpret family narratives. Coders can be reliably trained to code scales that logically cluster on two of our proposed dimensions. The third dimension of beliefs about relationships must be kept subdivided into separate scales for beliefs about the current family, family of origin, and the social world as represented by the interviewer. The next big question to address is whether these scales are related to other aspects of family functioning.

Validity of Narrative Dimensions

The validity of our narrative assessment should be determined by its relation to other dimensions of family life. The data from the four sites in our collaborative effort allowed us to examine the relation of the narrative scales to other behavior of the whole family, to the husband's and wife's behavior as a couple, to other individual characteristics of the husband and wife, and to the developmental progress of their children.

Family Level

Because we are proposing that the assessment of family narratives is an important aspect of family life, it is important that the narrative dimensions show such empirical relations in the data sets. The Washington, DC, Providence, and Syracuse studies included other measures of family functioning that permitted an examination of this issue. The findings from the separate sites are summarized in Table 24. For ease of presentation we have included the self-report measures of family of origin closeness from the Washington, DC, sample, the structured interview of family functioning from the Providence site, and the summary measures of dinnertime affect collected in the Syracuse and Providence studies.

In terms of narrative coherence, the Providence sample provided the most consistent findings. In addition to the family traditions interview used in the FNC analysis, each of the families in the Providence study was rated by an interviewer in a group format, observed at a family dinner, and the

TABLE 24

CROSS-SITE SUMMARY OF NARRATIVE CONSORTIUM SCALES AND FAMILY FUNCTIONING

	Study Site				
	DC Positive Family	DC Close to Mother	DC Close to Father	Providence McSiff	Syracuse Dinner Behavior	Providence Dinner Behavior
Narrative Scale						
Wife Coherence	.43[a]**		.44[a]**	.43**		.44**
Husband Coherence				.48**		.58**
Narrative Interaction			−.29[b]*		.39[c]** −.45[d]***	.41**
Current Relationship Beliefs Wife				.61**	.57[c]*** −.53[d]	.57**
Current Relationship Beliefs Husband				.56**	.61[c]*** −.67[d]***	.57**
Relationship Beliefs Family of Origin Wife	.47***	.47***		.45**	.35[c]*	.45**
Relationship Beliefs Family of Origin Husband	.49***	.31*	.34*	.49**	−.36[d]*	.49**
Interviewer Intimacy			.33*		.38[c]** −.38[d]**	.31*

[a]Congruence of Content and Affect subscale.
[b]Men's Confirmation/Disconfirmation subscale.
[c]Positive affect.
[d]Negative affect.
* $p < .05$.
** $p < .01$.
*** $p < .001$.

parents filled out questionnaires about family functioning in addition to the family narrative. These family measures incorporated multiple indicators of behaviors including affect expression, communication, role-taking, and problem-solving. Dinnertime behavior and an assessment of overall family functioning taken from the independent interview were consistently related to narrative coherence for husbands and wives. In the Washington, DC, sample, women's report of the family of origin as cohesive and affectively expressive provided more coherent accounts of their family relationships. The same pattern was not reliable in the Syracuse sample. The corroborative evidence from the Washington, DC, and Providence samples provide preliminary evidence that narrative coherence as measured in this study is related to reports and observations of family functioning. The extensive nature of the assessment of family functioning in Providence, as contrasted to the single observation in Syracuse, may have provided more reliable estimates of family functioning.

In Providence, the three FNC dimensions had significant correlations with each of the other assessments of family behavior. Higher levels of family functioning in the interview, better family functioning at dinnertime, and higher scores on the parent's family functioning questionnaires were related to greater narrative coherence and more positive relationship belief scores on the narrative assessment. Interestingly, the dinnertime observation was more strongly connected to the FNC interaction dimension. This result could be the consequence of shared behavioral component of the two interaction measures. Taken together, these results are strong indicators of the validity of the narrative dimensions as a measure of family functioning.

In the Syracuse study, interactions around dinnertime were observed on a more restricted range of dimensions than in Providence. These included overall positive and negative family affective expression during dinnertime, summary variables considered central to understanding child adjustment in the family context (Katz & Gottman, 1994). Interestingly, these observed affective dimensions were related to the interaction and belief dimensions, but not the FNC coherence scales. The coherence dimension seems to be more related to family role-taking and problem-solving as measured in the Providence study, whereas the interaction and belief dimensions were more closely related to affect regulation and the emotional climate of family interaction as observed in the Syracuse study. These findings suggest that affective features of family life maintain family practices and that family representations involve problem-solving and role-taking dimensions. It is likely that family representations are reaffirmed through family practices and that the affective tone of family practices contributes to the construction of family representations.

We were struck with how consistent the strength of relation between the narrative interaction, relationship beliefs, and directly observed mealtime behavior was across the Providence and Syracuse sites. Using different rating scales of family mealtime behavior, both sites found that close to 20% of the variance was accounted for when correlating FNC interaction scales from the interview setting and family mealtime behavior. The behaviors evidenced by the couple in constructing their stories were consistent with the behaviors observed during a mealtime. This relation may be a consequence of observing families only at mealtimes where coordination of the efforts of multiple family members, confirmation of comments of others, and collaboration are required for effective meals. Whether a similar pattern holds when observing the family in other contexts such as problem-solving or conflict resolution still needs to be determined.

At Providence and Syracuse, over 25% of the variance was found in the relation between mealtime behavior and narrative representations of family relationships. This consistency points to the potential transactive nature between family representations and behavior. Although we cannot directly test our hypothesis in the two cross-sectional studies, the findings do suggest that representations of relationships as recounted by husbands and wives individually are related to how the family interacts when gathered together as a group. Just as with the findings on narrative interaction, whether the same pattern holds in different interactional contexts is yet to be determined. Another possibility is that the narrative assessment and mealtime behaviors may be linked through a common third variable that was not evaluated in any of these studies.

Couple Level

Our primary measure of couple behavior was self-reports of marital satisfaction. Although this measure is only one view of couple functioning, data were collected with this measure in all the studies. We believed that a measure of satisfaction with the marital relation would correlate most highly with the FNC relationship belief and interaction dimensions. In general, we did find positive correlations between marital satisfaction and rater codings for some of the narrative dimensions. The findings were not uniform, however, across sites or narrative dimensions. Summaries of these findings are presented in Table 25.

The most consistent findings across sites were the significant correlations between relationship beliefs and marital satisfaction and the likelihood that the couples would remain together (relationship fate in the Washington, DC, sample). Husbands' and wives' narrative accounts of their current family relationships were tied to how satisfied they were with each other. Relationship stability in the Washington, DC, site also was strongly related to expectations about relationships. Couples who described relationships as trustworthy and

TABLE 25

CROSS-SITE SUMMARY OF NARRATIVE CONSORTIUM, SCALES AND MARITAL SATISFACTION[1]

	Study Site					
Narrative Scales	DC (DAS) N = 53	DC (Instability) N = 48	DC Relationship Fate F(1,48)	Syracuse (DAS) N = 50	Minn. (PSI) N = 27	Providence (DAS) N = 43
Coherence						
Total						
Wife					.47[d]*	.39**
Husband						.33*
Affect Congruence						
Wife						
Husband				.37*		.32*
Narrative Interaction	.33[a]* .36[b]***	−.29[c]*				
Relationship Beliefs						
Current Wife		−.31*				.48**
Current Husband	.42**	−.32*	5.43*	.34*		.30*
Family of Origin Wife				.42***		.45**
Family of Origin Husband				.44***		.44**

[1]Correlations for all measures except DC Relationship Fate which is F-ratio for group comparisons.
[a]Coordination Subscale.
[b]Women's Confirmation/Disconfirmation Subscale.
[c]Men's Confirmation/Disconfirmation Subscale.
[d]Based on differences in coherence between individual and couple interviews.
* $p < .05$.
** $p < .01$.
*** $p < .001$.

expected to be rewarded in future relationships were more likely to remain together as couples and less likely to dissolve their relationship 1 year after the interview. It can be questioned whether lessened expectations for satisfaction led to couple breakup or whether poor interaction patterns confirmed the couple's belief that relationships are not rewarding. Again, the interplay between representations and practices can be seen when examining narratives about family relationships.

Findings at the Providence and Syracuse sites support the contention that family of origin representations may be related to current marital relationships. At both sites, relationship beliefs about the family of origin were related to marital satisfaction of husbands and wives. This pattern did not hold true for the Washington, DC, site. The young Washington, DC, couples may not clearly distinguish between their family of origin and current family situation. Until there has been adequate history in a relationship to create a distinct identity, the family of origin is the most salient reference point and overlaps significantly with representations of the current family.

The narrative interaction dimension assessed how the couple worked together and was expected to be related to self-report measures of marital satisfaction. Overall our findings in this area were relatively weak. The strongest findings were at the Washington, DC, site, where marital satisfaction, stability of the relationship over time, and the likelihood that the couple would stay together was related to FNC interaction scales. It was only by examining the individual subscales at the Syracuse and Providence sites that relations with marital satisfaction could be found. The strongest findings in the Syracuse and Providence sites were between the FNC confirmation scale and marital satisfaction. These subscales were drawn from established measures of marital interaction (i.e., Gottman, 1983; Julien et al., 1987) and include behaviors that have been found to be related to marital distress in married couples (Gottman, 1993; Markman et al., 1988). Discounting another's comment, sarcastic responses, and put-downs are markers of poor marital communication often leading to divorce. In the Washington, DC, sample, confirmation was moderately related to satisfaction but not to endurance of the relationship. Rather, it was the couple's ability to present as a team and demonstrate connectedness in the narrative that was related to stability. Negotiation of roles and finding a balance between individual and group needs may be important aspects of newly formed relationships (Fitzpatrick, 1988) in contrast to long-standing relationships that have already established group rules.

We had lower expectations that the coherence dimension would be related to marital satisfaction, because it is more distal to the couple's experience and may be based on individual cognitive processes. The congruence between affect and content is less cognitively based and was found to be related to marital satisfaction for husbands at the Providence and Syracuse sites. The analysis presented by the Minnesota site points to how narrative coherence may be related to a supportive partner in the marital relationship. For wives, the expression of greater coherence in the couple interview than when interviewed alone was related to greater marital satisfaction. That is, when wives created a more coherent account of family relationships when in their husband's presence, they were more likely to report more satisfied marriages. This pattern also was noted in relation to the observed interaction between husbands and wives. Although narrative coherence may be more distal to the couple's experience, it may be affected by couple practices and interaction patterns. This is another example where narrative representations and practices are seen to be related to each other.

Our analyses of couple level associations and the narrative assessments were restricted to self-reports of marital satisfaction. Marital satisfaction is but one aspect of healthy couple relationships. Indeed, just as we found the narrative process to be composed of different dimensions the assessment of marital relationships may also include multiple aspects (Weiss & Heyman, 1997). Future efforts are warranted to consider how different aspects of marital health may be accessed through a narrative assessment.

Individual Level

Individual differences in parent level variables were available to us in the Minnesota and Providence studies and the findings are summarized in Table 26. Adoption was the issue at Minnesota, and we investigated the degree to which level of disclosure was related to the family narratives. Because disclosure is a more representational than behavioral interaction variable, in that it deals with the restriction of information that can be shared, we expected that there would be stronger relations to the coherence dimension. The data provided support for this expectation, and the husbands' and wives' coherence scores, in both the individual and couple interviews, were significantly different across the three disclosure conditions. Coherence was lowest in the confidential adoptions, in which there was the least sharing of information, and highest in the fully disclosed adoptions, in which there was the most. In this study we were struck with how the manner in which the adoption was handled was related to the family members' construction of a coherent family story.

In the Providence study, we were concerned with how a mother's diagnosis of a major affective disorder would be related to her own and her spouse's narrative performance. Overall, women diagnosed with depression presented a less coherent account of family relationships. Although husbands whose wives were depressed tended to construct less coherent stories, this did not reach statistical significance. Further efforts with larger samples may be able to more accurately detect the ways in which mental illness in one spouse may affect the narrative process in the healthy spouse.

The effects of maternal depression also were related to the relationship belief dimension. Wives held more negative beliefs about current family relationships if they had a lifetime diagnosis or were currently depressed. A similar pattern held for husbands for both groups of wives. Finer discriminations could be made when considering narratives about the family of origin. Wives who currently had symptoms of depression cast their family of origin in the least positive light. Lifetime diagnosis also was associated with lowered

TABLE 26

CROSS-SITE SUMMARY OF NARRATIVE CONSORTIUM SCALES AND TESTS OF GROUP DIFFERENCES

	Group Comparison	
Narrative Scales	Minnesota Openness in Adoption $F(2,24)$	Providence Psychiatric Illness $F(2,40)$
	Individual Couple	Couple
Coherence		
Wife	13.79***; 8.70**	3.58*
Husband	6.85**; 5.36*	
Narrative Interaction		
Relationship Beliefs		
Current Wife		6.41**
Current Husband		4.44*
Family of Origin Wife		10.03**
Family of Origin Husband		3.21*

* $p < .05$.
** $p < .01$.
*** $p < .001$.

expectations for rewarding relationships in the family of origin, but to a lesser degree. For husbands, however, only wives' current symptoms were associated with lower expectations about family of origin relationships. We can only speculate whether this is a spillover effect generalizing from their current situation or a precursor that led to assortative mating to a depressed woman.

The individual difference data provided a view on how both external and internal factors can constrain family narratives. At Minnesota, the need for secrecy or lack of information in the confidential adoptions was related to the way parents talked about their families and constricted the degree of coherence they could provide in their narrative constructions. At the Providence site, the constricted internal emotional functioning accompanying depression was similarly related to the mothers' narratives. These data gave another dimension to the validity of the narrative assessments we had conducted.

Child Level

For developmentalists, the validity of the narrative assessments resides in the degree to which they are predictive of the fate of children in the family. Although there is a distal relation between the form of parental representational processes and the content of child behavior, studies using the adult attachment interviews had provided support for such a connection (van IJzendoorn, 1995). In two of our studies, we had information about child adjustment from the Child Behavior Checklist (CBCL; Achenbach & Edelbrook, 1983) that could be related to the narrative scores.

The data from the Providence site were not very satisfying in this respect. Child behavior data collected for the 2½ year-olds in each family were not significantly correlated with any of the narrative dimensions. The children all had two-parent families, which may have restricted the range of scores to the high end of mental health functioning. In addition to measurement issues, the young age of the children in this study may have limited the potential for strong findings between parent narratives and child adjustment. In order for the child to share in the representational world of the parent, and thus be more directly affected by it, the child should be an active contributor to the process. The limited cognitive skills of 2½ year olds may have precluded an active involvement of the child in the parent's construction of family narratives. Previous work in the area of attachment points to a more direct link between maternal attachment representations and child attachment classifications (Main & Goldwyn, 1984). In the Providence study, parent's general representations about family relationships were not as directly related to child behavior, a longer chain of causal links.

The Syracuse data were more satisfying in connecting family narratives to child behavior. In this larger sample of older children, significant correlations were found between all three narrative dimensions and child behavior scores. The relations were stronger for externalizing than internalizing behavior, but this is not surprising, given the difficulties in parent report of emotional states as compared to observable conduct (Achenbach et al., 1991). The Syracuse data analysis went further and successfully demonstrated that different mediation models were found for husbands and wives. For mothers, the relation between the FNC current family relationship beliefs and child behavior was mediated by the behavioral expression of negative affect at dinnertime. For fathers, however, the relationship between negative dinnertime affect and child behavior problems was mediated by relationship beliefs.

The inconsistent findings between the narrative scores and child behavior are a major limitation of the consortium's effort to link narrative processes with developmental outcomes. The consortium was successful in linking markers of family functioning that should affect child behavior with the narrative measures. The measurement of child behavior and developmental processes, however, was limited to parental reports of child behavior. On the one hand, it is possible that such a link cannot be found and that even with further study and larger samples a direct relation between child behavior and family narrative measures will not be revealed. On the other hand, reports using attachment classifications have found a connection between narrative markers and child adaptation. The narrative measures constructed as a part of this consortium focus on interactional process and relationship representation. A more relationship-focused measure of child behavior, such as attachment, may be a more valid approach in attempting to link narratives and child adjustment.

Families Have Meaning

Both the academic and popular press confront us daily with information that today's children are under siege. On the social side there are increasing incidents of delinquency and problem behavior (Dryfoos, 1991), on the family side there are increasing levels of family instability (Hetherington & Camara, 1984), and on the individual side children are increasingly diagnosed with problems of depression and inattention (Cross-National Collaboration Group, 1992). One of the common explanations of such changes is the declining economic circumstance of middle-class families and the concentration of poverty in inner-city ghettos and rural America. Yet, within the poorest neighborhoods and among the poorest families, children are being raised who are achieving in school, have high levels of self-esteem and efficacy, and are optimistic about their chances for a productive and happy life (Furstenberg, Cook, Eccles, Elder, & Sameroff, 1998).

What distinguishes the development of children who are making it from those who aren't? One answer is that success is intrinsic to the natures of the children themselves. Those that have individual characteristics of intelligence, sociability, and perseverance will succeed in any context. Studies of children growing up under conditions of multiple family and social adversities, however, have found that the most positive individual characteristics cannot overcome the combined burden of social, economic, and family risk factors (Sameroff, 1996; Sameroff, Bartko, Baldwin, Baldwin, & Seifer, 1998).

The important point here is that it is not any single factor alone that distorts the development of children, but rather the unrelenting accumulation of negative influences that permit no opportunity for a haven or escape route. Conversely, there are a variety of promotive and protective factors that render children immune from many of the ravages of economic distress and family instability. The one we have highlighted in this monograph is the meaning system of the family. Our hypothesis is that where family meaning is coherent, family life is more successful in terms of dyadic adjustment, parent mental health, and child mental health. Where family meaning is lacking, where there is inconsistency in thought, incongruence between words spoken and the emotions expressed, and a lack of trust in relationships, both parents and children show the negative effects. This description is, of course, consistent with one that family therapists have been advocating for years. Families that have created meaningful stories about their relationships and in which they are happy in their marriages have children who are well-adjusted (Boszormenyi-Nagy & Ulrich, 1981; Imber-Black, 1988; Kerr, 1981; White & Epston, 1990). The findings from this study do not necessarily extend what we know is healthy for families and children, but rather provide a methodology to gain entry into the insider's view of the family. From this perspective, clinicians may find themselves better equipped to listen to the family's stories as well as consider that there are multiple ways to gain access to the meaning of family stories.

The use of preexisting interviews may have also limited our examination of how the presence of children in the storytelling task may affect narrative processes. Only the Syracuse site included children in the interview process and these children were relatively young (5 to 7 years old). It is still unclear whether having more active participants in the storymaking process may influence the types of relations found between child development and family narratives. Future efforts are warranted to include children of different ages in the storytelling task to further examine this question.

The way couples organize their family representations is related to many aspects of their family practices. We were struck by the apparent interplay between family representations and practices. In some cases, the observable behavior of the family was moderated by the beliefs they held about family relationships, for example, the relation between dinnertime behavior and relationship expectations in the Syracuse study and the scaffolding effect of husband presence on wife coherence in the Minnesota study. In other cases, the family's practices were confirmed through the representations, for example, the likelihood that couples would remain together if they expected rewarding relationships and engaged in coordinated efforts in constructing their stories in the Washington, DC, study. It is probable that family representations and practices do not operate in isolation from each other but indeed are part of a transactive process in which both influence child development.

The analysis of *narrative coherence* provided evidence that we could use this dimension independent of the specific content of the narrative. It should be noted, however, that all of the interviews shared a common focus on family relationships, often evoking powerful and emotional images of family life. By extension, other studies with family narratives would be able to apply this methodology for scoring narrative coherence, even though their contents were different. A focus on how families make meaning out of their personal experiences can be distinguished from other strategies that rely on generating lists of family activities or availability of support.

The narrative beliefs dimension was regarded as part of the family's representation of relationships and expectations for satisfactory encounters with the current family, family of origin, and the social world. Interestingly, the findings using this dimension were relatively consistent and strong across the sites. When considering how representations influence child-rearing, it will be important to determine the different types of relationships that influence child development. In our study, we found that family of origin representations, although often distal to the child's experience, influenced satisfaction in the marriage, which in turn may influence child development. More proximal to the child's experience are beliefs about current relationships, which would potentially include the child as an active contributor. These beliefs may be more proximal to the child's experience and were found to be related to current child behavior and family interaction. Beliefs regarding the outside social world may be important to consider when the family is faced with negotiating interchanges between family and social context such as schools, medical institutions, and the legal system. Central to the various belief systems is an emphasis on how meaning is transmitted to the child and may serve as regulator of the child's beliefs about relationships in the future.

Constraints on meaning-making were evident in our findings. Individual characteristics such as maternal depression and institutional constraints, such as openness in adoption, point to how the context in which meaning is made and can potentially influence the relative coherence of the narrative. In this regard, coherence is about relationships in context, not a unidimensional trait inherent to the individual. Future efforts to determine the contextual influences on coherence could point to how overcoming adversity is often linked to forming a coherent story about stressful conditions (Baumeister, Stillwell, & Wotman, 1990; Cohler, 1991).

We began this collaborative endeavor to gain a better understanding of how families come to place meaning on their personal experiences. We found that this is not a simple or unidimensional process. Some families struggled with putting together their story, stumbling over central pieces of information, often leaving the interviewer confused. Raising a child in a system that has difficulty in explaining personal experiences may leave the child more vulnerable to the stress of daily living. All families experience change and all families must confront difficult situations. Families that experience multiple insults to their integrity are often ill-equipped to deal with the challenges of raising healthy children (Sameroff et al., 1998). Families that are able to make sense of their experiences, pleasant or challenging, however, provide their children with a meaning-making system that can better prepare them for an unpredictable world. When reporters in Chicago (*Chicago Journal*, May 26, 1982) asked a group of urban school children what would happen if there were no stories in the world, one child responded, "People would die of seriousness," and another answered, "There wouldn't be a world, because stories make the world." Coherent and meaningful family stories may allow children to thrive and face adverse conditions in ways that will better serve their development, and perhaps that of their children as well.

APPENDIX A

INTERVIEW FORMATS[1]

SYRACUSE DINNERTIME PROJECT
DINNERTIME INTERVIEW (1990)
BARBARA FIESE, JULIE POEHLMANN, AND DOUG DUFORE

Syracuse Dinnertime Project

The interview followed the family viewing the videotape of their meal-time. Prior to the interview, the family was asked to stop the tape at any time to comment on typical and/or unusual mealtime behaviors or conversations.

Questions were addressed to all family members present. Interviewer encouraged everyone to participate.

1. Now that you have had a chance to watch your family at dinnertime, was there anything that surprised you or you hadn't noticed before?

2. For some families dinnertime is a time to get fed and get on with other activities, and for some other families dinnertime is a special event. How do you think dinnertime defines you as a family?

3. How do you think dinnertime in your family compares to other families that you know?

4. For each of you, what was your favorite part of the tape?

5. (Question addressed to parents separately) How does your current dinner-time compare to dinnertime when you were growing up?

6. I would like for you to think back to a dinnertime when you were growing up and tell [child's name] a story about that time. You may want to think about who was typically there, where people sat, what people talked about, and anything else that comes to your mind. Take a few moments to try and create what dinnertime was like in your family when you were growing up and tell your child a story.

---

[1]The interview for the Washington, DC, Couple study may be found in Wamboldt and Wolin, 1989.

124

MINNESOTA/TEXAS ADOPTION RESEARCH PROJECT
ADOPTIVE PARENT INTERVIEW (1989)
HAROLD D. GROTEVANT & RUTH G. McROY

Code number: _____

Interviewer Name: _____

Date of Interview: _____

Note to interviewers: Ask questions in the order in which they are written; ignore the fact that question numbers are often out of sequence. Begin the interview process by reviewing with the parent the number of adopted children s/he has, their names and ages. Also be sure to clarify who the target child is and that the responses here should primarily refer to the target child's adoption. If you talk about more than one adopted child for comparative purposes, be sure that it is clear who you are talking about.

BACKGROUND REGARDING ADOPTION

1. Could you begin by telling me a little bit about why you decided to adopt? (If infertility is mentioned, PROBE for specifics.)

2. Whom did you talk to about adoption before you reached your decision? What advice did you receive?

3. What did you expect the adoption process to be like?

4. Please explain the process you went through to adopt _____ (target child)?

5. How did you feel going through the process?

6. Did you rename the baby?

7. Do you know what name the birthmother originally gave to the baby? What was it?

8. Was it a requirement of the agency that you be infertile? If so, what kind of information did you submit with your application?

9. What, if any, counseling did you receive from the agency? PROBE: in which of the following did they participate: preadoption seminars, parenting classes, marital/family or genetic/medical counseling?

10. Were you adopted? If yes,

    a. How old were you when you were adopted?

    b. What type of adoption did you have? (traditional, semi-open, fully disclosed)

    c. What information do you have about your birth parents?

d. When were you told you were adopted?

e. How were you told?

f. What was your reaction to the news?

g. Did you discuss your adoption with your adoptive parents?

h. What sort of impact do you think your experiences with adoption had on your choice of an adoption plan for your child?

11a. Do any of your friends or acquaintances have adopted children?

11b. If "yes," what has been the quality of their experiences?

11c. When you began to consider adoption, did these friends influence your decision?

12a. Do any of your relatives have adopted children?

12b. If "yes," what has been the quality of their experiences?

12c. When you began to consider adoption, did these relatives influence your decision?

13. What age or sex preference for a child did you have when you applied to adopt _____ (target child)?

14a. (If more than one adopted child in the family) Are any of your adopted children related to each other biologically?

14b. If "yes," please specify how.

15a. Are any of the adopted children related to either adoptive parent?

15b. If "yes," please specify how.

Now I'd like to ask you a few questions about _____'s (child's) birthparents? Given what you know about the birthparents both at the time of placement and perhaps more recently, can you please give me the following information about both the birthmother and birthfather?

(NOTE: Have respondent give details, *NOT* just whether they know the information or not.)

	Birthmother	*Birthfather*
16. Age at birth of child		
17. Occupation		
18. Education		
19. Marital status		
20. Racial/ethnic background		
21. Special interests or talents		
22. Medical history		
23. Reason for relinquishing child		
24. Physical or emotional problems		
25. Circumstances of pregnancy and delivery		

26. What do you know about the prenatal care of the birthmother?

27. What was _____'s (child's) birth weight?

28. Do either of the birthparents have any other children? If "yes," please describe.

29. Is _____ (child) aware of them?

30. What other placements had _____(target child) experienced before coming to your family? (Begin with birthparents.)

Type of Placement (hospital > week, birthparents, foster, adopt, etc.)

	Length	**Quality**
a.		
b.		
c.		
d.		

31. Was _____ (child) ever abused or neglected in any of these placements? If so, please describe.

30b3. How old was your child when he/she was placed in your home?

32. When did you tell _____ (child) s/he was adopted?

33. Have you had any problems, regarding the adoption, since your adoption?

34. How old were you when _____ (child) was adopted?

35a. How did your relatives react to your decision to adopt?

35b. What are their more recent feelings concerning your decision to adopt?

36. In what ways is _____ (child) like you (temperament, appearance)?

37a. In what ways is _____ (child) dissimilar to you (temperament, appearance)?

37b. How well do you feel your child fits into your family?

38. Did you anticipate that the arrival of _____ (child) would mean making changes in your lifestyle? If so, what changes did you anticipate?

39. How did you and your spouse prepare for the arrival of _____ (child) (e.g., reading, talking with each other or to others, preparing siblings, etc.)?

40. Did you and your spouse talk about how your relationship might change? How did you plan to handle the changes?

How did your relationship *actually* change after the adoption of your child?

41a. Please describe the time around the arrival of _____ (child) in your family. (PROBE for specific events and behaviors rather that global evaluations.)

41b. How would you describe _____'s (child's) early behavior (PROBE: pleasant, easy, fussy, difficult, etc.)?

41c. What were some of the satisfactions and problems you encountered in the first 3 years?

41d. What was your relationship like with _____ (child) during those early years?

41e. Were there any other significant life circumstances going on at the time of the adoption? If "yes," what were they?

KNOWLEDGE ABOUT DEGREES OF OPENNESS IN ADOPTION

42. What options did your adoption agency offer regarding open or closed adoptions (nonidentifying information, photos of birthparents, continued sharing of information, meeting parents, ongoing contact, etc.)?

43. Had you heard of open adoptions before you adopted _____ (target child)?

44. If so, what did you think the term meant?

45. What does the term "semi-open adoption" mean to you?

46. What does the term "confidential or closed adoption" mean to you?

47. Describe the process you went through before deciding what form of openness for _____ (target child's) adoption?

48. If you did make a choice, what option did you choose?

49. If you did make a choice, why did you choose this option?

***********(INTERVIEWER NOTE: GIVE OUR DEFINITIONS FROM THE MANUAL OF CONFIDENTIAL, SEMI-OPEN, AND FULLY DISCLOSED NOW)*********

50. What do you see as the advantages and the disadvantages of:

    a. confidential "closed" adoption

    b. semi-open adoption

    c. fully-disclosed adoption

**IF FAMILY CHOSE A CONFIDENTIAL (CLOSED) ADOPTION,
CONTINUE DIRECTLY ON TO THE *PINK* SECTION, PAGES *8–9*.**

**IF FAMILY CHOSE TO SHARE INFORMATION ONLY,
NOW GO TO THE *GREEN* SECTION, PAGES *10–11*.**

IF FAMILY CHOSE TO MEET THE BIRTHPARENTS, NOW GO TO THE *YELLOW* SECTION, PAGES *12–13*.

IF FAMILY CHOSE TO MEET THE BIRTHPARENTS AND SHARE INFORMATION, NOW GO TO THE *TAN* SECTION, PAGES *14–17*.

IF FAMILY RESPONDENT CHOSE TO HAVE ONGOING FACE TO FACE CONTACT, NOW GO TO THE *BLUE* SECTION, PAGES *18–21*.

IF FAMILY INITIALLY CHOSE A LESS OPEN OPTION AND LATER CHANGED TO A MORE OPEN OPTION, NOW GO TO THE *ORANGE* SECTION, PAGES *22–26*.

IF FAMILY CHOSE CONFIDENTIAL (CLOSED) ADOPTION . . .

51. How do you plan to talk with your child about adoption? (Or, for older children, how have you talked with your child about adoption?)

    a. Now?

    b. In middle childhood?

    c. In adolescence?

52. Does _____ (child) know what "birthmother" means?

53. What does _____ (child) call his/her birthmother?

54. What does _____ (child) call his/her birthfather?

55. How do you feel about this?

56a. How comfortable is _____(child) with talking about his/her adoption?

56b. Does s/he initiate conversations with you about it? If "yes," how frequently?

57. Does _____ (child) ever try to use his/her adoption as a lever to get his/her way? If so, please describe.

58. If there are other siblings in the household, do they ever try to use _____ (child's) adoption against him/her? If so, please describe.

59. What kinds of information do you think adoptive parents should have about their child's background? Why?

60. What kinds of information do you think adopted children should have about themselves?

pink

61. What kinds of information do you think birthparents should have about their children after they have been placed?

62. How would you handle it if _____ (child) decided to search for his/her birthparent(s)? Why?

63. How would you handle it if your agency notified you that your child's birthmother wished to share information or pictures through the agency?

162. Do you think the birthmother wishes she could reclaim your child? Why or why not?

64. What is the meaning of "open adoption" to you?

What do you think the consequences of open adoption would be for the:

    a. adoptive parent?
    b. adopted child?
    c. birthparent(s)?

65. Have you ever regretted making the decision to have a confidential or closed adoption?

66. We've talked about quite a few things, but I wonder if there might be something that we have skipped which you might feel to be important to understanding you and your family. Is there anything that you would like to add to what we have discussed?

BRING PARENTS BACK TOGETHER AND COMPLETE THE COUPLES INTERVIEW

pink

IF FAMILY CHOSE TO SHARE INFORMATION ONLY . . .

67. How often do you share information with birthparents? Who initiates each exchange? (PROBE for the history of sharing.)

68. For what period of time will you be sharing information (few years, until adulthood, forever)?

69. What kind of information do you share (pictures, gifts, etc.)?

70. What do the birthparents share with you?

71. How do you present this information (pictures, gifts, etc.) to your child?

72. How do you feel after you have received a letter, picture, gift, etc., from the birthparents?

73. Is there a written or verbal agreement for this kind of sharing? How binding do you feel this agreement is?

74. Have the birthparents changed their agreement with you in terms of sharing information? How does this make you feel?

75. What impact do you think sharing information will have on:

a. your child?

b. you and your spouse?

c. birthparents?

d. other children in the family (if applicable)?

green

76. Do you think _____ (child) will initiate a search for his birthparents when he/she reaches adulthood? Why or why not?

77. Do you think _____ (child's) birthparents will initiate a search for _____ (child) when he/she reaches adulthood? Why or why not?

162. Do you think the birthmother wishes she could reclaim your child? Why or why not?

172. Has she ever said or written anything that indicated she regrets her her decision to terminate her parental rights? If yes, what?

78. Have you ever regretted making the decision to share information with the birthparents?

79. How would you handle it if the birthparents requested a meeting with you and/or your child?

(FOR OLDER CHILDREN:)

80. What impact has this sharing had on:
   a. the child?
   b. you and your spouse?
   c. birthparents?
   d. other children in the family (if applicable)?

81. We've talked about quite a few things, but I wonder if there might be something that we have skipped which you might feel to be important to understanding you and your family. Is there anything that you would like to add to what we have discussed?

BRING PARENTS BACK TOGETHER AND COMPLETE THE COUPLES INTERVIEW

green

IF FAMILY CHOSE TO MEET BIRTHPARENTS . . .

82a. Describe the circumstances of your *FIRST* meeting with the birthparent(s).

82b & c. (If not specified in 82) When and where did the first meeting take place?

83. How did you feel during the meeting?

84. How did you feel about the birthparents? Has that feeling changed since then? If so, how?

85. Did you exchange identifying information (first or last name, address, telephone number, etc.)? Why or why not?

86. What else did you talk about?

87. How do you think the birthparents felt about you?

88. Have you had any more meetings with the birthparents? If "yes," how are these meetings initiated and arranged?

89. How do you think they feel about you now?

90. Do you plan to have continued contact?

91. What kind of an impact did the meeting(s) have on you?

yellow

92. What kind of an impact do you think the meeting(s) have on the birthparent(s)?

93. What kind of an impact do you think such meetings will have on _____ (child)?

94. What kind of an impact do you think such meetings will have on other children in your family?

95. What kind of a difference do you think this meeting will have on your family in the future?

96. Do you think _____ (child) will initiate a search for his birthparents when he/she reaches adulthood? Why or why not?

97. Do you think _____ (child's) birthparents will initiate a search for _____ (child) when he/she reaches adulthood? Why or why not?

162. Do you think the birthmother wishes she could reclaim your child? Why or why not?

172. Has she ever said or written anything that indicated she regrets her decision to terminate her parental rights? If yes, what?

98. Have you ever regretted your decision to meet the birthparents?

99. We've talked about quite a few things, but I wonder if there might be something that we have skipped which you might feel to be important to understanding you and your family. Is there anything that you would like to add to what we have discussed?

BRING PARENTS BACK TOGETHER AND COMPLETE COUPLES INTERVIEW

yellow

IF FAMILY CHOSE TO SHARE INFORMATION AND MEET BIRTHPARENTS . . .

Your family shares information and has met with the birthparent(s). First, let's discuss the sharing of information, and then we'll talk about the actual meeting(s) with the birthparents.

67. How often do you share information with birthparents? Who initiates each exchange? (PROBE for the history of sharing.)

68. For what period of time will you be sharing information (few years, until adulthood, forever)?

69. What kind of information do you share (pictures, gifts, etc.)?

70. What do the birthparents share with you?

71. How do you present this information (pictures, gifts, etc.) to your child?

72. How do you feel after you have received a letter, picture, gift, etc., from the birthparents?

73. Is there a written or verbal agreement for this kind of sharing? How binding do you feel this agreement is?

74. Have the birthparents changed their agreement with you in terms of sharing information? How does this make you feel?

tan

75. What impact do you think sharing information will have on:

    a. your child?

    b. you and your spouse?

    c. birthparents?

    d. other children in the family (if applicable)?

78. Have you ever regretted making the decision to share information with the birth parents?

Now we will begin the discussion of the meeting(s) you've had with the birthparent(s).

82a. Describe the circumstances of your *FIRST* meeting.

82b & c. (If not specified in 82) When and where did the first meeting take place?

83. How did you feel during the meeting?

84. How did you feel about the birthparents? Has that feeling changed since then? If so, how?

85. Did you exchange identifying information (first or last name, address, telephone number, etc.)? Why or why not?

86. What else did you talk about?

87. How do you think the birthparents felt about you?

88. Have you had any more meetings with the birthparents? If "yes," how are these meetings initiated and arranged?

tan

89. How do you think they feel about you now?

90. Do you plan to have continued contact?

91. What kind of an impact did the meeting(s) have on you?

92. What kind of an impact do you think the meeting(s) have on the birthparent(s)?

93. What kind of an impact do you think such meetings will have on _____ (child)?

94. What kind of an impact do you think such meetings will have on other children in your family?

95. What kind of a difference do you think this meeting will have on your family in the future?

96. Do you think _____ (child) will initiate a search for his birthparents when he/she reaches adulthood? Why or why not?

97. Do you think _____ (child's) birthparents will initiate a search for _____ (child) when he/she reaches adulthood? Why or why not?

162. Do you think the birthmother wishes she could reclaim your child? Why or why not?

tan

172. Has she ever said or written anything that indicated she regrets her decision to terminate her parental rights? If yes, what?

98. Have you ever regretted your decision to meet the birthparents?

99. We've talked about quite a few things, but I wonder if there might be something that we have skipped which you might feel to be important to understanding you and your family. Is there anything that you would like to add to what we have discussed?

BRING PARENTS BACK TOGETHER AND COMPLETE COUPLES INTERVIEW

tan

IF FAMILY CHOSE TO HAVE ONGOING FACE–TO–FACE CONTACT . . .

100. Describe the circumstances of your *FIRST* meeting with the birthparent(s). When and where did it occur?

101. How did you feel during the meeting?

102. How did you feel about the birthparents?

103. How do you think the birthparents felt about you?

104. Did you exchange identifying information (first or last name, address, telephone number etc.)? Why or why not?

105. What else did you talk about?

106. Do you plan to have continued contact? Why or why not?

107. What other contacts have you had with the birthparent(s)? How are these contacts initiated and arranged?

170. Is the birthmother ever alone with your child?

108. Is there a written or verbal agreement for these meetings?

109. How binding do you feel this agreement is?

blue

110. Have the birthparents changed their agreement with you in terms of frequency or kinds of contact between you and the adoptive family. If so, how did this make you feel?

111. How would you describe your relationship with the birthparents? (PROBE: as a relative, friend, etc.)

112. What has been the impact of these meetings on the child?

113. What has been the impact of these meetings on other children in the family?

114. What do you think the impact will be as _____ (child) grows up?

115. What do you think the impact of these meetings has been on you?

116. What do you think the impact will be on your family? (PROBE for each family member.)

117. How do you feel after a visit? Have your feelings changed over time?

118. Are any of the birthparents' relatives involved in _____ (child's) life (grandparents, aunts, uncles, etc.)?

119. Do you ever fear that _____ (child) might wish to live with his/her birthmother?

blue

120. What kind of role do you want the birthparent to play in your family's life in:

    a. 5 years?

    b. 10 years?

    c. after the child reaches adulthood?

121. Do you ever seek the birthparents' advice? In what areas?

122. What is the most satisfying aspect of your relationship with the birthparents?

123. What is the most difficult aspect of this relationship?

124. Describe the birthparents' relationship(s) with:

    a. your child.

    b. you.

    c. your spouse.

    d. other children in the family.

125. Has the birthparents' relationship towards you changed at all since placement? Why or why not? Describe.

126. Do you behave differently with your child in the presence of the birthparent? Describe.

127. What kinds of joint activities do you participate in with the birthparent?

blue

128a. Has the birthmother ever said or written anything that indicated she regrets her decision to terminate her parental rights? If so, what?

128b. Do you think she wishes she could reclaim your child? Why or why not?

129. Have you ever regretted making the decision to have a fully disclosed adoption?

174. If you lose contact with the birthmother, do you think your child will initiate a search for her when he/she reaches adulthood? Why or why not?

175. If you lose contact, do you think the birthmother will initiate a search for _____ (child) when he/she reaches adulthood? Why or why not?

130. We've talked about quite a few things, but I wonder if there might be something that we have skipped which you might feel to be important to understanding you and your family. Is there anything that you would like to add to what we have discussed?

BRING PARENTS BACK TOGETHER AND COMPLETE COUPLES INTERVIEW

blue

IF FAMILY INITIALLY HAD A LESS OPEN OPTION AND LATER CHANGED TO A MORE OPEN OPTION . . .

131. In the beginning, how often did you share information with birthparents? Who initiated each exchange?

132. What kind of information did you share (pictures, gifts, etc.)?

133. What did the birthparents share with you?

134. Was there a written or verbal agreement for this kind of sharing? How binding do you feel this agreement is?

135. How did the change in openness come about? Whose idea was it to change?

136. Describe the changes that took place.

137. How did you feel about the decision to change?

138. What kinds of contacts have you had with the birthparents since the change in openness? How are these contacts initiated and arranged?

139. Describe the circumstances of your first meeting. When and where did it occur? What happened?

140. How did you feel during the meeting?

orange

141. How do you think the birthmother felt about you?

142. Did you exchange identifying information (first or last name, address, telephone number etc.)? Why or why not?

143. What else did you talk about?

144. Did you plan to have continued contact? Why or why not?

145. What kind of an impact did this first meeting have on you?

146. What kind of an impact did this first meeting have on the birthmother?

147. How would you describe your relationship with the birthmother?

148. Do you ever feel in competition with your child's birthmother? Do you think she feels in competition with you?

149. What has been the impact of this first, or any subsequent, meetings on _____ (child)?

150. What do you think the impact of these meetings will be as _____ (child) grows up?

151. What do you think the impact of any subsequent meetings has been on the birthmother?

152. What do you think the impact of these meetings has been on you?

orange

153. What do you think the impact will be on you and your family in the future? (PROBE for each family member.)

154. How do you feel after a visit?

155. Does your child know what "birthmother" means?

156. What does the child call his/her birthmother?

157. How do you feel about this?

158. What would you like for him/her to call the birthmother?

159. What does the child call you?

160. How do you feel about this?

161. Are any of the birthmother's relatives involved in _____'s (child's) life?

162. Do you think the birthmother wishes she could reclaim your child? Why or why not?

172. Has she ever said or written anything that indicated she regrets her decision to terminate her parental rights? If so, what?

orange

163. What kind of role do you want the birthmother to play in your child's life in:

     a. 5 years?

     b. 10 years?

     c. 15 years?

     d. after the child reaches adulthood?

164. Does the birthmother ever seek your advice? On what issues or questions?

165. Do you view the birthmother as being a part of your family?

166. What is the most satisfying aspect of your relationship with your child's birthmother?

167. What is the most difficult aspect of your relationship with your child's birthmother?

168. Has the birthmother's relationship towards you changed at all since placement?

     a. Why or why not?

     b. Describe.

169. How do you behave with your child while in the presence of his/her birthmother?

170. Is the birthmother ever alone with your child?

orange

171. How do you view the birthmother in relation to your family? (PROBE: as relative, as friend, etc.)

173. Have you ever regretted making the decision to have an open adoption?

174. If you lose contact with the birthmother, do you think your child will initiate a search for her when he/she reaches adulthood? Why or why not?

175. If you lose contact, do you think the birthmother will initiate a search for _____(child) when he/she reaches adulthood? Why or why not?

176. How happy do you think your child is in your family?

177. How satisfied are you in your role as adoptive parent?

178. Would you like to have other meetings with your child's birthmother? Why or why not?

179. We've talked about quite a few things, but I wonder if there might be something that we have skipped which you might feel to be important to understanding you and your family. Is there anything that you would like to add to what we have discussed?

BRING PARENTS BACK TOGETHER AND COMPLETE COUPLES INTERVIEW

PROVIDENCE FAMILY STUDY
FAMILY TRADITIONS INTERVIEW (12/91)
ARNOLD J. SAMEROFF, SUSAN DICKSTEIN, AND RONALD SEIFER

Current Family Section. For Questions 59–66, interview both parents together:

59. (To father): What would you say it meant to be a member of the family you grew up in—the [Father's Last Name] family? (*Give time to answer before probing: For example, "We were the kind of family that believed everyone had to carry their own weight," or "everyone in our family was an athlete." We are looking for your views on the kinds of people you were or the kinds of things you did.*)

60. (To mother): What would you say it meant to be a member of the family you grew up in—the [Mother's Maiden Name] family? (*Same probes as above.*)

61. What does it mean to be a member of the [Current Family Name] family now?

62. Do you or your family ever talk about things like this?

63. When you got married, did you hope that your new family would be similar to the families you grew up in? *Probe: In what way? Did you work to make it happen? How has it worked out over the years?*

64. When you got married, did you hope that your new family would be different from the families you grew up in? *Probe: In what way? Did you work to make it happen? How has it worked out over the years?*

65. Compared to the good times that most families experience together, how good does it get with your family?

66. Compared to the difficult times most families experience, how difficult does it get with your family?

Child Agendas Section. "Okay (Dad), I'm going to give you a short break while I ask (Mom) some questions about your children. Then I'm going to ask you the same questions."

Start with Mother. Once Father leaves the room, ask questions 67–80 for each child.

67. Let's talk about your child(ren) now. Which one would you like to start with?

68. Why did you choose that name? Is there anything significant about it?

69. Please give me a couple of adjectives to describe [Child]. *Get at least two adjectives.*

70. You described [Child] as being ADJECTIVE 1; can you recall an instance that would be an example of that? *Probe for detailed example. Repeat for remaining adjectives.*

71. Some parents have an idea about what their children will grow up to be. Have you thought about how [Child] will grow up? *Wait before probing: What occupation do you hope (Child) will have? What kind of personality do you think (Child) will have?*

72. How do you feel [Child] is turning out? *Wait before probing: How smart? How sociable? How emotional?*

73. Is [Child] turning out to be what you expected?

74. Did you hope that [Child] would turn out to be like anyone in particular?

75. Do you see any physical resemblance between [Child] and anyone in your family?

76. Do you see any personality resemblance between [Child] and anyone in your family?

77. (If not mentioned already): Did you hope that [Child] would turn out to be the same or different from: Yourself or your spouse? (*Probe: In what way? How has that worked out?*) Your parents? (*Probe: In what way? How has that worked out?*)

78. Think about the hardest times with [Child]. Compared with the hard times most people have with their children, how hard are things with your child?

79. Think about the easiest times with [Child]. Compared with the easy times most people have with their children, how easy are things with your child?

80. Think about the times you felt closest to [Child]. Compared with how close most people feel to their children, how close do you feel with your child?

REPEAT QUESTIONS 67–80 FOR EACH CHILD.
THEN CONDUCT CHILD AGENDAS SECTION SEPARATELY WITH *FATHER.*

APPENDIX B

SCALE EXCERPTS FROM CODE BOOK

This Appendix includes abstracted descriptions of the FNC narrative scales. A complete manual is available that provides information for training raters, detailed descriptions of each scale, systematized note-taking procedures, and decision rules for each scale. This Appendix is included for illustrative purposes only. Readers interested in receiving a copy of the entire coding manual may contact Barbara H. Fiese, 430 Huntington Hall, Department of Psychology, Syracuse University, Syracuse, NY 13244 [e-mail: bhfiese@psych.syr.edu].

INTERNAL CONSISTENCY

	SCALE LEVEL	INDICATORS
1.	No Theory	**No theory can be identified.** Multiple unacknowledged contradictions, without personalized examples. May include descriptions.
2.	Unsupported Theory	**May include some minor unacknowledged contradictions.** Descriptive statements about family functioning without generalizations or synthesizing explanations.
3.	Theory With Some Support	**Respondent may make generalizations** about his/her experience (relating to world or society in general but not giving personal details). Contradictions may be recognized, but not explained.
4.	Theory in Process	**Emergent theory; supported evidence but not integrated.** Usually does not include unexplained contradictions. Examples can be either personalized or specific but not both.
5.	Well Documented Theory	**Must have all indicators** (no unexplained contradictions; specific and personal examples, synthesizing explanations).
8.	Can't Code due to Mechanical Problems	
9.	Unclear/Can't Code	

ORGANIZATION

	SCALE LEVEL	INDICATORS
1.	Poor Organization	**Rater has no clear picture of story.** Individual does not put pieces of narrative together. Many/mostly markers of disorganization; especially stops and starts, scattered with no transitions, thought blockage, and ambiguous referents.
2.	Moderately Poor Organization	**Rater understands most of narrative, with effort or with assistance from interviewer or other family member.** Individual puts some of story together but not all of story. Some markers of disorganization, typically stops and starts, or incomplete thoughts.
3.	Moderate Organization	**Rater can understand story but there may still be some markers of disorganization.** Individual does put story together but with difficulty.
4.	Moderately Good Organization	**Rater can understand story clearly with rare incidence of markers of disorganization.** Individual puts story together and self-corrects.
5.	Good Organization	**Individual puts story together in succinct and direct fashion.** Use of orienting statements.
8.	Can't Code due to Mechanical Problems	
9.	Unclear/Can't Code	

FLEXIBILITY

	SCALE LEVEL	INDICATORS
1.	Low Flexibility/Rigid	**Individual narrative strongly adheres to one perspective.** Issues are all one-sided.
2.	Moderately Low Flexibility	**Individual narrative adheres to one perspective with minimal recognition of alternative views.** Alternatives may be mentioned but dismissed as not valid or wrong.
3.	Moderate Flexibility	**Individual clearly recognizes more than one perspective.** Valid alternatives mentioned. (Action mentioned if appropriate, given interview.)
4.	Moderately High Flexibility	**Individual elaborates two or more perspectives to issue.** (Possible alternatives elaborated if appropriate given interview.)
5.	High Flexibility/Balanced	**Individual integrates and resolves two or more perspectives.** May discuss implications for action, if appropriate given the interview. Both sides evaluated and elaborated. No rigid statements.
8.	Can't Code due to Mechanical Problems	
9.	Unclear/Can't Code	

CONGRUENCE OF AFFECT AND CONTENT

	SCALE LEVEL	INDICATORS
1.	Low Congruence	**Clear mismatch between expressed affect and content of narrative** (e.g., laughter when discussing emotionally negative event such as loss, divorce, illness). Intensity of affect does not match content.
2.	Moderately Low Congruence	**Content of narrative and expressed affect frequently do not match.**
3.	Moderate Congruence	**Content and expressed emotions occasionally mismatch.**
4.	Moderately High Congruence	**Content of actions and expressed emotion rarely mismatch.**
5.	High Congruence	**No mismatch.** Affect and content always match and are well modulated.
8.	Can't Code due to Mechanical Problems	
9.	Unclear/Can't Code	

SCALE LEVEL	INDICATORS
1. Disengaged	**Content.** There are major disagreements or differences of opinion expressed to the extent that one *cannot discern the family's story*, only the stories of different individuals. Or, *parallel stories* are told containing the same overall facts and time sequences but with one person telling his/her story, then the other telling his/her story in sequence with little or no comments on the other's version. **Process.** The interaction is decidedly *cool and distant*. There is little affect of any type expressed. Family members' *behavior shows disengagement* (e.g., looking away or closing eyes when someone else is speaking). There may be *a few episodes* of mild, quickly abated anger/rejection/conflict. *No* evidence of moderate to severe rejection/conflict.
2. Conflictual-Disruptive	**Content.** There are major disagreements or differences of opinion expressed, to the extent that one *cannot discern the family's story*, only the stories of different individuals. **Process.** The interaction is *hot and negative*. There are several episodes of moderate-to-high-intensity anger/rejection/conflict that lingers in the interaction (for at least 2 turns) or *at least 1 episode* of intensely negative interaction (severe denigration, shouting, hitting).
3. Conflictual-Contained	**Content.** Couple produces a conjoint story in which there are *some discrepancies* or *differences of opinions*. These may or may not be resolved within the narrative, but they are *not major disruptions* to the story as a whole. **Process.** The interaction is conflictual but socialized. There are a *few episodes* of mild, quickly abated anger/rejection/conflict, or a *few episodes* of moderate-to-high-intensity anger/rejection/conflict (e.g., put-downs, character assaults, sarcasm) that linger (i.e., are responded to in kind across at least the next two turns of interaction). However, the couple manages to keep the conflict relatively well contained and continue the narrative.
4. Cooperative	**Content.** Couple produces a conjoint *story that hangs together well*, containing similar facts, sequences, perspectives, etc. However, there is little augmentation and expansion, as well as little disagreement or fragmentation of the story. **Process.** Interaction is quite pleasant, with couple being engaged with each other. May be a few episodes of mild, quickly abated anger/rejection/conflict, such as teases, whines, interruptions, disagreements about facts, etc. Quickly abated means that while the remark may be responded to in the next speaker's turn, it is dropped thereafter. *No* evidence of moderate to severe rejection/conflict such as put-downs, character assaults, sarcasm, etc.
5. Collaborative	**Content.** The *story told conjointly is richer* than the individuals would have told alone. Family members contribute different pieces of the story that fit together nicely as an integrated whole. **Process.** Interaction is *highly collaborative*, with some indicators such as the presence of synthetic, synergistic exchanges in which new words and/or frames of reference are introduced and accepted into the story, thereby improving the overall narrative (completion of others' sentences in a spiraling, facilitative manner; *presence* of joy and positive affect during interaction; *absence* of conflict and/or disconfirmation).
8. Can't Code due to Mechanical Problems	
9. Unclear/Can't Code	

COORDINATION SCALE

SCALE LEVEL	INDICATORS
1. Very Low	**Family members present as separate and unrelated individuals.** Family presents almost entirely separate threads of opinions. There is usually lack of confirmation of others' opinions.
2. Low	**Some separateness among family members.** Family presents some separate threads of opinions. There is some lack of confirmation of others' opinions.
3. Balanced	**There is balance between separateness and connectedness in family relationships.** Balanced team effort in interview. Family members have an opportunity to present their opinions. Polite turn-taking is evident.
4. High	**Family presents itself as a group.** Members respect each other's opinions and call for individual input. A member may comment on another member's statement, but group needs predominate.
5. Very High	**Family presents as an overinvolved group.** Members almost always actively call for input from others. One member will usually comment on another member's statement and/or ask for clarifications.
8. Can't Code due to Mechanical Problems	
9. Unclear/Can't Code	

CONFIRMATION/DISCONFIRMATION

SCALE LEVEL	INDICATORS
1. Overtly Disconfirming	**Major restrictions and/or denial of other's right to think, feel, or speak; or, insists on other's inferiority, immaturity, or craziness.** May include: • rigid commands ("Shut up!") • strong power moves with major put-downs of other ("What you've just heard is a fantasy, but I'll tell you the real story") • harsh sarcasm, name calling, or malicious teasing
2. Moderately Disconfirming	**Moderate restriction of other's right to** think, feel, or speak; or emphasis on their inferiority, immaturity, or craziness. May include: • intense bragging without major put-downs ("Of course, for a question like that you must want me to answer") • prolonged withdrawal from the narrative (leaving room, refusing to look at partner, staring at the ceiling, prolonged silence)
3. Occasionally Disconfirming	**Occasional mild disconfirmation.** May include: • mild sarcasm, name calling, or teasing • low grade power moves (noncollaborative interruptions, topic shifts) • some nonverbal disconfirmation (poor eye contact, eye rolls, finger taps)
4. Occasionally Confirming	*Neutral* **polite conversation with no** evidence of disconfirmation, but not more than occasional confirmation. Most confirmations are low-level speech encouragers ("uh huh").
5. Actively Confirming	**Evidence of active confirmation/validation. No disconfirmation.** May include: • respectful disagreement ("Okay, but I don't see it that way") or comment on the nature of prior statement ("That seems unclear to me") • recognition, acknowledgement, and endorsement of other • relevant, clear verbal and nonverbal responses to other's comments; laughter with but not at partner • nonverbal behavior is appropriate (turns towards partner, directs remarks to other, makes frequent but not constant eye contact, not engaged in other tasks) • contribution to give-and-take of conversation (speaks when reply is appropriate and expected, alternates listening/speaking, relevant comments on prior communication, requests clarification or otherwise encourages partner to talk)
8. Can't Code due to Mechanical Problems	
9. Unclear/Can't Code	

RELATIONSHIP EXPECTATIONS

	SCALE LEVEL	INDICATORS
1.	Very Low	**Expect relationships to be dangerous, threatening, or overwhelming.** Family talks about relationships as a source of fear and may believe that others willfully harm each other. Family cannot understand motives of others. Talk of relationships is marked by statements of confusion and dissatisfaction.
2.	Low	**Relationships are seen as precarious, trying, or unreliable.** Family talks about past disappointments in relationships and considers almost everyone not to be worthy of trust. The family's general tone regarding relationships is dissatisfaction.
3.	Moderate	**Relationships may be met with success, but family tends to categorize into good or bad, black or white.** There are still instances of being dissatisfied, and the sense that some people can be trusted but others can't.
4.	High	**Relationships are relatively understandable, safe, successful, usually rewarding and reliable.** There may be isolated references to dissatisfying relationships.
5.	Very High	**Relationships are safe, reliable, rewarding, and fulfilling.** The family feels confident and positive enough about its understanding of relationships to embrace opportunities to establish relationships with others. Relationships are seen as opportunity to feel successful and satisfied.
8.	Can't Code due to Mechanical Problems	
9.	Unclear/Can't Code	

INTERVIEWER INTIMACY

	SCALE LEVEL	INDICATORS
1.	Hostile	At least one member of the family is overtly hostile to interviewer, refuses to answer question, or leaves room inappropriately.
2.	Cold	Family members present just the facts, little attempt to engage interviewer. Talks past interviewer.
3.	Stoic	Family is polite and responsive but responses appear to be well rehearsed with few intimate details.
4.	Moderately Warm	Family provides a few details on sensitive or affectively charged experiences. Pleasant and cooperative with interviewer.
5.	Warm and Inviting	Family actively includes interviewer in conversation. Provides several examples of affectively charged material, elaborates "insider" information.
8.	Can't Code due to Mechanical Problems	
9.	Unclear/Can't Code	

REFERENCES

Abidin, R. R. (1986). *Parenting stress index*. Charlottesville, VA: Pediatric Psychology Press.

Abramson, L. Y., Seligman, M. E. P., & Teasdale, J. (1978). Learned helplessness in humans: Critique and reformulation. *Journal of Abnormal Psychology, 87*, 49–74.

Achenbach, T. M. (1988). *Child behavior checklist for ages 2–3*. Burlington, VT: University of Vermont.

Achenbach, T. M. (1995). Developmental issues in assessment, taxonomy, and diagnosis of child and adolescent psychopathology. In D. Cicchetti & D. J. Cohen (Eds.), *Handbook of developmental psychopathology: Vol 1. Theory and methods*. New York: Wiley.

Achenbach, T. M., & Edelbrock, C. (1983). *Manual for the Child Behavior Checklist*. Burlington, VT: Department of Psychiatry, University of Vermont.

Achenbach, T. M., Howell, C. T., Quay, H. C., & Conners, C. K. (1991). National survey of competencies and problems among 4- to 16-year-olds: Parents' reports for normative and clinical samples. *Monographs of the Society for Research in Child Development, 56* (3, Serial No. 225).

Agar, M., & Hobbs, J. R. (1982). Interpreting discourse: Coherence and the analysis of ethnographic interviews. *Discourse Processes, 5*, 1–32.

American Psychiatric Association. (1987). *Diagnostic and Statistical Manual for Mental Disorders* (3rd. ed., rev.). Washington, DC: Author.

Antonovsky, A. (1979). *Health, stress, and coping*. San Francisco: Jossey-Bass.

Bakeman, R., & Gottman, J. M. (1987). Applying observational methods: A systematic view. In J. Osofsky (Ed.), *Handbook of infant development* (2nd ed.). New York: Wiley.

Barnett, P. A., & Gotlib, I. H. (1988). Psychosocial functioning and depression: Distinguishing among antecedents, concomitants, and consequences. *Psychological Bulletin, 104*, 97–126.

Baron, R. M, & Kenny, D. A. (1986). The moderator-mediator variable distinction in social psychological research: Conceptual, strategic, and statistical considerations. *Journal of Personality and Social Psychology, 51*, 1173–1182.

Baumeister, R. F., & Newman, L. S. (1994). How stories make sense of personal experiences: Motives that shape autobiographical narratives. *Personality and Social Psychology Bulletin, 20*, 676–690.

Baumeister, R. F., Stillwell, A., & Wotman, S. R. (1990). Victim and perpetrator accounts of interpersonal conflict: Autobiographical narratives about anger. *Journal of Personality and Social Psychology, 59*, 994–1005.

Bell, D. C., & Bell, L. G. (1989). Micro and macro measurement of family system concepts. *Journal of Family Psychology, 3*, 137–157.

Belsky, J., & Pensky, E. (1988). Marital change across the transition to parenthood. *Marriage and Family Review, 12*, 133–156.

Belsky, J., Spanier, G. B., & Rovine, M. (1983). Stability and change in marriage across the transition to parenthood. *Journal of Marriage and the Family, 45*, 567–577.

Bengston, V. L., & Kuypers, J. A. (1971). Generational differences and the developmental stake. *Aging and Human Development, 2*, 249–260.

Bengston, V. L., & Schrader, S. S. (1982). Parent-child relations. In D. J. Mangen & W. A. Peterson (Eds.), *Research instruments in social gerontology: Vol. 2. Social roles and social participation.* Minneapolis: University of Minnesota Press.

Bennett, L. A., Wolin, S. J., & McAvity, K. J. (1988). Family identity, ritual and myth: A cultural perspective on lifecycle transitions. In C. J. Falicov (Ed.), *Family transitions.* New York: The Guilford Press.

Bennett, L. A., Wolin, S. J., Reiss, D., & Teitelbaum, M. A. (1987). Couples at risk for transmission of alcoholism: Protective influences. *Family Process, 26*, 111–129.

Benoit, D., & Parker, K. C. H. (1994). Stability and transmission of attachment across three generations. *Child Development, 65*, 1444–1456.

Benoit, D., Vidovic, D., & Roman, J. (1991, April). *Transmission of attachment across three generations.* Paper presented at the Biennial Meeting of the Society for Research in Child Development, Seattle, Washington.

Berger, P. L., & Kellner, H. (1964). Marriage and the construction of reality: An exercise in the microsociology of knowledge. *Diogenes, 46*, 1–24.

Billings, A. G., & Moos, R. H. (1983). Comparisons of children of depressed and non-depressed parents: A social-environmental perspective. *Journal of Abnormal Child Psychology, 11*(4), 463–486.

Bollen, K. A. (1988). *Structural equations with latent variables.* New York: Wiley.

Booth, A., Johnson, D., & Edwards, J. N. (1983). Measuring marital instability. *Journal of Marriage and the Family, 45*, 387–394.

Bossard, J., & Boll, E. (1950). *Ritual in family living.* Philadelphia: University of Pennsylvania Press.

Boszormenyi-Nagy, I., & Ulrich, D. (1981). Contextual family therapy. In A. S. Gurman & D. Kniskern (Eds.), *Handbook of family therapy.* New York: Brunner/Mazel.

Bowen, M. (1966). The use of theory in clinical practice. *Comprehensive Psychiatry, 7*, 345–374.

Bowen, M. (1978). *Family therapy in clinical practice.* New York: Aronson.

Bowlby, J. (1969/1982). *Attachment and loss: Vol. 1. Attachment.* New York: Basic Books.

Bowlby, J. (1973). *Attachment and loss: Vol. 2. Separation: Anxiety and anger.* New York: Basic Books.

Bowlby, J. (1980). *Attachment and loss: Vol. 3. Loss.* New York: Basic Books.

Brody, G. H., & Forehand, R. (1986). Maternal perceptions of child maladjustment as a function of the combined influence of child behavior and maternal depression. *Journal of Consulting and Clinical Psychology, 54*, 237–240.

Bronfenbrenner, U. (1977). Toward an experimental ecology of human development. *American Psychologist, 32*, 513–531.

Bruner, J. (1986). *Actual minds, possible worlds.* Cambridge, MA: Harvard University Press.

Bruner, J. (1987). Life as narrative. *Social Research, 54*, 11–32.

Bruner, J. (1990). *Acts of meaning.* Cambridge, MA: Harvard University Press.

Buehlman, K. T., Gottman, J. M., & Katz, L. F. (1992). How a couple views their past predicts their future. *Journal of Family Psychology, 5*, 295–318.

Burke, K. (1950). *A rhetoric of motives.* New York: Prentice Hall.

Byng-Hall, J. (1988). Scripts and legends in families and family therapy. *Family Process, 27*, 167–179.

Carpenter, P. J. (1984). The use of intergenerational family ratings: Methodological and interpretive considerations. *Journal of Clinical Psychology, 40*, 505–512.

Chodorow, N. (1978). *The reproduction of mothering.* Berkeley: University of California Press.

Christensen, A., & Arrington, A. (1987). Research issues and strategies. In T. Jacob (Ed.), *Family interaction and psychopathology*. New York: Guilford.

Cohler, B. J. (1991). The life story and the study of resilience and response to adversity. *Journal of Narrative and Life History, 1*, 169–200.

Cohn, D. A., Silver, D. H., Cowan, C. P., Cowan, P. A., & Pearson, J. (1992). Working models of childhood attachment and couple relationships. *Journal of Family Issues, 13*, 432–449.

Conrad, M., & Hammen, C. (1989). Role of maternal depression in perceptions of child maladjustment. *Journal of Consulting and Clinical Psychology, 57*, 663–667.

Costell, R., Reiss, D., Berkman, H., & Jones, C. (1981). The family meets the hospital: Predicting the family's perception of the treatment program from its problem-solving style. *Archives General Psychiatry, 38*, 569–577.

Cowan, P. A. (1991). Individual and family life transitions: A proposal for a new definition. In P. A. Cowan & M. Hetherington (Eds.), *Family transitions*. Hillsdale, NJ: Lawrence Erlbaum Associates.

Cowan, P. A., Cohn, D. A., Cowan, C. P., & Pearson, J. L. (1996). Parents' attachment histories and children's externalizing and internalizing behaviors: Exploring family systems models of linkages. *Journal of Consulting and Clinical Psychology, 64*, 53–63.

Cowan, C. P., Cowan, P. A., Heming, G., & Miller, N. (1991). Becoming a family: Marriage, parenting, and child development. In P. A. Cowan & M. Hetherington (Eds.), *Family transitions*. Hillsdale, NJ: Lawrence Erlbaum Associates.

Coyne, J. C., & Downey, G. (1991). Social factors and psychopathology: Stress, social support, and coping processes. *Annual Review of Psychology, 42*, 401–425.

Crane, D. R., Allgood, S. M., Larson, J. H., & Griffin, W. (1990). Assessing marital quality with distressed and nondistressed couples. *Journal of Marriage and the Family, 52*(1), 87–93.

Crockenberg, S., Lyons-Ruth, L., & Dickstein, S. (1993). The family context of infant mental health, part II: Infant development in multiple family relationships. In C. Zeanah (Ed.), *Handbook of infant mental health*. New York: Guilford Press.

Cross-National Collaborative Group. (1992). The changing rate of major depression: Cross-national comparisons. *Journal of the American Medical Association, 268*, 3098–3105.

Crowell, J. A. (1990). *Current Relationships Interview*. Unpublished manuscript, State University of New York at Stony Brook.

Crowell, J. A., & Feldman, S. S. (1988). Mothers' internal models of relationships and children's behavioral and developmental status: A study of mother-child interaction. *Child Development, 59*, 1273–1285.

Cummings, E. M., & Cicchetti, D. (1990). Toward a transactional model of relations between attachment and depression. In M. T. Greenberg, D. Cicchetti, & E. M. Cummings (Eds.), *Attachment in the preschool years: Theory, reseach and intervention*. Chicago: The University of Chicago Press.

Cummings, M. (1995). Security, emotionality, and parental depression: A commentary. *Developmental Psychology, 31*, 425–427.

Daly, K. J. (1992). Toward a formal theory of interactive resocialization: The case of adoptive parenthood. *Qualitative Sociology, 15*, 395–417.

Deal, J. E., Halverson, C. F., & Wampler, K. S. (1989). Parental agreement on child-rearing orientations: Relations to parental, marital, family, and child characteristics. *Child Development, 60*, 1025–1034.

Dickstein, S., Hayden, L. C., Schiller, M., Seifer, R., & San Antonio, W. (1994). *Providence Family Study mealtime family interaction coding system. Adapted from the McMaster Clinical Rating Scale*. East Providence, RI: E. P. Bradley Hospital.

Dickstein, S., Seifer, R., Hayden, L., Schiller, M., Sameroff, A. J., Keitner, G., Miller, I., Rasmussen, S., Matzko, M., & Dodge-Magee, K. D. (1998). Levels of family assessment, II:

151

Impact of maternal psychopathology on family functioning. *Journal of Family Psychology, 12*, 23–40.

Dishion, T. J., French, D. C., & Patterson, G. R. (1995). The development and ecology of antisocial behavior. In D. Cicchetti & D. Cohen (Eds.), *Handbook of developmental psychopathology: Vol. 2. Risk, disorder and adaptation*. New York: Wiley.

Downey, G., & Coyne, J. C. (1990). Children of depressed parents: An integrative review. *Psychological Bulletin, 108*, 50–76.

Dryfoos, J. G. (1991). Adolescents at risk: A summation of work in the field: Programs and policies. *Journal of Adolescent Health, 12*, 630–637.

Egeland, J. A., Gerhard, D. S., Pauls, D. L., Sussex, J. N., Kidd, K. K., Allen, C. R., Hostetter, A. M., & Housman, D. E. (1987). Bipolar affective disorders linked to DNA markers on chromosome 11. *Nature, 325*, 783–787.

Eichberg, C. G. (1987, April). *Quality of infant-parent attachment: Related to mother's representation of her own relationship history*. Paper presented at the biennial meeting of the Society for Research in Child Development, Baltimore, MD.

Eisenberg, N., & Fabes, R. A. (1992). Emotion, regulation, and the development of social competence. In M. S. Clark (Ed.), *Review of personality and social psychology: Vol. 14. Emotion and social behavior*. Newbury Park, CA: Sage.

Emde, R. N. (1994). Individuality, context, and the search for meaning. *Child Development, 65*, 719–737.

Epstein, N. B., Baldwin, L. M., & Bishop, D. S. (1983). The McMaster family assessment device. *Journal of Marital and Family Therapy, 9*, 171–180.

Epstein, N. B., & Bishop, D. S. (1981). Problem-centered systems therapy of the family. In A. S. Gurman & D. P. Kniskern (Eds.), *Handbook of family therapy*. New York: Brunner/Mazel.

Epstein, N. B., Bishop, D. S., & Baldwin, L. M. (1982). McMaster model of family functioning: A view of the normal family. In F. Walsh (Ed.), *Normal family processes*. New York: Guilford Press.

Epstein, N. B., Bishop, D. S., & Levin, S. (1978). The McMaster model of family functioning. *Journal of Marriage and Family Counseling, 4*, 19–31.

Erikson, E. H. (1963). *Childhood and society*. New York: Norton.

Fendrich, M., Warner, V., & Weissman, M. M. (1990). Family risk factors, parental depression, and psychopathology in offspring. *Developmental Psychology, 26*, 40–50.

Fiese, B. H. (1992). Dimensions of family rituals across two generations: Relation to adolescent identity. *Family Process, 31*, 151–162.

Fiese, B. H. (1995). Family rituals. In D. Levinson (Ed.), *Encyclopedia of marriage and the family*. New York: MacMillan.

Fiese, B. H., Hooker, K. A., Kotary, L., & Schwagler, J. (1993). Family rituals in the early stages of parenthood. *Journal of Marriage and the Family, 55*, 633–642.

Fiese, B. H., Hooker, K. A., Kotary, L., Schwagler, J., & Rimmer, M. (1995). Family stories in the early stages of parenthood. *Journal of Marriage and the Family, 57*, 763–770.

Fish, B., Marcus, J., Hans, S. L., Auerbach, J. G., & Perdue, S. (1992). Infants at risk for schizophrenia: Sequelae of a genetic neurointergrative defect. *Archives of General Psychiatry, 49*, 221–235.

Fitzpatrick, M. (1988). *Between husbands and wives: Communication in marriage*. Beverly Hills, CA: Sage.

Fivush, R. (1991). Gender and emotion in mother-child conversations about the past. *Journal of Narrative and Life History, 1*, 325–341.

Fleiss, S. L. (1981). *Statistical methods for rates and proportions*. New York: Wiley.

Fonagy, P., Steele, H., & Steele, M. (1991). Maternal representations of attachment during pregnancy predict the organization of infant-mother attachment at one year of age. *Child Development, 62*, 891–905.

Fravel, D. L., & Boss, P. (1992). An in-depth interview with parents of missing children. In J. Gilgun, K. Daly, & G. Handel (Eds.), *Qualitative methods in family research* (pp. 126–145). Newbury Park, CA: Sage.

Furstenberg, F. F., Jr., Cook, T. D., Eccles, J., Elder, G. H., Jr., & Sameroff, A. J. (1998). *Managing to make it: Urban families and adolescent success.* Chicago: University of Chicago Press.

George, C., Kaplan, N., & Main, M. (1985). *Adult attachment interview.* Unpublished manuscript, University of California at Berkeley.

Gergen, K. J., & Gergen, M. M. (1988). Narrative and the self as relationship. In L. Berkowitz (Ed.), *Advances in experimental social psychology.* San Diego, CA: Academic Press.

Gilligan, C. (1982). *In a different voice: Psychological theory and women's development.* Cambridge, MA: Harvard University Press.

Goldstein, M. J., & Strachan, A. M. (1987). The family and schizophrenia. In T. Jacob (Ed.), *Family interaction and psychopathology.* New York: Plenum Press.

Gottman, J. M. (1983). *Rapid couples interaction coding system.* Unpublished manuscript, University of Illinois.

Gottman, J. M. (1993). The roles of conflict engagement, escalation, and avoidance in marital interaction: A longitudinal view of five types of couples. *Journal of Consulting and Clinical Psychology, 61*, 6–15.

Gottman, J. M. (1994). *What predicts divorce?* Hillsdale, NJ: Lawrence Erlbaum Associates.

Gottman, J. M., & Levenson, R. W. (1992). Marital processes predictive of later dissolution: Behavior, physiology, and health. *Journal of Personality and Social Psychology, 63*, 221–233.

Grotevant, H. D. (1993). The integrative nature of identity: Bringing the soloists to sing in the choir. In J. Kroger (Ed.), *Discussions in ego identity* (pp. 121–146). Hillsdale, NJ: Lawrence Erlbaum Associates.

Grotevant, H. D., & McRoy, R. G. (1997). The Minnesota/Texas Adoption Research Project: Implications of openness in adoption for development and relationships. *Applied Developmental Science, 1*, 168–186.

Grotevant, H. D., McRoy, R. G., Elde, C. L., & Fravel, D. L. (1994). Adoptive family system dynamics: Variations by level of openness in the adoption. *Family Process, 33*, 125–146.

Gubrium, J. F., Holstein, J. A., & Buckholdt, D. R. (1994). *Constructing the life course.* Dix Hills, NY: General Hall.

Halliday, M. A. K. (1973). *Explorations in the functions of language.* London: Edward Arnold.

Hammen, C. (1991) Generalization of stress in the course of unipolar depression. *Journal of Abnormal Psychology, 100*, 555–561.

Harvey, D. M, Curry, C. J., & Bray, J. H. (1991). Individuation and intimacy in intergenerational relationships and health. *Journal of Family Psychology, 5*, 204–236.

Hayden, L. C., Schiller, M., Dickstein, S., Seifer, R., & Matzko, M., (1994). *The McMaster Clinical Rating Scale Providence Family Study Revisions.* Providence, RI: E. P. Bradley Hospital.

Hetherington, M. V. (1991). The role of individual differences and family relationships in children's coping with divorce and remarriage. In P. Cowan & M. Hetherington (Eds.), *Family transitions.* Hillsdale, NJ: Lawrence Erlbaum Associates.

Hetherington, M. V., & Camara, K. A. (1984). Families in transition: The process of dissolution and reconstitution. In R. D. Parke (Ed.), *Review of Child Development Research: Vol. 7. The family.* Chicago: University of Chicago Press.

Hollingshead, A. B. (1975). *A four-factor index of socio-economic status.* Unpublished manuscript, New Haven, CT.

Hooley, J. M., & Teasdale, J. D. (1989). Predictors of relapse in unipolar depressives: Expressed emotion, marital distress, and perceived criticism. *Journal of Abnormal Psychology, 98*, 229–235.

Howard, G. S. (1991). Culture tales: A narrative approach to thinking, cross-cultural psychology, and psychotherapy. *American Psychologist, 46*, 187–197.

Imber-Black, E. (1988). Ritual themes in families and family therapy. In E. Imber-Black, J. Roberts, & R. Whiting (Eds.) *Rituals in families and family therapy*. New York: Norton.

Jacobson, N. S., Dobson, K., Fruzetti, A. E., Schmaling, K. B., & Salusky, S. (1991). Marital therapy as a treatment for depression. *Journal of Consulting and Clinical Psychology, 59*, 547–557.

Julien, D., Markman, H. J., Lindahl, K., Johnson, H. M., & Van Widenfelt, B. (1987). *Interactional dimensions coding system: Researcher's manual*. Unpublished manuscript, University of Denver, Colorado.

Kaslow, N., Warner, V., John, K., & Brown, R. (1992). Intrainformant agreement and family functioning in depressed and nondepressed parents and their children. *American Journal of Family Therapy, 20*(3), 204–217.

Katz, L. F., & Gottman, J. M. (1993). Patterns of marital conflict predict children's internalizing and externalizing behaviors. *Developmental Psychology, 29*, 940–950.

Katz, L. F., & Gottman, J. M. (1994). Patterns of marital interaction and children's emotional development. In R. D. Parke & S. G. Kellam (Eds.), *Exploring family relationships with other social contexts* (pp. 49–74). Hillsdale, NJ: Lawrence Erlbaum Associates.

Katz, L. F., & Gottman, J. M. (1995). Marital interaction and child outcomes: A longitudinal study of mediating and moderating processes. In D. Cicchetti & S. L. Toth (Eds.), *Emotion, cognition, and representation. Rochester symposium on developmental psychopathology* (pp. 301–342). Rochester, NY: University of Rochester Press.

Keitner, G. I., Miller, I. W., Ryan, C. E., Bishop, D. S., & Epstein, N. B (1990, May). *Compounded depression and family functioning*. Paper presented at the First International Conference on The McMaster Model of Family Functioning, Providence, Rhode Island.

Keitner, G. I., Ryan, C. E., Miller, I. W., Epstein, N. B., & Bishop, D. S. (1990, May). *Family functioning and recovery from depression*. Paper presented at the First International Conference on The McMaster Model of Family Functioning, Providence, Rhode Island.

Kerig, P. K., Cowan, P. A., & Cowan, C. P. (1993). Marital quality and gender differences in parent-child interaction. *Developmental Psychology, 29*, 931–939.

Kerr, M. E. (1981). Family systems theory and therapy. In A. S. Gurman & D. P. Kniskern (Eds.), *Handbook of family therapy*. New York: Brunner/Mazel.

Kobak, R. R., Cole, H. E., Ferenz-Gillies, R., Fleming, W. S., & Gamble, W. (1993). Attachment and emotion regulation during mother-teen problem solving: A control theory analysis. *Child Development, 64*, 231–245.

Kowalik, D. L., & Gotlib, I. H. (1987). Depression and marital interaction: Concordance between intent and perception of communication. *Journal of Abnormal Psychology, 96*, 127–134.

Kurdek, L. (1991). Predictors of increases in marital disinterests in newlywed couples: A 3-year prospective longitudinal study. *Developmental Psychology, 27*, 627–636.

Labov, W., & Waletzky, J. (1967). Narrative analysis: Oral versions of personal experience. In J. Helm (Ed.), *Essays in the verbal and visual arts*. Seattle: University of Washington Press.

Lamb, M. E. (1979). The effects of social context on dyadic social interaction. In M. E. Lamb, S. T. Suomi, & G. R. Stephenson (Eds.), *Social interaction analysis: Methodological issues*. Madison: University of Wisconsin Press.

Landesman, S., Jaccard, J., & Gunderson, V. (1991). The family environment: The combined influence of family behavior, goals, strategies, resources, and individual experiences.

In M. Lewis & S. Feinman (Eds.), *Social influences and socialization in infancy*. New York: Plenum.

Larson, J. H., & Holman, T. B. (1994). Premarital predictors of marital quality and stability. *Family Relations, 43*, 228–237.

Lehnert, W. G., & Vine, E. W. (1987). The role of affect in narrative structure. *Cognition and Emotion, 1*, 299–322.

Levy, S. Y., Wamboldt, F. S., & Fiese, B. H. (1997). Family of origin experiences and conflict resolution behaviors with young adult dating couples. *Family Process, 36*, 297–310.

Lewis, M., & Feiring, C. (1982). Some American families at dinner. In L. Laosa & I. E. Sigel (Eds.), *Families as learning environments for children* (pp. 115–146). New York: Plenum Press.

Loehlin, J. C. (1987). *Latent variable models: An introduction to factor, path, and structural analysis.* Hillsdale, NJ: Erlbaum.

Main, M. (1991). Meta-cognitive knowledge, meta-cognitive monitoring, and singular (coherent) vs. multiple (incoherent) model of attachment: Findings and directions for future research. In P. Marris, J. Stevenson-Hinde, & C. Parkes (Eds.), *Attachment across the lifecycle*. New York: Rutledge.

Main, M., & Goldwyn, R. (1984). Predicting rejection of their infant from mother's representation of her own experience: Implications for the abused and abusing intergenerational cycle. *Child Abuse and Neglect, 8*, 203–217.

Main, M., & Goldwyn, R. (1996). *Adult Attachment Interview.* Unpublished manual.

Main, M., Kaplan, N., & Cassidy, J. (1985). Security of attachment in infancy, childhood and adulthood: A move to the level of representation. In I. Bretherton & E. Waters (Ed.), *Growing points in attachment theory. Monographs of the Society for Research in Child Development, 50*.

Mandler, J. M., & Johnson, N. S. (1977). Remembrance of things passed: Story structure and recall. *Cognitive Psychology, 9*, 111–151.

Markman, H. J. (1992). Marital and family psychology. *Journal of Family Psychology, 5*, 264–275.

Markman, H. J., Floyd, F., Stanley, S., & Storaasli, R. (1988). The prevention of marital distress: A longitudinal investigation. *Journal of Consulting and Clinical Psychology, 56*, 210–217.

Markus, H. R., & Kitayama, S. (1991). Culture and the self: Implications for cognition, emotion, and motivation. *Psychological Review, 98*, 224–253.

Martin, P., Hagestad, G. O., & Diedrick, P. (1988). Family stories: Events (temporarily) remembered. *Journal of Marriage and the Family, 50*, 533–541.

McAdams, D. P. (1988). Biography, narrative, and lives: An introduction. *Journal of Personality, 56*, 1–17.

McAdams, D. P. (1989). The development of a narrative identity. In D. M. Buss & N. Cantor (Eds.), *Personality psychology: Recent trends and emerging directions* (pp. 160–174). New York: Springer-Verlag.

McAdams, D. P. (1993). *The stories we live by: Personal myths and the making of the self.* New York: William Morrow & Co., Inc.

McCabe, A., Capron, E., & Peterson, C. (1991). The voice of experience: The recall of early childhood and adolescent memories by young adults. In A. McCabe & C. Peterson (Eds.) *Developing narrative structure.* Hillsdale, NJ: Lawrence Erlbaum Associates.

McCabe, A., & Peterson, C. (1991). Getting the story: A longitudinal study of parental styles in eliciting narratives and developing narrative skill. In A. McCabe & C. Peterson (Eds.), *Developing Narrative Structure.* Hillsdale, NJ: Lawrence Erlbaum Associates.

McCall, R., & Appelbaum, M. I. (1991). Some issues of conducting secondary analysis. *Developmental Psychology, 27*, 911–917.

155

McNeil, T. F., & Kaij, L. (1987). Offspring of women with nonorganic psychosis: Early sample characteristics and mental disturbance at six years of age. *Schizophrenia Bulletin, 13*, 373–381.

Miller, I., Bishop, S., Norman, W. H., & Maddever, H. (1985). The modified Hamilton rating scale for depression: Reliability and validity. *Psychiatry Research, 14*, 131–142.

Miller, I. W., Epstein, N. B., Bishop, D. S., & Keitner, G. I. (1985). The McMaster family assessment device: Reliability and validity. *Journal of Marital and Family Therapy, 11*(4), 345–356.

Miller, P. J., Wiley, A. R., Fung, H., & Liang, C-H. (1997). Personal storytelling as a medium of socialization in Chinese and American families. *Child Development, 68*, 557–568.

Minuchin, S. (1974). *Families and family therapy.* Cambridge, MA: Harvard University Press.

Moos, R., & Moos, B. (1986). *Family Environment Scale Manual* (2nd ed.) Palo Alto, CA: Consulting Psychologists Press.

Murray, H. A. (1938). *Theories of personality.* New York: Oxford University Press.

Neisser, U. (1994). Self-narratives: True and false. In U. Neisser & R. Fivush (Eds.), *The remembering self: Construction and accuracy in the self-narrative.* Cambridge: Cambridge University Press.

Nurcombe, B., Seifer, R., Scioli, A., Tramontana, M. G., Grapentine, W. L., & Beauchesne, H. C. (1989). Is major depressive disorder in adolescence a distinct diagnostic entity? *Journal of the American Academy of Child and Adolescent Psychiatry, 28*, 333–342.

Oliveri, M., & Reiss, D. (1981). A theory based empirical classification of family problem-solving behavior. *Family Process, 20*, 409–418.

Oppenheim, D., Nir, A., Warren, S., & Emde, R. N. (1997). Emotion regulation in mother-child narrative co-construction: Associations with children's narratives and adaptation. *Developmental Psychology, 33*, 284–294

Oppenheim, D., Wamboldt, F. S., Gavin, L. A., Renouf, A. G. & Emde, R. N. (1996). Couples' co-constructions of the story of their child's birth: Associations with marital adaptation. *Journal of Narrative and Life History, 6*, 1–21.

Owens, G., Crowell, J., Pan, H., Treboux, D., O'Connor, E., & Waters, E. (1995). The prototype hypothesis and the origins of attachment working models: Adult relationships with parents and romantic partners. In E. Waters, B. E. Vaughn, G. Posada, & K. Kondo-Ikemura (Eds.), Caregiving, cultural and cognitive perspectives on secure base behavior and working models. *Monographs of the Society for Research in Child Development*, 60 (2–3, Serial No. 244).

Papero, D. V. (1990). *Bowen family systems theory.* Boston: Allyn and Bacon.

Parke, R. D., & Bhavnagri, N. P. (1989). Parents as managers of children's peer relationships. In D. Belle (Ed.), *Children's social networks and social supports.* New York: Wiley.

Parke, R. D., & Kellam, S. G. (1994). *Exploring family relationships with other social contexts.* Hillsdale, NJ: Lawrence Erlbaum Associates.

Parke, R. D., Power, T. G., & Gottman, J. M. (1979). Conceptualization and quantifying influences patterns in the family triad. In M. E. Lamb, S. J. Suomi, & G. R. Stephenson (Eds.), *Social interaction analysis: Methodological issues.* Madison: University of Wisconsin Press.

Patterson, G. R. (1982). *Coercive family process.* Eugene, OR: Castalia.

Patterson, J. M., & Garwick, A. W. (1994). Levels of meaning in family stress theory. *Family Process, 33*, 287–304.

Peterson, C., & Seligman, M .E. P. (1984). Causal explanations as a risk factor for depression: Theory and evidence. *Psychological Review, 91*, 347–374.

Phares, V. (1992). Where's Poppa? *American Psychologist, 47*, 656–664.

Phares, V., & Compas, B. E. (1992). The role of fathers in child and adolescent psychopathology: Make room for daddy. *Psychological Bulletin, 111*, 387–412.

Plomin, R. (1986). *Development, genetics, and psychology,* Hillsdale, NJ: Lawrence Erlbaum Associates.

Polkinghorne, D. E. (1988). *Narrative knowing and the human sciences.* Albany: State University of New York Press.

Polkinghorne, D. E. (1991). Narrative and self-concept. *Journal of Narrative and Life History, 1,* 135–153.

Quinton, D., Rutter, M., & Liddle, C. (1984). Institutional rearing, parenting difficulties and marital support. *Psychological Medicine, 14,* 107–124.

Radke-Yarrow, M., Nottelman, E., Martinez, P., Fox, M. B., & Blemont, B. (1992). Young children of affectively ill parents: A longitudinal study of psychosocial development. *Journal of the American Academy of Child and Adolescent Psychiatry, 31,* 68–77.

Reiss, D. (1981). *The family's construction of reality.* Cambridge, MA: Harvard University Press.

Reiss, D. (1989). The practicing and representing family. In A. J. Sameroff & R. Emde (Eds.), *Relationship disturbances in early childhood* (pp. 191–220). New York: Basic Books.

Richters, J., & Pelligrini, D. (1989). Depressed mothers' judgments about their children: An examination of the depression-distortion hypothesis. *Child Development, 60,* 1068–1075.

Rickard, K. M., Forehand, R., Wells, K. C., Greist, D. L., & McMahon, R. J. (1981). A comparison of mothers of clinic-referred deviant, clinic-referred nondeviant, and nonclinic children. *Behavior Research and Therapy, 19,* 201–205.

Riessman, C. K. (1993). *Narrative analysis.* Newbury Park, CA: Sage.

Riskind, J. H., Beck, A. T., Berchick, R. J., Brown, G., & Steer, R. A. (1987). Reliability of DSM-III diagnoses for major depression and generalized anxiety disorder using the Structured Clinical Interview for DSM-III. *Archives of General Psychiatry, 44,* 817–820.

Rounsaville, B. J., Prusoff, B. A., & Weissman, M. M. (1980). The course of marital disputes in depressed women: A 48-month follow-up study. *Comprehensive Psychiatry, 21*(2), 111–118.

Russell, G., & Radojevic, M. (1992). The changing role of fathers? Current understandings and future directions for research and practice. *Infant Mental Health Journal, 13*(4), 296–311.

Sameroff, A. J. (1987). The social context of development. In N. Eisenberg (Ed.), *Contemporary topics in developmental psychology* (pp. 273–291). New York: Wiley.

Sameroff, A. J. (1996, Fall). Democratic and Republican models of development: Paradigms or perspectives. *Developmental Psychology Newsletter,* 1–9.

Sameroff, A. J., Bartko, W. T., Baldwin, A., Baldwin, C., & Seifer, R. (1998). Family and social influences on the development of child competence. In M. Lewis & C. Feiring (Eds.), *Families, risk, and competence.* Mahwah, NJ: Lawrence Erlbaum Associates.

Sameroff, A. J., & Fiese, B. H. (1990). Conceptual issues in prevention. In D. Schafer, I. Philip, & N. Enzer (Eds.), *Prevention of mental disorders, alcohol use and other drug use in children and adolescents.* OSAP Prevention Monograph No 2. Rockville, MD: Office of Substance Abuse Prevention.

Sameroff, A. J., & Fiese, B. H. (1992). Family representations of development. In I. Sigel, A. V. McGillicuddy-DeLisi, & J. J. Goodnow (Eds.), *Parent belief systems: The psychological consequences for children* (pp. 347–369). Hillsdale, NJ: Lawrence Erlbaum Associates.

Sameroff, A. J., Seifer, R., Baldwin, A., & Baldwin, C. P. (1993). Stability of intelligence from preschool to adolescence: the influence of social and family risk factors. *Child Development, 64,* 80–97.

Sarbin, T. R. (1986). *Narrative Psychology: The storied nature of human conduct.* New York: Praeger.

Seifer, R., Sameroff, A. J., Anagnostopolou, R., & Elias, P. K. (1992). Mother-infant interaction during the first year: Effects of situation, maternal mental illness and demographic factors. *Infant Behavior and Development, 15*, 405–426.

Seifer, R., Sameroff, A. J., Dickstein, S., Hayden, L., Keitner, G., Miller, I., Rasmussen, S., & Hayden, L. C. (1996). Parental psychopathology, multiple contextual risks, and one-year outcomes in children. *Journal of Clinical Child Psychology, 25*, 423–435.

Sigafoos, A., Reiss, D., Rich, J., & Douglas, E. (1985). Pragmatics in the measurement of family functioning: An interpretive framework for methodology. *Family Process, 24*, 189–203.

Spanier, G. B. (1976). Measuring dyadic adjustment: New scales for assessing the quality of marriage and similar dyads. *Journal of Marriage and the Family, 38*, 15–28.

Spitzer, R. L., Williams, J. B. W., Gibbons, M., & First, M. B. (1990). *Structured clinical interview of DSM-III-R*. Washington, DC: American Psychiatric Press, Inc.

Sroufe, L. A. (1983). Infant-caregiver attachment and patterns of adaptation in preschool: The roots of maladaptation and competence. In M. Perlmutter (Ed.), *Minnesota symposium on child psychology* (Vol. 16). Hillsdale, NJ: Erlbaum.

Steinglass, P. (1987). A systems view of family interaction and psychopathology. In T. Jacob (Ed.), *Family interaction and psychopathology*. New York: Plenum.

Stephen, T. D., & Markman, H. J. (1983). Assessing the development of relationships: A new measure. *Family Process, 22*, 15–25.

Stern, D. N. (1985). *The interpersonal world of the infant*. New York: Basic.

Stern, D. N. (1989). The representation of relational patterns. In A. Sameroff & R. N. Emde (Eds.), *Relationships and relationship disorders*. New York: Basic Books.

Tannen, D. (1994). *Gender and discourse*. New York: Oxford University Press.

Thompson, L., & Walker, A. (1989). Gender in families: Women and men in marriage, work, and parenthood. *Journal of Marriage and the Family, 51*, 845–871.

Troll, L. E., & Bengston, V. L. (1982). Intergenerational relations throughout the life span. In B. B. Wolman (Ed.), *Handbook of developmental psychology*. Englewood Cliffs, NJ: Prentice Hall.

Tronick, E. Z., Cohn, J., & Shea, E. (1986). The transfer of affect between mothers and infants. In T. B. Brazelton & M. Yogman (Eds.), *Affective development in infancy*. Norwood, NJ: Ablex.

van IJzendoorn, M. H. (1995). Adult attachment representations, parental responsiveness, and infant attachment: A meta-analysis on the predictive validity of the Adult Attachment Interview. *Psychological Bulletin, 117*, 387–403.

van IJzendoorn, M. H., & Bakermans-Kranenburg, M. J. (1996). Attachment representations in mothers, fathers, adolescents, and clinical groups: A meta-analytic search for normative data. *Journal of Clinical and Consulting Psychology, 64*, 8–21.

Veroff, J., Sutherland, L., Chadiha, L. A., & Ortega, R. M. (1993). Predicting marital quality with narrative assessments of marital experience. *Journal of Marriage and the Family, 55*, 326–337.

Wagner, B. M., & Reiss, D. (1995). Family systems and developmental psychopathology: Courtship, marriage, or divorce? In D. Cicchetti & D. J. Cohen (Eds.), *Handbook of developmental psychopathology: Vol. 1. Theory and methods*. New York: Wiley.

Walsh, F. (1993). Conceptualizations of normal family process. In F. Walsh (Ed.), *Normal Family Processes* (2nd ed.). New York: Guilford.

Wamboldt, F. S., & Gavin, L. A. (1992). A reconsideration of the family-of-origin scale. *Journal of Marital and Family Therapy, 18*(2), 179–188.

Wamboldt, F. S., & Reiss, D. (1989). Defining a family heritage and a new relationship identity: Two central tasks in the making of a marriage. *Family Process, 28*, 317–335.

Wamboldt, F. S., & Reiss, D. (1991). Task performance and the social construction of meaning: Juxtaposing normality with contemporary family research. In D. Offer & M. Sabshin (Eds.), *The diversity of normal behavior.* New York: Basic Books.

Wamboldt, F. S., & Wolin, S. J. (1989). Reality and myth in family life: Changes across generations. *Journal of Psychotherapy and the Family, 4,* 141–165.

Wampler, K. S., Moore, J. J., Watson, C., & Halverson, C. F. (1989). *The Georgia Family Q-sort manual.* Unpublished manual, Texas Tech University, Lubbock, Texas.

Ward, M. J., Botyanski, N. C., Plunkett, S. W., & Carlson, E. A. (1991, April). *The concurrent and predictive validity of the AAI for adolescent mothers.* Paper presented to the Biennial meeting of the Society for Research in Child Development, Seattle, Washington.

Watzlawick, P., Beavin, J., & Jackson, D. (1967). *Pragmatics of human communication.* New York: Norton.

Wegner, D. M. (1991). Transactive memory in close relationships. *Journal of Personality and Social Psychology, 61,* 923–929.

Weiss, R. L., & Heyman, R. E. (1997). A clinical-research overview of couple interactions. In W. K. Halford & H. J. Markman (Eds.), *The clinical handbook of marriage and couple interventions.* New York: Wiley.

White, M., & Epston, D. (1990). *Narrative means to therapeutic ends.* New York: Norton.

Williamson, D. S. (1991). *The intimacy paradox: Personal authority in the family system.* New York: Guilford Press.

Wolin, S. J., & Bennett, L. A. (1984). Family rituals. *Family Process, 23,* 401–420.

Wolin, S. J., Bennett, L. A., Noonan, D. L., & Teitelbaum, M. A. (1980). Disrupted family rituals: A factor in the generational transmission of alcoholism. *Journal of Studies of Alcohol, 41,* 199–214.

Zeanah, C. H., & Barton, M. L. (1989). Introduction: Internal representations and parent-infant relationships. *Infant Mental Health Journal, 10,* 135–141.

ACKNOWLEDGMENTS

Address all correspondence to Barbara H. Fiese, 430 Huntington Hall, Department of Psychology, Syracuse University, Syracuse, N. Y. 13244-2340. E-mail bhfiese@psych.syr.edu

CHAPTER I

Fiese and Sameroff

The research reported in this chapter was supported by a grant to the Family Story Collaborative Project from the J. D. and Catherine T. MacArthur Foundation–Early Childhood Network directed by Robert Emde. David Reiss and Howard Markman served as consultants to the project. Preparation of this chapter was supported, in part, by a National Research Scientist award to Arnold Sameroff and a grant from the National Institute of Mental Health to Barbara Fiese. We gratefully acknowledge the assistance provided by Gemma Skillman and Paul ver Hagen in the LISREL analysis. Address all correspondence to Barbara H. Fiese, 430 Huntington Hall, Department of Psychology, Syracuse University, Syracuse, NY 13244. Email: bhfiese@psych.syr.edu.

CHAPTER II

Wamboldt

This work was supported in part by a grant to the Family Story Collaborative Project from the MacArthur Foundation and NIH grants K11-MH00607, R03-MH48683, R01-HL53391, and M01-RR00051 to Dr. Wamboldt. Special thanks to Ms. Santi Karamchetti for her diligent work as primary coder on the project—may all her stories end well! Address all correspondence to Frederick S. Wamboldt, National Jewish Center for

Immunology and Respiratory Medicine, Suite F301A, 1400 Jackson St., Denver, CO 80206.

CHAPTER III

Fiese and Marjinsky

An earlier version of this chapter was presented in B. H. Fiese (Chair), *A multidimensional view of family narratives: Coherence, interaction styles, and beliefs.* Symposium presented at the meeting of the Society for Research in Child Development, Indianapolis, March, 1995. The research reported in this chapter was supported by a grant from the MacArthur Foundation. Preparation of this chapter was supported, in part, by a grant from the National Institute of Mental Health to the first author. Address all correspondence to Barbara H. Fiese, 430 Huntington Hall, Department of Psychology, Syracuse University, Syracuse, NY 13244. Email: bhfiese@psych.syr.edu

CHAPTER IV

Grotevant et al.

An earlier version of this chapter was presented in B. H. Fiese (Chair), *A multidimensional view of family narratives: Coherence, interaction styles, and beliefs.* Symposium presented at the meeting of the Society for Research in Child Development, Indianapolis, March, 1995. Harold D. Grotevant and Ruth G. McRoy (Co–Principal Investigators) directed the larger project from which data for this study were drawn. We gratefully acknowledge funding for the parent project for the following sources: U.S. Office of Population Affairs, Hogg Foundation for Mental Health, National Institute of Child Health and Human Development, Minnesota Agricultural Experiment Station, and University Research Institute of the University of Texas at Austin. Address all correspondence to Harold D. Grotevant, Department of Family Social Science, University of Minnesota, 1985 Buford Avenue, St. Paul, MN 55108. Email: Hgrotevant@CHE2.CHE.UMN.EDU

CHAPTER V

Dickstein et al.

An earlier version of this chapter was presented in B. H. Fiese (Chair), *A multidimensional view of family narratives: Coherence, interaction styles, and beliefs.*

Symposium presented at the meeting of the Society for Research in Child Development, Indianapolis, March, 1995. This research was supported by Grant MH44755 from the National Institute of Mental Health. Address all correspondence to Susan Dickstein, Bradley Hospital, 1011 Veterans Memorial Parkway, East Providence, RI 02915. Email: Susan_Dickstein@ Brown.edu

COMMENTARY

WHAT WE TALK ABOUT WHEN WE TALK ABOUT FAMILIES

Philip A. Cowan

Researchers who collect and analyze stories are attracted to narratives because they are naturally occurring accounts of life experiences, organized, stored, and recounted in personally meaningful ways. In an unusual multisite multidisciplinary collaboration, the investigators in the Family Narrative Consortium (FNC) tell a very interesting interconnected set of stories about "The Stories that Families Tell." Four research teams with a shared theoretical focus examined narratives about couple and family life, using samples at different milestones or in different life circumstances. Premarital couples were asked about how they met and about their current relationship (Wamboldt). Couples with 5-year-old children commented on videotapes of a family dinner (Fiese & Marjinsky). Couples with an adopted child between the ages of 5 and 8 talked about the adoption process (Grotevant, Fravel, Gorall, & Piper). And couples from a study of depressed mothers with 2½-year-old children talked about their current family traditions and future expectations of family life (Dickstein, St. Andre, Sameroff, Seifer, & Schiller).

In all samples, the spouses were asked in different ways to compare and contrast their current families with their experiences in their families of origin. One immediately attractive aspect of this approach is that it appears to be ecologically valid. We all tell stories about our families. Marital partners frequently discuss their families with each other, and we all co-construct narratives with their friends and acquaintances when the topic of family arises. The investigators, then, are studying something that couples do in "real life."

In child development and family research it often is difficult to compare results across studies, because methods and measures vary so widely. It is refreshing to find here researchers from different sites working together to develop a coding system for narratives that yields comparable but certainly not identical results across research sites. This *Monograph* provides an excellent

163

example of how science can be advanced through a well-planned conjoint analysis of secondary data sets.

Three Narrative Dimensions: A Discussion of the Measures

Like the authors, I have already switched back and forth between "narratives" and "stories." The authors make a distinction: narratives refer to the form and stories refer to the content. People tell stories, and recount past events, within a narrative framework. In this *Monograph*, the investigators' analyses of the stories reflect this form-content distinction. The investigators delineate three narrative dimensions, each drawn from a different research tradition. The first dimension, Narrative Coherence, includes scales representing a formal analysis of how the narrative is constructed *by the individual*. Hallmarks of coherence include internal consistency, organization, flexibility, and congruence of affect and content. Although the evaluation of story coherence is a dimension of almost all discourse analysis, the focus on coherence in this study appears to come specifically from work on adult attachment (Main, Kaplan, & Cassidy, 1985). A basic assumption in Main's work is that beyond what is said, the organization of discourse provides an important window into the adult's working models of intimate family relationships.

The second dimension, described as Narrative Style, focuses on transactions *between partners* in the process of storytelling. Hallmarks of Narrative Style include active engagement, conflict, collaboration, and validation. The measures of Narrative Style reported in this *Monograph* are derived in part from clinical theories of marital and family functioning, and in part from some behavioral assessments of marital interaction developed by Gottman and Levenson (1986) and Markman (1992). Although not emphasized by the present authors, these measures emphasize the regulation of negative emotion when disagreements arise between partners.

The third dimension, Relationship Beliefs, refers to an *individual's* expectations about relationships. Hallmarks of this dimension include whether family relationships are seen as manageable, reliable, and safe, and whether the couple is open to collaboration with the interviewer; the interviewer is conceived as a representative of others outside the family. The authors cite Reiss's work on the family's construction of reality (1981) and his description of family paradigms as providing the conceptual framework for this narrative dimension. In my view, there is another source. The view of family relationships as predictable and safe may reflect that part of what Bowlby (1988) referred to as the central aspect of working models—the construct of a "secure base"—the expectation that an attachment figure will be available for nurturance and support in times of stress.

A confirmatory factor analysis of data across all four research sites supported the hypothesis that Narrative Coherence and Narrative Style can be thought of as separate measurement dimensions. Relationship Beliefs, however, did not constitute a third dimension in the overall model, probably because the two ingredients of this construct (whether family relationships are considered safe, and whether the couple could relate well to the interviewer) were more highly correlated with Coherence and Narrative Style than with each other (Table 6). It is not immediately clear what the problem is. It is possible, as the authors note, that a belief in whether relationships are safe is simply not in the same realm as whether the couples choose to engage with the interviewer. Because Relationship Belief scales are correlated with both Coherence and Narrative Style, it may be that the model should be collapsed into two dimensions, with beliefs incorporated somehow in a revised construct of coherence. This would make the coding system here closer to the Adult Attachment Interview (AAI) coding, in which adults with secure working models tell coherent stories, showing that they value intimate relationships.

The investigators are to be commended for systematically including husbands as well as wives as informants on the family. Having done so, they left themselves open to the question of what to do when measures from husbands and wives fail to show similar psychometric properties. Unfortunately, the four scales assumed to measure coherence were highly intercorrelated for men, but not for women. Perhaps, as the authors speculate, the narrative process is more homogeneous for men than for women. Perhaps, too, women are more differentiated about relationships than men. I wonder whether the findings are related to Gilligan's argument (1982) that men and women have different "voices" in their conceptualization of interpersonal issues.

The issue of gender differences in the coherence of measures requires further exploration. It would be possible to find out more about the meaning of the scales for women and men by examining not only their correlations with other narrative scales (this is done in Tables 7 and 8, Chapter 1), but also differences in their patterns of correlation with both self-report and behavioral observations. The first question to be answered would be whether the scales have different correlational patterns for men and women. The second question would be how to interpret the differences. And the third question would be, "Why do these differences occur?"

Epistemological Issues

As the authors point out, the study of narratives has a long history. Although narrative methods have held an honored place in a number of social science disciplines (linguistics, sociology, anthropology) and in clinical theory and research, the use of narratives in psychology has only recently been taken up with some enthusiasm. Within psychology, data obtained from any type of self-report, but especially narratives that are not highly structured by interviewers, often are treated with skepticism. I believe that narrative methods have been resisted even more strongly than other self-report instruments or techniques, because investigators who use them tend to endorse a set of epistemological assumptions that run counter to the logical positivist paradigm that shaped psychological research during the last half of the 20th century. In contrast with the logical positivist claim that self-reports are "biased" or "distorted," those who use narrative methods embrace story methods precisely because they tell us more about the story-teller than about the events that the storyteller is recounting. Thus, the use of narrative often pits a constructivist epistemology focused on the story-teller's truth as a set of subjective meanings (the insider view) against a posi-tivist epistemology focused on the observer's truth purported to present a set of objective facts (the outsider view).

The major contribution of this *Monograph* is that the investigators attempt, rather successfully, to have it both ways. They consider in some detail the relationship between insider perspectives on what Reiss (1989) has termed the "represented family," and outsider perspectives on what he has termed "the practicing family." Narratives usually are the products of individuals, but, in this set of studies, the stories were co-constructed by couples. This twist on narrative methods allows the investigators to examine each part-ner's contribution to the narrative description of couple and family life *and* to consider the observer's perspective on the process of interaction between the partners as they collaborate or fail to collaborate in telling their story.

The details of the findings vary across the four studies, but it seems to me that the investigators provide convincing evidence that the coherence of the narrative, the transactions involved in constructing the narrative, and general beliefs about relationships are correlated with (a) each other, (b) measures of self-reported individual and marital adaptation, (c) observational measures of family interaction, and (d) child outcomes, although this last conclusion is not as solid as the others. The fact that, of the four samples, the premarital cou-ples in Wamboldt's study had narratives with the lowest internal consistency, lowest between-partner correlations, and lowest correlations between coher-ence and other self-report measures of their relationship, only serves to rein-force the meaningfulness of the method. As Wamboldt states, premarital relationships are works in progress. If he's right, it even may be that increas-ing individual and between-partner coherence of co-constructions of family stories could serve as a measure of relationship development. Whereas we wouldn't want to substitute family narratives for all other assessments of family functioning, especially early in the couple relationship, we can be reassured that what established couples say about their families, and how they say it, have at least some systematic connection to the quality of relationships measured both by questionnaires and observations.

Context of Assessment, Focus of the Narrative, and Combinations of Perspectives

Formidable thickets cover the methodological terrain entered by the investigators. They state, quite correctly, that by examining narratives that are co-constructed by couples, they have "gone beyond" the individual to deal with how the family makes sense of the world. Although I agree with their claim, I would like to point out that this set of studies, like all other family studies, can be situated in a much more complicated methodological matrix. The selection of individual and couple narratives represents only one of many possible methods of moving from the individual to the family level of analysis.

Context of assessment. Until relatively recently, our major source of insider information on the family was an individual, usually a mother, sometimes a child, and even more rarely a father. It is possible to obtain data from a dyad—a couple, a parent-child, or a sibling pair as the investigators did here. But it also is possible, as Fiese and her colleagues did, to ask the family as a collective to construct a narrative, although, as I understand it, the coding included data from only the marital dyad.

Do family narratives obtained in different contexts produce the same data? A comparison of individually told and co-constructed narratives by Grotevant et al. found moderate positive correlations between the two, with the correlation between his and her coherence scores higher when they told the story together than when each told it alone. It is not clear whether this increase results from coder halo effects, or actually arises from the process of co-construction of the story.

Grotevant et al. emphasize the cross-context consistency of their findings. What may prove to be even more important is the fact that an individual sometimes had a different level of coherence when telling the story of the adoption to an interviewer than when constructing the story with his/her spouse. These differences seem to have had a marked effect. Wives who were able to construct a more coherent narrative in the presence of their husbands than when interviewed alone were more satisfied with their marital relationship than wives who were consistent across contexts. The authors interpret this result as evidence that the marital relationship is able to provide a scaffold that stimulates the development of more competent behaviors. This interpretation is consistent with other evidence that a good marriage can reduce an individual partner's vulnerability to psychological risk, with the buffering effect especially noted for wives (Cohn, Cowan, Cowan, & Pearson, 1992; Quinton, Rutter, & Liddle, 1984)

Focus of the narrative. In the studies reported here, the focus of the narrative was on dyads (the relation between the respondent and his/her parent, spouse, or child). The investigators could have asked participants in each context to construct narratives about individual family members, or about the family as a whole. The interviews did contain questions like these, but the answers were not coded separately. The fact that it is possible to ask individuals, dyads, or whole families to tell stories about individuals, dyads, or whole families means that there is a potential 3×3 matrix combining context and focus, from which any investigator selects one or more alternative combinations.

Combination of methods and perspectives. My point here is not that the present investigators used only three cells (individual, couple, whole family assessment contexts, each with a focus on dyads). Rather, I want to underline the fact that we don't yet know how or whether these possible methodological variations affect the data. It will be important to explore whether specific combinations of data sources and narrative focus might add unique information to our understanding of family process and children's developmental outcomes. For example, it is possible that narratives *about* whole families co-constructed *by* the whole family may be more predictive of variations in family structure and process, whereas narratives about individuals obtained in an individual setting might be more effective in predicting individual adaptation.

I want to make one further point about combining perspectives. Now that at least some studies of families have come to include data from and about fathers as well as mothers, there still is a curious omission in the analysis of data. Almost all studies, including those in this *Monograph*, analyze data from mothers and fathers separately. As these mothers and fathers are in couples, it is possible to ask whether information from both partners adds to our understanding of family processes. In my view, it is likely that the combination may be interactive rather than additive. That is, certain pairings of couples (e.g., high-coherent wife, low-coherent husband, or vice versa) may affect not only the quality of the marital interaction, but also the nature of family processes and the ultimate impact of parents' characteristics on children's development.

In sum, I want to commend the authors for moving from the individual to the dyadic level in both assessment context and focus, and at the same time point out that this is part of a larger array of methodological variations, appropriate when we move from the level of individual analysis to the study of the family.

The Issue of Linkage with Children's Adaptation

In two of the studies, the child's adaptation in terms of externalizing and internalizing problems was assessed by the Child Behavior Check List (CBCL; Achenbach & Edelbrock, 1983). The Dickstein et al. study obtained mothers' reports of their 2-year-olds' behavior problems, and the Fiese et al. study obtained both parents' reports of their 5 to 7-year-olds, behavior problems. Narrative measures were significantly correlated with children's outcomes only in the Fiese study.

Even if both studies had found links between family narratives and parents' descriptions of their children, further research would be needed in which independent observers reported on the child, in order to rule out the possibility that the association resulted from the fact that the same parent was the source of both kinds of data. Given the single source in the Dickstein et al. study, it is surprising that there were no connections between the narratives of depressed mothers and their descriptions of their children's behavior problems. The failure to find such links is not likely to lie with the narrative measures. These measures, especially Coherence, demonstrated impressive links with diagnostic status of the parents, and observed family interaction during a meal. I believe that the problem lies with the measure of children's adjustment. First, despite the fact that Achenbach has created norms for 2-year-olds, the scale is overloaded with problem items and contains few items assessing competence. Dickstein et al. argue that this scale may not be appropriate for a sample with very low frequencies of serious disturbance, and I agree. Second, it is not at all clear that any assessment technique can diagnose externalizing and internalizing problems accurately in 2-year-olds, and distinguish them from the 2-year-olds' normative tendencies to be oppositional and often shy. It is now time to replicate the investigators' approach using a broader range of assessment instruments, focusing on a wider sample of behavior, observed by informants both inside and outside the family.

In the present *Monograph*, there is a large conceptual leap from the marital satisfaction and family dinner table interactions assessed by the investigators to the prediction of children's outcomes. Even if there were broader measures of children's adaptation, the investigators would not necessarily find direct links with family processes without assessing the intermediate links provided by mothers' and fathers' parenting of each child, not only in the whole-family dinner time interaction, but in dyadic interaction.

Family Narratives and Family Functioning

Family researchers are intent on demonstrating that there is consistency of functioning across individual and family domains. We take pride in using

complex regressions or path models to show that there is a web of associations (paths) linking personality or adjustment in parents to marital conflict,
marital conflict to parent-child relationship quality, and parent-child relationship quality to children's outcomes (e.g., Conger & Elder, 1994; Cowan,
Cohn, Cowan, & Pearson, 1996). Near the end of this *Monograph*, the authors attempt to weave together the strands of their investigation: "Our hypothesis is that where family meaning is coherent, family life is more
successful in terms of dyadic adjustment, parent mental health, and child
mental health. Where family meaning is lacking, where there is inconsistency in thought, incongruence between words spoken and the emotions expressed, and a lack of trust in relationships, both parents and children show
the negative effects. This description is, of course, consistent with what family therapists have been advocating for years." (p. 120–121).

How far have the investigators come in providing evidence for this conclusion? Part way, and this is in itself a considerable achievement. Some measures of individual and family adaptation were related to one or more of the
three major narrative dimensions (coherence, interactive style, beliefs) in
one or more of the studies. At the individual level of analysis, low Narrative
Coherence was associated with partners' experience of closed rather than
open adoption (Grotevant et al.) and with a diagnosis of depression
(Dickstein et al.). Beliefs that past and current family relationships are not to
be relied on also were associated with depression (Dickstein et al.). At the
couple level of analysis, high Narrative Coherence measured in the
Grotevant and Dickstein studies was related to marital satisfaction, and so
were secure base Relationship Beliefs in the Wamboldt, Fiese, and Dickstein
studies. At the family level of analysis, Narrative Coherence in the Dickstein
study was associated with more positive and less negative observed family interaction at dinner time, as were Narrative Interaction and Relationship Beliefs in both Fiese and the Dickstein studies. With these findings, the authors
are entitled to claim support for their hypotheses. If we take account of the
number of predicted correlations across all studies that were not statistically
significant, however, it is clear that the glass is partially empty as well as partially full. Because this is a new and interesting venture, I want to give the authors credit for creating the glass, and for obtaining at least some support
for their predictions across measures, methods, and samples.

The authors naturally placed family narratives at center stage, because
that is the focus of their work, so their conclusion, quoted above, begins with
coherent family meanings. This placement suggests that narratives may be
the engine driving the family system. It seems to me that the data are not
strong enough to support this position.

First, within their discussion of narratives and the presentation of results the authors appear to place their conceptual focus on Coherence and
Narrative Interaction, but it is my impression that the Relationship Beliefs

dimension showed some of the most consistent correlations with marital quality and family interaction. Rather than three parallel dimensions of narratives (Coherence, Narrative Interaction, and Beliefs), it is possible that there is a hierarchical ordering. General beliefs about the safety of relationships may provide a filter affecting how family stories are told and how partners approach interactions with each other and with their children.

Second, as I noted above, the fact that there were not always correlations between measures of narratives relating to families of origin and the current family suggests that there may be some advantage in treating these two domains separately, in order to understand the contribution of each to our understanding of family processes.

Third, as I also noted above, although two of the authors examined parent-child interaction in the context of the family (at dinner), the investigators did not consider either representations or observations of mother-child or father-child interactions. In addition, with the exception of the interaction between the couples and the interviewers, there were no assessments of relationships between family members and outsiders. I recognize that the authors had a great many issues to deal with, and in this seminal study of family narratives had to make choices.

A theoretical story that is consistent with the authors' general formulation, but has a slightly different focus, could be constructed from the significant findings. I begin by taking a cue from the authors' emphasis on the importance of studying both the represented and the practicing family (Reiss, 1989). Let us assume that these two perspectives, encompassing both insider and outsider views on the family, are relevant to every domain of family life. Because the correlations between scores derived from narratives describing the family of origin and the couples' current family are low, and correlations between narratives and observed behavior are moderate, let us also assume that we need information about representation and behavior in each family domain. We could then use narratives to assess the insider perspective on (a) men's and women's families of origin, (b) themselves, (c) their marriage, (d) their relationships with their children, and (e) their connection or lack of connection with people and institutions outside the family. I should note here that in the present study, some of the children were too young to tell stories, but that children's perspectives on themselves and their families can in fact provide useful information about family functioning (Measelle, Ablow, Cowan, & Cowan, 1998; Steele & Steele, 1994). Using the co-construction approach, narratives also can be used as one of many methods to assess behavior in each of these domains.

The "full model" of the represented and practicing family, then, would include two parallel streams of data from each domain of family life. For example, we could ask whether and how narratives focused on the family of origin and observations of grandparent-parent interaction combine to predict

Coherence and Narrative Style determined from co-constructed stories about the marriage. We could then ask whether and how these four measures combine to predict Coherence and Narrative Style in stories co-constructed by each parent and child. And, finally, we could examine the direct and indirect connections among all of these measures and assessments of children's cognitive, social, and emotional development. The question of whether and how "working models" and behavior in one domain combine to predict working models and behavior in other domains could then help to integrate the self-report and observational traditions in family research.

Narrative Representations as Explanations of Cross-Domain Continuity and Discontinuity

The authors have provided some information about continuity between representations and behavior, and between adaptive functioning across family domains. The most important unresolved question before us now is to identify the processes or mechanisms responsible for the fact that adaptive functioning in one domain is associated with adaptive functioning in another, and to identify systematic conditions governing discontinuities across family domains.

Although it makes intuitive sense, for example, that depression in mothers might be related to the quality of their marriage, it is not immediately obvious why this connection should occur. A number of possible mechanisms are offered as explanations of linkage, including genetics, reinforcement and modeling, and emotional "spillover." The present authors offer a different alternative. They argue that the represented family, in the form of internal working models of relationships in the family of origin and the current family, function as schemas that guide our interpretations of what our loved ones do, and our general expectations about the nature and quality of intimate relationships (whether they can be relied upon in a crisis). Owens and colleagues (1995), in describing research on adult attachment, refer to this formulation as a "template" theory.

In its strong form, template theory would predict that a single working model, based on constructions of early childhood relationships, guides behavior in all intimate relationships. I have noted that the correlations between narratives focused on the family of origin and the current family are low enough to cast doubt that these narratives support the strong form of template theory. This pattern is consistent with other studies showing significant but far from perfect correspondence between adult attachment security and quality of marital interaction (Cowan et al., 1996; Owens, Crowell, Treboux, Pan, & O'Connor, 1995) and between adult attachment and the quality of parent-child relationships (van Ijzendoorn, 1992).

We are left, then, with the possibility that narrative representations may explain some of the continuity between generations, and between domains of family life, but there must certainly be other factors involved. In writing about the AAI (Cowan et al., 1996), my colleagues and I argued that the telling of family stories often raises emotional issues, and that maintaining coherence while recounting a narrative to an interviewer provides a good test of the interviewee's emotion regulation strategies. Research by Gottman, Katz, and Hooven on "meta-emotion" (1987) shows that parents' strategies for regulating their child's negative emotion, assessed in parent interviews, are correlated with measures of emotion regulation obtained from behavioral observation of parent-parent, parent-child, and child-peer interaction, and from psychophysiological measures of the child's ability to self-soothe when upset. This line of reasoning is as yet highly speculative, but it seems to me that the "active ingredient" in family narratives that promotes cross-domain consistency may not be cognitive schemas of relationships, but rather effectiveness in staying on track while completing an emotionally arousing task. The individual and co-constructed narratives described by the present authors would provide ideal contexts in which to examine the role of individual and interpersonal regulation of emotion in promoting both continuity and discontinuity of adaptation across family domains.

A Few Implications for Clinical Theory and Practice

Fortunately for most adults, despite a tendency toward continuity between narrative representations of the family of origin and one's current love relationship, and between these representations and observed patterns of interaction, it appears possible to interrupt the cycle in which negative patterns are transmitted across the generations. It is beyond the scope of this *Monograph* to determine the conditions under which both continuity and discontinuity occur, but this is a central question for the fields of developmental psychopathology, prevention science, and psychotherapy.

As the authors point out, the importance of patients' stories about their families has long been accepted by individual therapists and family therapists. The emphasis on both the represented and the practicing family in this *Monograph* indicates that the meanings family members place on family events are important in explaining patterns of family interaction. This formulation is quite consistent with a cognitive-behavioral approach to understanding and treating couple relationships (e.g., Baucom & Epstein, 1990) and family systems (e.g., Epstein, Schlesinger, & Dryden, 1988).

Over the last decade, narrative therapies for individuals and families have attempted to focus on what the correlational data here suggest—changing individual and couple narratives as a way of improving intrapsychic well-being and altering maladaptive patterns of interaction. This idea still needs systematic testing through intervention research. This research certainly could determine the impact, if any, of changes in narratives on changes in relationship transactions. In addition, it could provide some answers to the question of direction of effects. Do representations of family relationships shape behavior and experience? Do changes in behavior and experience alter family representations? Is the connection bidirectional? Only with an experimental design that tests the difference between intervention and controls will we learn whether the correlations between the stories families tell have a causal connection to the patterns of couple and family interaction we observe.

Conclusions

What do the stories in this *Monograph* tell us, and what do we still need to know? The psychometric properties of the narrative coding system look promising. The authors demonstrate that the narrative scales can be reliably coded. There is reasonable internal consistency in Coherence and Narrative Interaction scales, with lower consistency for Relationship Beliefs. It will be important in future research to track down the meaning of the fact that the interrelation of scales is different for men and women, and whether this finding indicates that there are fundamental gender differences in the ways that family narratives are constructed.

In answer to questions of validity—whether the narrative dimensions were related to other aspects of the behavior or family members—the authors have begun to find encouraging answers. They have shown that there are systematic correlations between narrative codes and both self-reported and observed marital and family interaction. The ties between co-constructed narratives and children's developmental outcomes require much more systematic research. I have suggested one possible "full model" that might provide such linkage, but there are bound to be others stimulated by this innovative and important set of studies.

I believe that this *Monograph* makes a significant contribution to both method and theory in the field of family research. In their focus on stories families tell, the investigators show us that a method central to attachment research can be used productively to elucidate family members' understanding of family relationships and processes. In their use of co-constructed narratives, the investigators show us that it is possible to use the narrative context to obtain detailed observations of how family members work together on an emotionally meaningful task. In these ways, the authors have made a significant step forward in our understanding of the links between the represented and practicing family.

REFERENCES

Achenbach, T. M., & Edelbrock, C. S. (1983). *Manual for the Child Behavior Checklist.* Burlington, VT: Queen City.

Baucom, D. H., & Epstein, N. (1990). *Cognitive-behavioral marital therapy.* New York: Brunner/Mazel.

Bowlby, J. (1988). *A secure base: Clinical applications of attachment theory.* London: Routledge.

Cohn, D. A., Cowan, P. A., Cowan, C. P., & Pearson, J. (1992). Mothers' and fathers' working models of childhood attachment relationships, parenting styles, and child behavior. *Development and Psychopathology, 4,* 417–431.

Conger, R. D., & Elder, G. H. Jr. (Eds.). (1994). *Families in troubled times: Adapting to change in rural America.* New York: Aldine de Gruyter.

Cowan, P. A., Cohn, D. A., Cowan, C. P., & Pearson, J. L. (1996). Parents' attachment histories and children's internalizing and externalizing behavior: Exploring family systems models of linkage. *Journal of Consulting and Clinical Psychology, 64,* 53–63.

Epstein, N., Schlesinger, S. E., & Dryden, W. (Eds.). (1988). *Cognitive-behavioral therapy with families.* New York: Brunner/Mazel.

Gilligan, C. (1982). *In a different voice: Psychological theory and women's development.* Cambridge, MA: Harvard University Press.

Gottman, J. M., Katz, L. F., & Hooven, C. (1987). *Meta-emotion: How families communicate emotionally.* Mahwah, NJ: Lawrence Erlbaum Associates.

Gottman, J. M., & Levenson, R. W. (1986). Assessing the role of emotion in marriage. *Behavioral Assessment, 8,* 31–48.

Main, M., Kaplan, N., & Cassidy, J. (1985). Security in infancy, childhood, and adulthood: A move to the level of representation. In I. Bretherton & E. Waters (Eds.), *Growing points of attachment theory and research. Monographs of the Society for Research in Child Development, 50* (1–2, Serial No. 209).

Markman, H. J. (1992). Marital and family psychology: Burning issues. Special Issue: Diversity in contemporary family psychology. *Journal of Family Psychology, 5,* 264–275.

Measelle, J. R., Ablow, J. C., Cowan, P. A., & Cowan, C. P. (1998). Assessing young children's views of their academic, social, and emotional lives: An evaluation of the self-perception scales of the Berkeley Puppet Interview. *Child Development, 69,* 1556–1576.

Owens, G., Crowell, J., Pan, H., Treboux, D., O'Connor, B., & Waters, E. (1995). The prototype hypothesis and the origins of attachment working models: Child-parent relationships and adult-adult romantic relationships. In E. Waters, B. Vaughn, G. Posada, & K. Kondo-Ikemura (Eds.), *Caregiving, cultural, and cognitive perspectives on secure base behavior and working models: New growing points of attachment theory and research. Monographs of the Society for Research in Child Development, 60* (2–3, Serial No. 244).

Owens, G., Crowell, J., Treboux, D., Pan, H., & O'Connor, B. (1995, March). Multiple versus single working models of attachment: Relations between models of child-parent relationships and later romantic relationships. Paper given in a poster symposium presented at the Biennial Meeting of the Society for Research in Child Development, Indianapolis, IN.

Quinton, D., Rutter, M., & Liddle, C. (1984). Institutional rearing, parenting difficulties, and marital support. *Psychological Medicine, 14,* 107–124.

Reiss, D. (1981). *The family's construction of reality.* Cambridge, MA: Harvard University Press.

Reiss, D. (1989). The practicing and representing family. In A. J. Sameroff & R. Emde (Eds.), *Relationship disturbances in early childhood.* New York: Basic Books.

Steele, H., & Steele, M. (1994). Intergenerational patterns of attachment. In K. Bartholomew & D. Perlman (Eds.), *Attachment processes in adulthood:* Vol. 5. *Advances in personal relationships.* London: Jessica Kingsley.

van IJzendoorn, M. H. (1992). Intergenerational transmission of parenting: A review of studies in nonclinical populations. *Developmental Review, 12,* 76–99.

CONTRIBUTORS

Susan Dickstein (Ph.D., 1990, University of Illinois–Urbana-Champaign) is an Assistant Professor in the Department of Psychiatry and Human Behavior at Brown University, E. P. Bradley Hospital. She is affiliated with Bradley Hospital Early Childhood Center and Bradley Developmental Psychopathology Research Center. Her research centers on intergenerational attachment relationships, developmental psychopathology, and family functioning in high-risk contexts.

Barbara H. Fiese (Ph.D.,1987, University of Illinois–Chicago) is an Associate Professor of Psychology and Director of Clinical Training at Syracuse University. Her research interests include generational processes that affect child development and focuses on the study of family rituals and stories.

Deborah Lewis Fravel (Ph.D., 1995, University of Minnesota) is an Assistant Professor, Department of Applied Health Sciences, Indiana University. Her research interests include family stress, boundary ambiguity, adoptive families, families with missing children, adult interpersonal relationships, and narrative coherence.

Dean Gorall (M.S., 1992, Oklahoma State University) is a doctoral student in Family Social Science at the University of Minnesota.

Harold Grotevant (Ph.D., 1977, University of Minnesota, Institute of Child Development) is Professor of Family Social Science and Adjunct Professor of Child Psychology at the University of Minnesota. His research interests include adoptive family relationships, the development of identity, parent-adolescent relationships, and family assessment.

Kathleen A. T. Marjinksy (Ph.D., 1996, Syracuse University) is Director of School Psychology and Assistant Professor of Psychology at Marywood

College. Her research interests include adolescent adjustment, parent-adolescent conflict resolution, and family assessment.

Joyce Piper (Ph.D., 1995, University of Minnesota) works with families as a parish pastor (ELCA-Lutheran) and pastoral family therapist in rural southwest Minnesota. Her dissertation research was a cross-cultural study of "Work Stress Among Lutheran Clergy Women in the USA and Norway." Her clinical and research interests focus on clergy family issues.

Arnold J. Sameroff (Ph.D., 1965, Yale University) is a Professor of Psychology and a Research Scientist at the Center for Human Growth and Development at the University of Michigan. His theoretical interests have been in understanding the biological, psychological, and social influences on human development. His research program has included a number of longitudinal studies of children at developmental risk because of either parental psychopathology or environmental adversity.

Masha Schiller (Ph.D., 1994, University of Rhode Island) is a staff psychologist and research associate at E. P. Bradley Hospital, Brown University. She is the clinic coordinator for the Early Childhood Center at Bradley Hospital. Her research interests include family functioning, attachment, and developmental psychopathology in early childhood.

Ron Seifer (Ph.D., 1981, University of Rochester) is an Associate Professor in the Department of Psychiatry and Human Behavior at Brown University, E. P. Bradley Hospital. His research interests include development of relationship processes in children at risk for developmental psychopathology, the development of temperament, and attachment relationships.

Martin St. Andre (C.M., M.D., FRCPC) is Assistant Clinical Professor at the Hospital Sainte-Justine, University of Montreal. His research and clinical interests include infant psychiatry and obstetrical consultation-liaison.

Frederick S. Wamboldt (M.D., 1981, University of Wisconsin-Madison) is an Associate Faculty Member of the Department of Medicine at the National Jewish Center for Immunology and Respiratory Medicine and an Associate Professor of Psychiatry at the University of Colorado Health Sciences Center. His research interests include marital and family development in nonstressed as well as challenged (e.g. severe, chronic medical illness) populations.

Philip A. Cowan (Ph.D., 1963, University of Toronto) is professor of psychology and director of the Institute of Human Development at the University of California, Berkeley. For the past 25 years he has been collaborating with Carolyn Pape Cowan on two longitudinal studies of families. The first, focused on the transition to parenthood, has been summarized in *When Partners Become Parents: The Big Life Change for Couples.* Papers describing the second study, focused on the first child's transition to school, are in preparation. Both studies emphasize the role of the parents' marital quality in influencing parent-child relationships and children's development, and the importance of intervention studies for testing correlational models of family process and children's outcomes.

STATEMENT OF EDITORIAL POLICY

The *Monographs* series is intended as an outlet for major reports of developmental research that generate authoritative new findings and use these to foster a fresh and/or better-integrated perspective on some conceptually significant issue or controversy. Submissions from programmatic research projects are particularly welcome; these may consist of individually or group-authored reports of findings from some single large-scale investigation or of a sequence of experiments centering on some particular question. Multiauthored sets of independent studies that center on the same underlying question can also be appropriate; a critical requirement in such instances is that the various authors address common issues and that the contribution arising from the set as a whole be both unique and substantial. In essence, irrespective of how it may be framed, any work that contributes significant data and/or extends developmental thinking will be taken under editorial consideration.

Submissions should contain a minimum of 80 manuscript pages (including tables and references); the upper limit of 150–175 pages is much more flexible (please submit four copies; a copy of every submission and associated correspondence is deposited eventually in the archives of the SRCD). Neither membership in the Society for Research in Child Development nor affiliation with the academic discipline of psychology is relevant; the significance of the work in extending developmental theory and in contributing new empirical information is by far the most crucial consideration. Because the aim of the series is not only to advance knowledge on specialized topics but also to enhance cross-fertilization among disciplines or subfields, it is important that the links between the specific issues under study and larger questions relating to developmental processes emerge as clearly to the general reader as to specialists on the given topic.

The corresponding author for any manuscript must, in the submission letter, warrant that all coauthors are in agreement with the content of the manuscript. The corresponding author also is responsible for informing all coauthors, in a timely manner, of manuscript submission, editorial decisions, reviews received, and any revisions recommended. Before publication, the corresponding author also must warrant in the submission letter that the study has been conducted according to the ethical guidelines of the Society for Research in Child Development.

Potential authors who may be unsure whether the manuscript they are planning would make an appropriate submission are invited to draft an outline of what they propose and send it to the Editor for assessment. This mechanism, as well as a more detailed desctiption of all editorial policies, evaluation processes, and format requirements, is given in the "Guidelines for the Preparation of *Monographs* Submissions," which can be obtained by contacting the Editor-Elect, Willis Overton, Department of Psychology, 567 Weiss Hall, Temple University, Philadelphia, PA 19122 [e-mail: overton@vm.temple.edu].